Reciprocity, U.S. Trade Policy,
and the GATT Regime

Reciprocity, U.S. Trade Policy, and the GATT Regime

Carolyn Rhodes

Cornell University Press

Ithaca and London

First published 1993 by Cornell University Press.
Second printing 1995.

Library of Congress Cataloging-in-Publication Data

Rhodes, Carolyn, 1952–
    Reciprocity, U.S. trade policy, and the GATT regime / by Carolyn Rhodes.
      p.   cm.
    Includes bibliographical references and index.
    ISBN 0-8014-2864-5
    1. United States—Commercial Policy. 2. Reciprocity—United States.
3. United States—Foreign economic relations. 4. General Agreement on Tariffs and Trade (Organization)   I. Title
HF1455.R46   1993
382′.3′0973—dc20   93-17892

Printed in the United States of America

⊗ The paper in this book meets the minimum requirements
of the American National Standard for Information Sciences—
Permanence of Paper for Printed Library Materials, ANSI Z39.48-1984.

To my parents,
Keith and Rhea Rhodes

Contents

Tables

Preface

I first became interested in this project in 1982, when I was struggling to understand whether fair trade enforcement efforts encouraged cooperation in trade and maintained an essentially liberal regime under the General Agreement on Tariffs and Trade (GATT) or whether such efforts merely served to disrupt trade and incite conflict. On the one hand, anti-appeasement advocates had argued since the 1930s that to tolerate illegal international behavior was to encourage it, and more recently game theorists argued that free-riding on collective goods undermines the maintenance of those goods. International political economists have extended this latter argument to GATT trade relations where global market access depends on the cooperation of individual nation-states. These arguments indicated that using retaliation against unfair behavior and bilaterally enforcing agreements could be beneficial—not only to bilateral trade cooperation but also to the integrity and longevity of the international trading regime.

On the other hand, classical free trade economists and multilateralists at the GATT made clear their fear that emphasizing reciprocal compliance with fair trade rules and reciprocal access to markets threatens to undermine the international trading regime, not enforce it. They worried that special bilateral agreements would proliferate, allowing importing nations to exploit the vulnerabilities of exporting nations and encouraging discriminatory practices that placed politics above economic efficiency. In particular these analysts were concerned that reciprocity would not only fail to enforce trade cooperation but would also actually undermine the regime based on multilateral expectations of liberal, nondiscriminatory trade. If trade policy continued to emphasize reciprocity and retaliation was increasingly employed by GATT member nations, the risk, they argued, was a retaliatory spiral that would plunge the world economy into a 1930s-style trade war. Moreover, hegemonic stability theory appeared to indicate that cooperation in trade would decrease as the United States declined in its ability to maintain a position of leadership and cost absorption in the post–World War II trade regime. This created a certain urgency about discovering why these contradictory interpretations could coexist and whether under scrutiny one held more sway than the other.

I began my investigation with an in-depth study of the emergence of this contradiction in the original GATT norms, rules, and procedures. I discovered that the GATT itself—and U.S. trade law before it—embodied the expectation that nations would not discriminate in their trade with one another but at the same time would expect reciprocal treatment. This fundamental tension within the regime itself indicated that the debate over reciprocity was not a new phenomenon, and so I searched U.S. trade policy history to discover its origins, its character, and how it had evolved over time. This historical analysis proved very useful in defining reciprocity and explaining its role in the U.S. trade policy context since the 1880s. I discovered that after 1934 reciprocity and liberalization were partners in producing trade expansion, whereas before that date reciprocity had been thwarted or distorted in the hands of protectionist interests, which indicated that even though protectionists might attempt to manipulate it for restrictive purposes, reciprocity could perform a useful role in encouraging trade cooperation.

It was clear that the tension between reciprocity and nondiscrimination in a liberal trading context was inherent in the normative and procedural approaches established by the United States in creating the GATT regime. This tension worsened during the 1970s and 1980s, when surplus capacity threatened established industries in the United States as new competitors clamored for access to the global market. To discover whether the mounting bilateral pressures for reciprocity and the proliferation of retaliatory activity during this period contributed to the enforcement or decline of the GATT, I conducted an empirical investigation of the actual playing out of bilateral trade relations during this period. I sought "most likely" cases where I expected the rules of the GATT regime to govern trade between well-established trading partners of the United States and where reciprocity, as well as liberalism and nondiscrimination, was a mutually accepted norm of the countries involved.

After examining U.S. trade relations in steel, autos, and wheat flour, I concluded that reciprocity, where the cooperative regime is well established and where it is pursued in accordance with delineated GATT rules, does serve a useful enforcement role. As was true before 1934, however, industrial interests will attempt to exploit reciprocity for their own protectionist purposes. The most interesting result of this study is that when nations have to take into account reciprocal relations, including retaliatory threats, this has a constraining effect on the protectionist actions. Even though voluntary restraint agreements (VRAs) proliferated during this period, in violation of GATT Article 11, trade flows were maintained and bilateral cooperation on market access was reinforced. Only in the wheat flour sector, where a cooperative regime had not been established and where retaliatory threats were less directly applied, did reciprocity fail to encourage cooperation.

Another element that became clear from the historical and case studies is that reciprocity has two faces. One consists of the GATT-legitimized enforcement of fair trade rules, such as countervailing duties, that buttress the trade regime. The other consists of the more loosely applied expectation of bilateral cooperation that bypasses GATT rules while reinforcing mutual accommodation in the form of VRAs or other bilaterally cooperative arrangements. Neither face represents a return to the unilateral protectionism of the pre-1934 period, and both indicate that reciprocity provides an incentive to maintain cooperative relations with trading partners, even when it requires a violation of GATT nondiscrimination rules.

Preface

This book contains information that has previously appeared under my authorship in other places. Chapter 5 includes material from "Managed Steel Trade, the GATT Subsidies and Countervailing Duty Code, and the 1979 United States Trade Act." This article was originally published in *World Competition* 12 (December 1988), and portions are reprinted with the kind permission of its publisher. Small portions of "Reciprocity in Trade: The Utility of a Bargaining Strategy," *International Organization* 43 (Spring 1989), are utilized in Chapter 1, also with the kind permission of the publisher.

In writing this book I had the support of many individuals and institutions. First, I thank Robert Keohane for inspiring my work on reciprocity and for continually supporting my effort. His critiques and his encouragement were instrumental in taking me from my first paper on reciprocity through to the book. His mentorship is greatly appreciated, and I cannot thank him enough.

I also recognize those who have helped me to formulate my arguments and who influenced me directly in their own contributions to the field. Beth and Robert Yarbrough deserve special thanks for their encouragement, ideas, and interest. Their work on self-enforcing agreements has been especially helpful to me, as has been their enthusiasm for my project. John Odell, Bruce Bueno de Mesquita, Stephen Krasner, Gilbert Winham, and David Richardson also took an interest in my work early on and helped me hone my ideas and clarify my arguments. Others who commented on the manuscript, its components, or earlier papers and who contributed to its development are Renée Marlin-Bennett, Helen Milner, David Lake, Richard Blackhurst, Gerard Curzon, the late Jan Tumlir, and two anonymous reviewers. Research assistance was contributed by Kristin Trenholm, Shannon Peterson, Chun-Tsung Chin, and Matt Shill. I also thank Linda Speth, Deborah Gessaman, and Cindy Nielsen for their editorial assistance, and Candace Witmer Crist, Cindy Nielsen, Jan Peterson, Kelly Glenn, and Paul Cook for their help in preparing the manuscript.

Research support for this project was provided by the Albert Gallatin Fellowship in International Affairs and the Graduate Institute of International Studies, Geneva, Switzerland, as well as by the Graduate School at Brandeis University. Support for preparation of the book manuscript came from the Milton R. Merrill Endowment and the Department of Political Science at Utah State University.

I am also indebted to the numerous individuals from the GATT Secretariat, the Department of Commerce, and the U.S. Trade Representative's Office whom I interviewed and who provided me with much of the information necessary to complete the research for this project. Finally, I thank my husband, Tod Shenton, for believing in me and expecting the best from me. His encouragement and input were vital to the success of this project.

CAROLYN RHODES

Logan, Utah

1

Reciprocity and Cooperation in Trade

The concept of reciprocity has received considerable attention in U.S. trade relations in recent years. It refers to the maintenance of balance in trading relationships where partners exchange access to the U.S. market for access abroad and establish mutually agreeable rules of fair trade. This notion implies that any perceived imbalance or rule violation may warrant retaliation in a tit-for-tat strategy to maintain balance. A component of U.S. trade policy for decades, reciprocity attracted increasing attention in the 1970s and 1980s, when domestic interests demanded its enforcement and critics decried its restrictionist character.

Perceptions of imbalances in market access, the emerging U.S. trade deficits, and the evident decline in U.S. hegemony contributed to the debate over bilateral reciprocity and over its potential effect on cooperation in the post–World War II trade regime based on the General Agreement on Tariffs and Trade (GATT). Controversy has centered on two general concerns: first, whether the increasingly popular use of reciprocal policies by the United States efficaciously achieved specific trade policy objectives and, second, whether reciprocal policies have enforced or undermined cooperation in the liberal trade regime.

Given these contradictory claims, I launched this study to identify the virtues and shortcomings of reciprocity in U.S. trade policy. First, I aim to define and explore the conceptual and substantive evolution of such reciprocity over the past century in order to

1

establish whether, and in what respects, recent strategies differ from earlier ones. Second, I evaluate reciprocity as a strategy to encourage and enforce trade policy objectives within differing international contexts. Third, I explore the effect that the U.S. use of reciprocity has had on the international trade regime, distinguishing reciprocal policies from unilateral protectionist actions.

Critics of Reciprocity

Critics of reciprocity worry that bilateral expectations of balance and fair trade are too often subjective and too easily abused by protectionist interests. Moreover, maintenance of reciprocity may require retaliation to restore balance to the bilateral trading relationship. This, it is argued, risks catalyzing counterretaliation, which can escalate into feuds between nations and potentially precipitate conflict with other nations, in turn producing detrimental effects on every trading nation by erosion of the collective liberal regime that has facilitated trade cooperation since 1948.[1]

The rationale for this perspective—that retaliation is a protectionist, discriminatory scheme that catalyzes similar protective reactions elsewhere—raises immediate concern that retaliation impedes efficiency and raises consumer prices by utilizing trade-restrictive actions to punish importers. Critics of reciprocal trade policies also fear that unilateral retaliations and enforcement of bilateral balances in trade cause conflict and encourage others to pursue similar trade-restricting arrangements.[2] Anne Krueger, for

---

1. Many economists are concerned that departures from most-favored-nation treatment outside the areas specified by GATT would lead to a spiral of protectionism and economic conflict. See Fritz Leutwiler et al., *Trade Policies for a Better Future: Proposals for Action* (Geneva: GATT Secretariat, 1985); Richard Blackhurst, "The Twilight of Domestic Economic Policies," *World Economy*, December 1981, 357–73; Jan Tumlir, "The Unworkable Reciprocity" (Paper JT/mre/ig prepared for GATT Secretariat 22 March 1982); Keith A. J. Hay and Andrei Sulzenko, "U.S. Policy and 'Reciprocity,'" *Journal of World Trade Law*, November–December 1982, 471–79; R. J. Wonnacott, *Aggressive U.S. Reciprocity* (Montreal: Institute for Research on Public Policy, 1984); and William R. Cline, *Reciprocity: A New Approach to World Trade Policy?* (Washington, D.C.: Institute for International Economics and MIT Press, 1983).

2. Robert E. Baldwin and T. Scott Thompson, "The Appropriate Response to

example, argues that "results-oriented aggressive bilateralism has scope for big disruptions of the international trading system and little potential for enhancing the efficient flow of goods and services in the international economy."[3]

Even as an incentive to induce mutually equivalent trade barrier concessions, reciprocity has been considered a problematic and subjective concept that can justify one nation's bullying another in a bargaining situation, thus breeding resentment, conflict, and trade closure.[4] Therefore, some argue that reciprocity is a counterproductive process that causes counterretaliation and risks a spiral of retaliatory behavior that reduces trade and encourages international conflict.

References to commercial lessons drawn from U.S trade policy during the period between 1880 and 1934, which is well known for its protectionist character, have often been used to support this conclusion. Arguing that reciprocity by its very nature protects and extorts, critics have drawn analogies with this earlier period to demonstrate that reciprocity leads to restrictive trade relations and international conflict.[5]

Proponents of Reciprocity

Proponents of reciprocity, however, contend that appeasing uncooperative behavior encourages bilateral imbalances in market access and free-riding on the GATT regime, which can also have a detrimental effect on the collective interest of international trade cooperation when no other means of effective enforcement exists. As Beth Yarbrough and Robert Yarbrough note, in the absence of punishment "an individual country may gain from 'opportunistic

---

Trade Barriers and 'Unfair' Trade Practices in Other Countries," *American Economic Review* 74 (May 1984): 271.

3. Anne O. Krueger, "Free Trade Is the Best Policy," in Robert Z. Lawrence and Charles L. Schultze, eds., *An American Trade Strategy: Options for the 1990s* (Washington, D.C.: Brookings Institution, 1990), 91.

4. Tumlir, "Unworkable Reciprocity."

5. William Cline, for example, has claimed that congressional proposals to use retaliation to induce trade liberalization by other countries and to punish unfair trade practices are dangerously similar to policies of the pre-1923 period. Cline, *Reciprocity*, 132.

protectionism' by failing to comply with negotiated trade-liber-alizing agreements if other countries continue to comply."[6]

Analysts have argued that this situation characterized the U.S. conditional most-favored-nation practice before 1923 because most of the country's trading partners extended unconditional most-favored-nation treatment while the United States refused equal access to its own market. This allowed the United States to free-ride on the collective provision of unconditional most-favored treatment by its trading partners.[7] David Lake, investigating the relationship between the international system and U.S. domestic pressures for protectionism between 1887 and 1939, discovered that "the opportunity to pursue both protection and export expansion was created by the position of the United States as an opportunist within an international economic structure of British hegemony."[8] According to his view, not until the British system of free trade began to collapse and the United States was expected to reciprocate in its trade policies toward other nations did this country begin to change its free-riding behavior.

In recent years, similar charges have been leveled at Japan for its unwillingness to shoulder a fair share of the burden of maintaining an open global trading system. Analysts, attempting to explain Japan's role in the global economy during the 1980s, have noted that a clear imbalance existed between export opportunities for Japan and import access for other nations to trade with Japan. They have argued that Japan persisted in exploiting the global trading system without altering domestic protectionist practices because no enforcement of liberalization caused behavior change. Until expectations of reciprocity abroad created specific, tangible pressures for liberalization, none was forthcoming.[9]

6. Beth V. Yarbrough and Robert M. Yarbrough, "Reciprocity, Bilateralism, and Economic 'Hostages': Self-enforcing Agreements in International Trade," *International Studies Quarterly* 30 (March 1986): 8.

7. Robert O. Keohane, "Reciprocity in International Relations," *International Organization* 40 (Winter 1986): 17.

8. David Lake, *Power, Protection, and Free Trade: International Sources of U.S. Commercial Strategy, 1887–1939* (Ithaca: Cornell University Press, 1988), 91.

9. One of the more carefully researched studies examines intra-industry

Reciprocity and Cooperation in Trade

Consequently, interest in the value of reciprocity for enforcing cooperative trade relations among U.S. policy-making circles has been a product of recent preoccupation with the "unfair" trade practices of major U.S. trading partners such as Japan and the European Community. Of particular concern has been the issue of whether some nations enjoy international market access without liberalizing their own markets reciprocally, while others, such as the United States, bear a disproportionately high political cost by keeping their own markets relatively open.[10] From this perspective, reciprocity in the form of retaliation plays an important role in enforcing trade agreements and in preventing such free ridership. These concepts have given rise to a new emphasis on reciprocity in U.S. trade policy.

For example, frustration with certain U.S. trade partners that fail to open their markets to U.S. exports fueled retaliatory fervor in Congress in 1988, paving the way for Section 301 trade act provisions, which strengthened the role of retaliation in enforcing

---

trade, demonstrating that Japan, despite its own export dependency, has refused to import at levels expected, given Japan's degree as an advanced industrial nation. This anomalous behavior, as explained by Edward J. Lincoln, *Japan's Unequal Trade* (Washington, D.C.: Brookings Institution, 1990), is attributable to cultural and decision-making characteristics that make liberalization very difficult. Lincoln concludes that persistent pressure must be applied to force liberalization; otherwise, Japan will continue to exploit markets abroad without reciprocally offering import access and will not have reason to change its behavior (see, in particular, 156–61). Kent Calder, who focuses on Japanese domestic institutions and traditional public policy formation, offers similar advice. See Calder, "Japanese Foreign Economic Policy Formation," *World Politics* 40 (July 1988): 528. See also the widely publicized book by Clyde V. Prestowitz, Jr., *Trading Places: How We Allowed Japan to Take the Lead* (New York: Basic Books, 1988). A brief recent appeal for a bilateral approach to trade negotiations with Japan was made by Rudiger W. Dornbusch, "Policy Options for Freer Trade: The Case for Bilateralism," in Lawrence and Schultze, eds., *American Trade Strategy*, 120–25.

10. This rationale is prominent in the omnibus trade bills passed since 1974, especially the so-called Super 301 legislation of the 1988 bill. It also has emerged in books dealing specifically with Japan. See, for example, Prestowitz, *Trading Places*. A more moderate but still supportive view of reciprocity is Lincoln's *Japan's Unequal Trade*, particularly 137. The best brief argument that retaliation can be a useful enforcement tool in American trade policy is Judith L. Goldstein and Stephen D. Krasner, "Unfair Trade Practices: The Case for a Differential Response," *American Economic Review* 74 (May 1984): 282–87.

"a level playing field" for U.S. producers.[11] Aimed primarily at Japan, Section 301 required retaliation against foreign countries whose trade barriers were considered unfair and illiberal but whose own exporters enjoyed asymmetrical access to the U.S. market. By passing this legislation, Congress sent a clear signal that management of U.S. trade relations had become a vital foreign policy goal and that free-riding on U.S. open markets would not be tolerated.[12]

Furthermore, theoretical literature in the field of international relations has suggested that reciprocity may actually encourage cooperative outcomes. Recent contributors who have focused on the value of reciprocity to achieve cooperation in this field argue that in the anarchic setting of world politics, in which self-help characterizes the behavior of sovereign nation-states, the strategy of matching comparable responses to the actions of other nations may over time educate them to cooperate, even in the absence of centralized enforcement. This conclusion is based to a large extent on game theoretic simulations of individual behavior in multiple encounters and on diplomatic lessons drawn by realists in international relations theory who observed the consequences of appeasement policy in the 1930s.[13] These ideas also draw from strategic trade theory and from the political economy of trade

11. Steven R. Phillips, "The New Section 301 of the Omnibus Trade and Competitiveness Act of 1988: Trade Wars or Open Markets?" *Vanderbilt Journal of Transnational Law* 22 (Spring 1989): 522.

12. Ira Wolf, "The Congressional Agenda for Japan," *Cornell University Law Journal* 22 (1989): 514.

13. For the game theoretic approach, see in particular Robert Axelrod, *The Evolution of Cooperation* (New York: Basic Books, 1984); Keohane, "Reciprocity in International Relations," 1–28; and Robert O. Keohane and Robert Axelrod, "Achieving Cooperation under Anarchy," in Kenneth A. Oye, ed., *Cooperation under Anarchy* (Princeton: Princeton University Press, 1985), 226–54 for specific examinations of the value of reciprocity for enforcing cooperation. For the best discussions of the appeasement lessons in security of the 1930s, see Ernest May, *Lessons of the Past* (New York: Oxford University Press, 1973); and Charles Maier, "The Historiography of International Relations," in Michael Kammen, ed., *The Past before Us* (Ithaca: Cornell University Press, 1980). As this applies to deterrence theory, see Anatol Rappaport, "System and Strategic Conflict," in Richard Falks and Saul Mendlovitz, eds., *The Strategy of World Order* (New York: World Law Fund, 1966).

literature, which recognize the value of reciprocity for engineering bilaterally acceptable trade agreements.[14]

These theoretical works indicate that bilateral trade relations are particularly well suited for evaluations of the general proposition that reciprocity may be a useful strategy for eliciting and maintaining cooperation. Because subjects can be chosen for their interdependence and for the likelihood of their continued interaction in the future, such choices enlarge the shadow of the future; each actor thus becomes aware that trading partners may retaliate against uncooperative behavior or may offer benefits when cooperation is secured. As Robert Keohane and Robert Axelrod have noted, in international political economy "retaliation for defection will almost always be possible [because of the interdependent and iterated character of relations in this area], and a rational player, considering defection, has to consider its probability and its potential consequences."[15]

Reciprocity in trade relations, it is argued, may be a partial answer to those who maintain that U.S. hegemonic decline is causing such deterioration in trade relations that destruction of the liberal trading regime seems probable.[16] A more optimistic view is that cooperative outcomes may continue to emerge in such areas as trade, even in the absence of a dominant hegemon, as long as regime norms and reciprocal relations encourage cooperation.[17] Armed with these various arguments for the value of reciprocity in international trade relations, advocates of tit-for-tat strategies directly contradict claims made by classical economists

14. See J. Richard Davidson, "The New Political Economy of Trade Policy," in Paul R. Krugman, ed., *Strategic Trade Policy and the New International Economics* (Cambridge: MIT Press, 1986), 274; and Yarbrough and Yarbrough, "Reciprocity ," 7–21.

15. Keohane and Axelrod, "Achieving Cooperation under Anarchy," 232–33.

16. The arguments of the two dominant hegemonic stability proponents can be found in Charles Kindleberger, "Dominance and Leadership in the International Economy," *International Studies Quarterly* 25 (June 1981): 242–54; and Robert Gilpin, *War and Change in World Politics* (Cambridge: Cambridge University Press, 1981). In the latter, see in particular 201 and 219–20 for the view that interdependence breeds conflict.

17. Robert O. Keohane, *After Hegemony* (Princeton: Princeton University Press, 1984), especially 75–78 and 214.

and multilateral purists that reciprocity creates conflict and risks escalatory trade contraction.

Analysts faced with evaluating the merits of these two lines of argument have had no systematic analysis of the use and effect of reciprocity in past U.S. trade relations to determine which outcome is likely. My book was launched to fill that void, to address empirical shortcomings in this area, and to elucidate the theoretical proposition that reciprocity can be a useful lever for producing cooperative outcomes in trade. To examine the role played by reciprocity in U.S. trade policy in this century, I focus on reciprocity as an instrument of protectionism before 1934, its use as an instrument of liberalism to establish and enforce the new global trading order after 1934, and its dichotomous role in U.S. trade relations since the liberal GATT regime was established. In particular, I examine U.S. bilateral relations to determine the character of reciprocal policies in relation to both protectionist and liberal motives and to determine the effect that reciprocity has had on the GATT regime in these situations. This dynamic will then be examined in the case studies presented in the latter part of the book.

Reciprocity Defined

Reciprocity refers to the maintenance of balance in trading relationships, where access to the domestic market is exchanged for access abroad and mutually agreeable rules of fair trade are established. Inherent in the reciprocal relationship is the expectation that when participants perceive imbalance or violate rules, then retaliation may be warranted to maintain balance.

This definition, although it draws on previous theoretical contributions, refers specifically to trade policy. As Keohane has noted, it assumes that "reciprocity refers to exchanges of roughly equivalent values in which the actions of each party are contingent on the prior actions of the others in such a way that good is returned for good and bad for bad."[18] Approximate equivalence forms a crucial component of reciprocity in trade because in

18. Keohane, "Reciprocity in International Relations," 8.

many situations equivalence cannot be measured and the acceptability of the proposed exchange cannot be predicted. Only in a few situations is equivalence exact and measurable, for example, in certain one-time-only market transactions or in the extension of reciprocal legal rights. Of necessity, equivalence must be recognized as a concept subject to the perceptions and particular requirements of the decision makers involved at a given time. An exchange of equivalent trade concessions, for instance, may be made in mutual good faith, even though the impact of those concessions may vary and occasionally be highly unbalanced.

Key to equivalence in trade relations is the concept that reciprocal treatment is assumed as long as both sides consider the exchange to be equivalent. Only when one side perceives a lack of balance will equivalence again become an issue, and even then the definition of equivalence in negotiations and agreements will result from opinion and domestic pressure rather than from measurement. Consequently, one actor may see his or her actions as reciprocal and retaliatory to redress a malignant imbalance with another actor, whereas the latter may perceive such action as harmful initiative to alter the previous bargain.

The concept of contingency poses similar problems. As in the example above, a government may take retaliatory action which it interprets as appropriate toward another government's wrongful action but which the latter views as nonreciprocal deviation from a cooperative relationship. This ambiguity figures commonly under circumstances in which one side sees itself playing by the rules of the game in a narrow sense while the other side takes a broader view. The trade relationship between the United States and Japan often fits this description. Whereas the Japanese government assumes that its trade surplus results from comparative advantage, the U.S. government argues that Japan's trade surplus may be possible only because Japan has more open access to other nations' markets than they do to Japan's market.[19] Thus, Japan claims fair behavior in its particular trade tactics under the

---

19. Stephen D. Cohen, *Uneasy Partnership: Competition and Conflict in U.S.-Japanese Trade Relations* (Cambridge, Mass.: Ballinger Press, 1985), 36–45. See also Chapter 6 regarding the U.S.-Japanese auto dispute and the larger issue of reciprocity.

GATT framework, whereas the United States claims that an accumulated imbalance has "delegitimized" those tactics.

Because such subjectivity is endemic to international relationships, including trade relationships, investigation of reciprocal strategies relies upon decision makers' perceptions and stated intentions to identify sequences of reciprocal and nonreciprocal actions. At times a specific set of interactions may have more than one interpretation; consequently, case analyses will include critical examinations of the motivations within their operational milieus.

The game theoretical condition of contingency may also present difficulties of interpretation for the actual interaction sequence. Axelrod's reciprocal "tit-for-tat" strategy outlines a "policy of cooperating on the first move and then doing whatever the other player did on the previous move";[20] but this game theoretic model becomes difficult in actual bargaining situations. A general reciprocity policy may at times include nonsequential conciliatory gestures that provide new momentum for stalemated negotiations. Strict tit-for-tat strategy is more likely to deteriorate into a feud. Therefore, if one actor should continue to defect from cooperation contingent upon its partner's continuance, the deadlock may actually be more productively broken by a very different accommodative initiative. This is especially true during periods of active bargaining, when settlement would return the trading partners to a cooperative norm. Thus, contingency becomes not only a logical component of reciprocity but also a broadly considered condition used to identify an overall policy rather than one strictly demanded in every instance for cooperation.

Tracing reciprocity in past U.S. trade relations indicates that decision makers manipulate definitions according to policy orientation. When reciprocity was used as an instrument of protectionist policy, its character and purpose were as trade-restrictive as the policy; used within the context of a liberal trade orientation, however, where internationalist policymakers dominated the foreign policy agenda, it was generally trade expansionary. Expecta-

---

20. Axelrod, *Evolution of Cooperation*, 13.

tions of contingency and equivalence have varied particularly with orientations of the dominant trade policymakers.

Reciprocity in U.S. trade relations before 1934, which was generally narrowly defined for an extremely limited effect, reflected the protectionist orientation of policymakers and explains in part free trade economists' concern about reciprocity in general. When the United States used reciprocity as a strategy before passage of the Reciprocal Trade Agreements Act, attitudes toward equivalence and contingency were based on extortionary expectations and nationalistic protectionism, not on mutual benefit and trade expansion. Other nations were unable to thwart the U.S. ability to extort preferential agreements under a reciprocal guise. Because it had developed no expectation that other nations would pursue reciprocal policies as well, the United States ignored such costs and benefits. Consequently, the few reciprocal trade agreements attempted were highly restrictive and coercive, reflecting the dominant view that U.S. manufacturing should not be subjected to foreign competition and that only very limited access to the U.S. market would be available in exchange for export markets abroad.

Keohane's definition of reciprocity—where balance, contingency, and interdependent relations are requisite—did not emerge in U.S. trade relations until internationalist officials and liberal economists successfully convinced the U.S. Congress in 1934 to reconsider protectionism. The visible consequences of U.S. restrictive trade policies, in the form of international retaliation against the Hawley-Smoot Tariff of 1930, as well as the depth of the Great Depression, proved to even the most die-hard protectionists that a more responsible, interdependent role was essential to economic well-being. Proponents based this new approach on the belief that free trade encourages economic growth at home and abroad and that reciprocally beneficial agreements, multilateralized by the unconditional most-favored-nation-treatment principle, would best achieve trade expansion. In chapters 2 and 3 I examine the evolution of U.S. trade policy through this period and compare the uses of reciprocity in the pre- and post-liberal eras.

Moreover, when the norm of free trade was not enough to ensure commitment to liberalism if adherence conflicted with other interests, fear of retaliation created a strong incentive for cooperative behavior. Negotiated under U.S. leadership in 1948, the GATT embodied the principles of most-favored-nation treatment and reciprocity, thus coupling the new liberal trading order with the reciprocity concept. As expectations of member states converged around these GATT norms, this liberal context, along with expectations of bilateral reciprocity, continued to influence trade policy decisions.

Consequently, the GATT embodies reciprocity as an *end* in the form of mutual benefit, where signatory nations expect equivalent treatment abroad for their producers in exchange for what they offer to other nations' producers; yet reciprocity also exists as a *means* to enforce balanced treatment and mutual benefit. When a nation fails to adhere to the GATT trade rules, other nations adversely affected by that behavior may retaliate to restore the relationship's balance. By the 1970s, pressure on U.S. hegemony placed new emphasis on reciprocity; protection of sovereign interests in balanced and fair treatment became even more important in enforcing trade agreements.

Cooperation, Regime Enforcement, and Regime Change

Explaining reciprocity's role in bilateral cooperation, particularly under the GATT regime, is a central goal of this book, in which I examine how reciprocal policies affect trading partners' immediate cooperation, as well as how reciprocal policies affect the larger trade regime. Crucial to an understanding of the causal relationship between reciprocity and cooperation generally and between reciprocity and the specific type of emergent cooperation, moreover, is how rules and norms governing reciprocity affect the expectations of trading partners and how departures from those expectations affect cooperative responses. Therefore, it is essential that cooperation be defined and understood within this context.

Cooperation under the GATT takes two forms. The first, which is most often associated with the GATT, involves institution and maintenance of liberal trade policies, whereas the second concerns compensation of GATT trading partners that experience illiberal actions. The cooperative ideal is collective trade liberalization by members in pursuit of their common well-being as defined by the GATT's normative framework; but individual nations that cannot maintain cooperative commitment to liberal trade must expect to compensate their injured partners. If compensation is not forthcoming or is considered inadequate, contracting members have the right under specific circumstances to take retaliatory action, which I discuss in detail in Chapter 4.

Inherent in GATT cooperation is the idea that members are expected to recognize the liberalizing efforts of their counterparts and to reciprocate. When disputes arise over equivalence of reciprocity or over new illiberal or illegal actions, parties are expected to negotiate a mutually acceptable settlement or to defer to previously negotiated guidelines for compensation. Most disputes are settled bilaterally to the common satisfaction of the nations involved, which makes it unnecessary to refer the dispute to the GATT contracting parties for collective recommendation. The GATT, which recognizes that disputants must both be satisfied before the matter can be practically resolved, encourages bilateral settlement.

It is very important to note, however, that cooperation between the United States and its trading partners has often taken the form of collusive arrangements aimed at maintaining acceptable mutual benefits via mechanisms that lie outside the GATT framework; voluntary export restraint agreements are cases in point. Although the overarching GATT regime influenced actors to resist trade closure and deeper conflict when protectionist or retaliatory impulses were strong, it did not prevent them from pursuing mutually accommodative arrangements that contradicted the GATT principles of nondiscrimination and free trade. This phenomenon has strongly pressured against strict interpretation of the nondiscrimination principle in the GATT, favoring bilaterally agreeable trade flows instead.

It is also important to understand the nature of cooperation as it evolved during this century. Before 1934, U.S. trade strategies differed from those after 1934 in the types of cooperative responses expected. In the earlier period, brief forays into international trade negotiations were characterized by protectionist-driven coercive strategies that were designed to obtain specific concessions for U.S. traders in exchange for limited access for noncompeting goods into the U.S. market.[21] Cooperative outcomes of these negotiations may or may not have provided a degree of mutual benefit, but even if so they were weighted heavily in favor of the United States. Had Congress approved them, these agreements would have had virtually no effect on liberalization of the U.S. market. Protectionism, coupled with a desire for access to certain foreign markets, drove trade policy before 1934.

Contingency was a very important requisite for limited U.S. cooperation, but equivalence was clearly distorted by U.S. protectionist preferences as well as the asymmetry of U.S. coercive power in comparison with that of its negotiation partners. In addition, the general U.S. orientation toward trade was autarky, and interest in trade expansion was just beginning to emerge. U.S. coercive protectionism effectively produced agreements to secure cooperation with U.S. policies; that cooperation, however, was not based on genuine expectations of mutual benefit but on U.S. dominance in compelling trading partners to accommodate. This form of cooperation, which can be characterized as *capitulation*, was the primary form of trade cooperation with the United States before 1934 and still occurs to some extent in the post-GATT period.

After 1934 the United States adopted a liberal reciprocal strategy that reflected an entirely different set of norms, including international cooperation, trade expansion, and even limited import liberalization. This contextual shift figured vitally in explaining why reciprocal policies after 1934 were characterized by expectations of mutual benefit and trade expansion rather than by autarky and coercive protectionism. These expectations, institutionalized in the GATT regime in 1948, generally affected the character of subsequent negotiations and dispute settlement. Cooperative outcomes often reflected these governing principles and

21. Noncompeting in this sense refers to goods that the United States either did not manufacture or did not consider a threat to key domestic industries.

rules, with equivalent mutual benefit as the overriding expectation.

Because the GATT tangibly reflects normative expectations for cooperation between major participants, GATT norms play a significant role in bilateral trade relations. Because reciprocity requires participants to be "nice" as well as "forgiving," the context of trade interactions becomes very important to understanding expectations of the GATT trading partners.[22] If all actors were to prefer autarky, then reciprocity would neither injure nor benefit others.

Where there are high potentials for future interactions and where expectations of actor behavior are defined by regime norms, short-term interests will be weighed against long-term interests, taking punishment or reward into account. Definitions about what constitutes cooperation and noncooperation, along with decisions to cooperate or not, are influenced by regime norms and rules as well as by each actor's perception of mutual vulnerabilities and interests immediately and over time.

Reciprocal responses could be mutual concessions aimed at trade expansion or retaliatory actions aimed at establishing (or reestablishing) a relationship based on mutual benefit. Thus the cooperative outcome within this particular context would be characterized by *fair mutual benefit* because both sides' expectations are governed by the established regime. When mutual benefit is the outcome but departs from regime rules, then cooperation becomes *collusion* against the established regime in favor of bilateral accommodation. Although bilaterally acceptable forms of cooperation, collusive arrangements may undermine general normative expectations as established under the GATT. Dispute settlements that provide bilateral management of trade shares, such as voluntary export restraint agreements, fall into this category. Their cooperative character and political attractiveness mean that collusive arrangements have proliferated, challenging regime rules about fair trade practices and nondiscrimination.

Finally, capitulation and collusion may result from reciprocal policies but also from coercive protectionism, given the tremen-

22. Axelrod, *Evolution of Cooperation*, 13.

dous U.S. leverage because of its consumer market and relative openness under the GATT regime. This raises an interesting analytical challenge: do differences in coercive enforcement strategies matter within the same regime context? And when regime contexts differ, do outcomes vary? Case studies in the latter part of this book provide empirical information to match strategies with outcomes within particular contextual settings to determine these answers. Clearly, cooperation takes different forms depending on the dispute context (regime as well as sectoral pressures), on trading partners' reactions, and on the strategies employed. Although asymmetry in the trading relationship affects strategies and outcomes, this alone cannot explain the presence or absence of cooperative outcomes or the form of cooperation produced.

Case Studies and Methodology

To identify and evaluate the effect that reciprocal policies have had in recent U.S. trade relations, I have developed a set of cases that focus on bilateral trading relationships for the United States and its three largest trading partners—Canada, Japan, and the European Community—between 1964 and 1985. I chose these trading relationships for suitability in meeting Keohane's theoretical conditions as outlined above. In addition to their two-way importance in U.S. trade and, therefore, the likelihood that these actors will continue to interact with the United States, these nations represent various interdependent relationships with the United States and different degrees of relative economic power.[23] A variety of bargaining circumstances allows focus on reciprocity's role in the interaction process across a range of relationships.

In determining how U.S. reciprocal policies have affected bilateral trade relations and how these have in turn affected the GATT regime, comparisons across these different relationships are useful. The degree and symmetry of interdependence between the United States and these three respective trade partners vary with each bilateral relationship, making possible comparisons that iso-

23. See Table 1.

16

Reciprocity and Cooperation in Trade

Table 1. Top three purchasers of U.S. exports and suppliers of U.S. imports in 1985

	Amount (millions of U.S. dollars)
Purchasers of U.S. exports[a]	
Canada	47,251
European Community	45,777
Japan	22,631
Suppliers of U.S. imports[b]	
Japan	72,380
Canada	69,427
European Community	67,818

[a]Exports = domestic and foreign merchandise, FAS (fee alongside ship).
[b]Imports = general imports, CIF (costs, insurance, freight).
Source. U.S. Department of Commerce, International Trade Administration, *1985 Foreign Trade Statistics* (Washington, D.C., 1986).

late from other factors the role played by reciprocity in dispute settlement and trade maintenance.

Although all these partners experience vulnerability to U.S. retaliatory threats, the depth of that vulnerability and the capability to exploit U.S. vulnerabilities differ. Variations in the use of counterreciprocal strategies help account for the ranges of emerging cooperation.

I selected industrialized long-term contracting parties to the GATT because they are governed by the same set of norms and rules (some exceptions exist for less-developed countries) and because they are highly integrated in the world political economy. This shared set of circumstances indicates a more consistent context for cooperation across relationships as well as expectations of continued interaction.

I made some effort to hold constant the sectors where these bilateral disputes emerged so that U.S. trade disputes with Canada, Japan, and the European Community (E.C.) are compared and contrasted within one sector whenever possible. I selected three different sectors—steel, automobiles, and wheat flour—because each has been characterized by fierce competition, strong domestic pressures to protect market interests, and charges of unfair trade against competitors.

Each sector contains sets of individual disputes that form the units of analysis for the comparative case study. Although the sectoral trade relationship may still be punctuated with discord, the bargaining and settlement of these encapsulated disputes provide a variety of different cases for comparative analysis.

Generally, the United States, Canada, Japan, and the European Community are treated as individual and rational unitary actors for the sake of abstraction and comparison. I give the decision-making process in the United States more detailed treatment, however, to demonstrate that decision makers often mediated conflicts between domestic interest groups and foreign interests and then modified national policies in reaction to foreign threats of retaliation. In the trade area, where many domestic actors and institutional arrangements compete with foreign interests for sympathetic decisions, policy making balances domestic demands against external factors. The general focus of this analysis, though, is on the bargaining dynamic that emerges between the United States and its trading partners rather than on that between the U.S. executive branch and domestic interest groups.

In each of these sectors, the United States attempted to use reciprocal policies to enforce GATT norms. What motivated these policies was the desire to maintain or initiate a bilateral relationship based on mutual benefit and balanced treatment when the trading partner's action threatened the U.S. position, which in turn opened the United States to reciprocal policies for similar ends. The resulting interactions and bargaining outcomes provide rich material to compare and evaluate the character and effect of reciprocity in U.S. bilateral trade relations.

What complicates the study is that the United States also pursued unilateral protectionist policies within two of the three sectors aimed not at enforcing fair trade rules but at securing a more comfortable position for domestic producers. Thus, the historical examination of sectoral trade disputes must distinguish between such unilateral protectionist actions and retaliation to untangle the web of interactions and bargaining dynamics from these different bilateral relationships. Specifically, in this book I determine what constitutes reciprocal actions and under what circumstances reciprocity does and does not prove useful in eliciting cooperative outcomes. I also analyze the role the GATT regime played in delineating acceptable bilateral outcomes and, in turn, the effect that reciprocal policies have on the GATT regime itself.

To accomplish this, I examine bilateral disputes in these three sectors, where departures from expected norms of behavior catalyzed international reactions, causing conflict between the United States and its three largest trading partners. The actions taken, both reciprocal and nonreciprocal, along with the outcomes, characterize emerging reciprocal policies in bilateral relationships across trade sectors. The cases not only specify circumstances under which reciprocal strategies and tactics emerge but also provide comparative information to distinguish U.S. reciprocal strategies from unilateral coercive protectionism. They also supply comparative information on whether the international context, including certain norms and rules, affects dispute outcomes in general and the efficacy of reciprocity as an enforcement strategy in particular.

This comparative case study approach then allows us to examine the broader effect that reciprocal policies have on the international trade regime. Has reciprocity enforced and confirmed the GATT norms or departed from and undermined them? Is the trend across sectors and bilateral relationships so evident that we can see the regime changing in a clearly discernible way? Does this change confirm the traditional free trade economists' bias against reciprocity or the political economists' view, or does it lie somewhere between them? This case study approach, which not only compares bilateral disputes in differing circumstances but also compares the policies and outcomes that emerge in the sectoral cases with the pre-1934 period in U.S. trade policy history, provides preliminary answers to these questions.

The case studies in Chapters 5, 6, and 7, combined with the historical treatment of U.S. trade policy from general protectionism to general liberalism in Chapters 2 and 3, allow evaluation of these more recent processes and outcomes as measured against pre-1934 and post-1934 trends and expectations. Chapter 4 buttresses analysis of GATT norms and member-state expectations, bridging both periods, to deepen understanding of the evolution of reciprocity in U.S. trade policy during the past century; facilitates critical assessment of its virtues and shortcomings as a trade strategy that achieves cooperation; and provides better insight into the interrelationship between reciprocal policies and regime context that determines the production and character of cooperative outcomes. We can then evaluate the effect that these outcomes have actually had on the trade regime.

This book is divided into two parts, the first of which examines reciprocity in U.S. trade relations before and after passage of the 1934 Reciprocal Trade Agreements Act. Chapter 2 analyzes the most restrictive era in U.S. trade history, 1885 to 1934, and determines that protectionism, not reciprocity, caused trade restrictions and bilateral conflict. Chapter 3 reviews changes with regard to reciprocity in the 1934 act and explains the crucial nature of the new liberal role for reciprocity to the success of the new trade program. This chapter also demonstrates that norms embodied in the act were incorporated in the GATT in 1948, including reciprocity as well as liberalism and most-favored-nation treatment. Chapter 4 describes how these dichotomous principles facilitated trade liberalization and cooperation under the GATT but also created pressures for bilateral collusion over nondiscriminatory multilateralism.

The second part of the book employs case studies. Chapter 5 focuses on steel trade relations, providing the richest set of cross-national comparisons. Chapter 6 traces bilateral dispute settlement in the automobile sector. This sectoral comparison is crucial in illustrating that a weaker nation can effectively utilize coercive and reciprocal strategies against a much stronger nation when market access is at stake. Chapter 7 examines bilateral conflict in wheat flour trade, where outcomes have proven very different from those produced by similar strategies in other sectors. This contrast provides a useful perspective on factors that make reciprocity a fruitful strategy. Chapter 8 then summarizes the comparisons of the pre-1934 period in U.S. trade policy with the later period, reviews the results of the case material, and compares strategies with outcomes to finally assess the virtues and shortcomings of reciprocity in trade.

2

Liberal Lore: Experience and Myth about Reciprocity, 1880–1933

Reciprocity in U.S. trade policy has historically been associated with protectionism and "fair trade." Before the 1934 reciprocal Trade Agreements Act passed, reciprocity had been used as an instrument of mercantilism. Even when multilateral liberalized trade became the foreign policy goal of the United States in 1934, reciprocity was retained as a means of bilaterally enforcing fair trade.[1] In recent years the principle has become prominent in U.S. trade policy as anti-dumping and countervailing duty suits have proliferated and congressional measures have increasingly stressed the expectation of reciprocity in particular bilateral trading relationships. Critics of this renewed emphasis on reciprocity warn that such practices threaten to plunge the United States into a new era of protectionism.

The history on which current analogies are based is poorly un-

---

1. Judith Goldstein usefully explains that the U.S. commitment to liberal trade after 1934 was coupled with a tradition of fair trade that encouraged state intervention to protect domestic industry from the "unfair" trading practices of foreign competitors. Goldstein, "Ideas, Institutions, and American Trade Policy," in G. John Ikenberry et al., eds., *The State and American Foreign Economic Policy* (Ithaca: Cornell University Press, 1988), 179–217. See also Beth V. Yarbrough and Robert M. Yarbrough, "Reciprocity, Bilateralism, and Economic 'Hostages': Self-enforcing Agreements in International Trade," *International Studies Quarterly* 30 (March 1986): 7–21. Thus U.S. trade policy couples liberal actions with bilateral mechanisms for enforcement and compensation. See Chapter 4.

derstood. The view prevailing among liberal economists about the period between 1880 and 1934 has been that experiments with reciprocity were abysmal failures; current directions in U.S. trade policy risk the same counterproductive consequences. These analysts, however, confuse the condition of reciprocity, which is an instrument of trade policy, with antiliberalism, which is a normative framework shaping the intent and purpose of trade policy.

Although liberalism, coupled with reciprocity, has generally guided U.S. trade policy since 1934 (with the exception of trade in the agricultural sector), earlier policy was flatly protectionist regardless of the instruments used. Protectionist sentiments and powerful protectionist interests undermined what limited efforts were made to link reciprocity and the reduction of the U.S. tariff. Whenever liberal reforms were advanced, whether as "reciprocity" or as "unconditional most-favored-nation treatment," the prevailing antiliberal view predominated.

Before 1934 a highly protectionist set of norms and beliefs yielded rules and policy actions that restricted imports and extorted export concessions from other nations, with little genuine regard for reciprocity. Even when the principle of most-favored-nation treatment was adopted in 1922 and hailed as a major advance in the trade relations of the United States, Congress retained its commitment to protectionism with one of the most restrictive tariff systems in its history. Only after the even more restrictive Hawley-Smoot Tariff in 1930 had provoked debilitating retaliation did an earnest experiment with reciprocity emerge.

In this chapter I trace the development of U.S. trade policy during this protectionist era. I focus in particular on debates between Democrats, who wanted to expand U.S. trade on a mutually beneficial basis with trading partners, and Republicans, who wanted to expand U.S. exports without risking new imports. Paradoxically, it was the Republican party that advanced the argument for reciprocal trade negotiations, but only as a means to extort concessions abroad without liberalizing in return. As we shall see, this manipulation of the concept of reciprocity to fit the protectionist designs of the Republican party has resulted in reciprocity's becoming associated with protectionism.

22

Reciprocity as an Instrument of Protectionism, 1880–1912

The most prominent early analyses of U.S. trade policy from 1880 to 1912 claimed that reciprocity, where trading arrangements are negotiated bilaterally on a reciprocal and exclusive basis, characterized American trade relations. Much of what is known about U.S. trade of the period has been drawn from these descriptions, which identified reciprocity as a limited, mutually acceptable effort to reach particular bilateral agreements on import liberalization. Critical of a mode of trade negotiation that is necessarily discriminatory and subjective, these analysts cited U.S. experiments with reciprocity to prove their case.[2] It is not the discriminatory and subjective nature of substantive reciprocity to which this historical examination takes exception, however, but the view that U.S. policy was based on reciprocity in the first place. Analysis of the character and outcome of the tariff acts of the period (see Table 2) shows that Congress rigidly held to an autonomous tariff policy, even when claims of reciprocity were made.

Before 1890, seven so-called reciprocal trade agreements were negotiated between the United States and other nations. Only two went into effect because Congress failed to ratify the others after agreements were reached.[3] The bills empowering the executive branch to enter into these reciprocal trade negotiations were, for the most part, highly protectionist measures aimed at reducing tariffs on U.S. goods exported abroad but offering few if any real concessions on foreign imports.

Under the Republican administration of President Chester Arthur, U.S. agricultural exports had declined by more than one-half

2. Hugh O. Davis, *America's Trade Equality Policy* (Washington, D.C.: American Council on Public Affairs, 1942), 16–17; and Henry J. Tasca, *The Reciprocal Trade Policy of the United States: A Study in Trade Philosophy* (Philadelphia: University of Pennsylvania Press, 1938), 101–2.

3. The exceptions were Canada in 1854, Hawaii in 1875, and a minor agreement with Spain for Cuba and Puerto Rico from 1883 to 1892. United States Tariff Commission, *Reciprocity and Commercial Treaties* (Washington, D.C., 1919), 21.

Reciprocity, U.S. Trade Policy, and the GATT Regime

Table 2. Major trade acts, 1880–1933

Act	Outcome
Trade Act, 1883: By all accounts "innocuous."	Maintained high levels of protection autonomously.
McKinley Tariff, 1890: Retaliatory punitive duties on key specified items unless acceptable concessions on U.S. exports made. Otherwise, all duty rates set autonomously by Congress.	Ten agreements completed.
Wilson-Gorman Act, 1894: Lowered tariff but abrogated agreements made under McKinley Tariff because of autonomous change in treatment of sugar imports.	McKinley Tariff agreements abrogated.
Dingley Tariff, 1897: Specified terms for limited reciprocal agreements exchanging duty reductions on argols, wines, statuary, and sugar for equivalent market access abroad. *Agreements limited in scope and economic effect.* Also set terms for future reciprocal negotiations on limited list of items.	No agreements resulted from reciprocal negotiations.
Payne-Aldrich Act, 1909: Dual tariff rates for favored and unfavored nations autonomously determined. Bilateral negotiations for nomination to one category or the other.	Resulted in all trading partners being placed on favored list, but all duty rates high.
U.S.-Canada Reciprocity Agreement, 1911: Limited reciprocity.	Voided by Canadian Parliament.
Underwood Tariff, 1913: Single tariff schedule somewhat liberalized. Reciprocal negotiations authorized.	No agreements resulted.
Fordney-McCumber Tariff, 1922: *Rejected reciprocity*, raised tariff autonomously, adopted *unconditional most-favored-nation* treatment, and specified special penalty duties for unfair trade.	Highly restrictive.
Hawley-Smoot Tariff, 1930: Raised tariff autonomously and added quotas.	Catalyzed global retaliation.

between 1879 and 1885. This precipitous decline was due to both the erection of foreign tariffs and mounting competition from abroad.[4] Consequently, President Arthur and his secretary of state, Frederick Theodore Frelinghuysen, sought negotiations that would lower barriers to U.S. agricultural products. Mindful, however, of an important constituency among industrial and investment sectors, they also sought reduced duties on exported manufactured goods and freer importation of goods in which U.S. investors held significant interests.

Their goal of expanding trade—particularly with Latin America—became increasingly manufacture-oriented, and as negotiations progressed the United States bargained with the offer of lower duties on certain farm products in exchange for reduced duties on U.S.-produced machinery. The aim of the Arthur administration was clearly to expand exports for U.S. products without offering in return access to the U.S. market that would put politically significant producers in competition with cheaper foreign goods. For example, the Mexican treaty, which was negotiated in 1882, put on the U.S. duty-free list only agricultural goods, and of these only a few items were products in which there was no significant U.S. investment in Mexico.

This pattern of lowering tariffs only on goods produced by U.S. investors abroad was true as well for the Cuban negotiations. The United States pursued reduced duties on U.S. flour and manufactured goods exported to Cuba and in return offered to put sugar on the duty-free list. As much of Cuban sugar production was American-dominated, this lower duty benefited the powerful sugar trust in the United States, although it put western beet sugar producers at a disadvantage.

In addition, the Arthur administration's approach to trade was characterized by a determination to make all negotiations strictly reciprocal and bilateral. There was much concern at the time that any concessions made to secure reduced tariffs abroad would be extended to third parties via the conditional most-favored-nation

4. Tom E. Terrill, *The Tariff, Politics, and American Foreign Policy, 1874–1901* (Westport, Conn.: Greenwood, 1973), 72–73, 79, 81.

clause in U.S. commercial treaties. Past practice with regard to this clause indicated that such fears were unfounded. Nevertheless, Congress insisted that the United States ensure that no concession be offered third-party states as a result of bilateral negotiations. Inserting the conditional clause in all the reciprocal treaties guaranteed that concessions would not be applied to other nations, regardless of their status, unless they met particular conditions set by the United States.

Despite the caution exhibited in these commercial arrangements, Congress still refused to ratify the agreements completed under President Arthur. Trade stagnated, and U.S. agriculture remained in serious trouble due to market surplus. The piecemeal approach to trade expansion had not lowered the general level of the tariff, and failure of even these minor efforts to gain congressional approval indicated that the United States wanted to benefit from expanded markets without incurring any costs of competition.[5] An 1884 bill to lower the tariff was soundly defeated by the Republicans, who controlled the Senate, along with an active minority of Democrats, who feared that tariff reduction would damage important sectors of their constituencies.

Grover Cleveland's election in 1884 brought a Democratic administration to the White House. The Senate remained in Republican hands and the House under Democratic leadership, as it had been during the Arthur administration. The protectionist faction within the Democratic party remained strong, but the recent "boom-bust" pattern in the U.S. economy led both Republicans and Democrats to conclude, as David Lake states, that the "United States urgently needed to expand its foreign trade in order to have continuous prosperity. Like many of their contemporaries, these politicians assumed that such economic expansion would naturally occur. However, important leaders and factions

5. The United States is well presented as a free rider on the world trading system by David Lake, who begins his analysis in 1887 but whose logic applies generally to the period from 1880 onward. See Lake, *Power, Protection, and Free Trade: International Sources of U.S. Commercial Strategy, 1887–1939* (Ithaca: Cornell University Press, 1988), particularly 91–118.

in both parties began to link the U.S. tariff to an enlarged foreign market."[6]

President Cleveland, recognizing the potential of this change of heart, pressed for a general reduction of the U.S. tariff. In 1887 in his annual message before Congress, he urged lowering duties, particularly on raw materials.[7] He grounded his reasoning in the belief that if the U.S. manufacturer could obtain the required raw materials at the cheapest possible price, the finished product would be more competitive abroad. "Thus," Cleveland argued, "our people might have the opportunity of extending their sales beyond the limits of home consumption, saving them from the depression, interruption in business, and loss caused by a glutted domestic market and affording their employees more certain and steady labor, with its resulting quiet and contentment."[8]

This "free trade" outlook departed significantly from the narrow approach of the previous administration. President Cleveland was not simply arguing that the United States needed more exports and thus that foreign trade barriers be reduced. He was advocating that the country reduce its own tariff to secure the most competitive supply of raw materials for U.S. industry. Manufacturers would benefit by comparative advantage in producing the most competitive finished product as long as export markets were also available.

By adapting this liberal position to the general philosophy of trade reciprocity, the head of the House Ways and Means Committee in 1888 offered a bill to lower the tariff and increase foreign trade. Unlike Cleveland's message, which touted only the benefits of securing for U.S. industry low-cost raw materials, this bill acknowledged that if other countries were to buy U.S. products, the United States would have to buy others' goods, which was especially important for U.S. farmers, who sought export markets. If Europeans were to buy large amounts of American farm produce and thus ease the American surplus, they would

6. Ibid., 10–11.
7. F. W. Taussig, *Free Trade, the Tariff, and Reciprocity* (New York: Macmillan, 1972), 253.
8. Grover Cleveland, as quoted in Terrill, *Tariff*, 96–97.

have to sell more manufactured goods to the United States. As President Cleveland observed, "They could not do this unless the United States lowered its tariff wall."[9]

This viewpoint allowed that trade flourished if reciprocated and that the process involved increasing imports as well as exports. Foreign buyers would be more likely to purchase U.S. goods that competed on the world market if Americans facilitated such purchases through willingness to buy abroad. In all likelihood, the one would follow the other as long as Americans manufactured products in the most efficient manner. Thus, President Cleveland's planned reduction of the tariff on raw materials persuaded others of this position.

Unfortunately for the advocates of trade liberalization via reciprocity, the so-called Mills Bill failed in Congress. The upcoming election that fall again placed the tariff issue before the public eye, and hard-core Republican protectionists raised the threat of free trade to domestic industry to gain voter loyalty. In need of an issue to discredit the Cleveland administration, Republicans rallied support within their own ranks to defeat the 1888 bill. Those who had previously believed that expanded trade would ensure greater prosperity returned to the more familiar belief that only export expansion, not genuine reciprocity, should be the responsibility of U.S. trade policy.

Fears of a flood of cheap foreign goods that would threaten business profits and jobs led to congressional defeat of the Mills Bill and to Cleveland's demise in the November elections. Although the strictly bilateral and special reciprocal trade agreement with Hawaii was renewed in 1887, Congress passed no further measures to facilitate trade in the ten years preceding the McKinley Tariff of 1890. Interpreting their 1888 victory as a mandate for erection of a new protective tariff, Republicans began work on legislation. Senator William McKinley, whose name would soon be synonymous with one of the most restrictive tariffs in American history, took the lead.

Initially, McKinley wanted to limit his tariff legislation to an autonomous new tariff that would not be subject to negotiation

9. Ibid., 128.

with America's trading partners. But Secretary of State James G. Blaine, an ardent protectionist as well as an enthusiastic advocate of export expansion, convinced the president to insert a clause that enabled the executive to negotiate the reduction of barriers to U.S. exports with some flexibility. Blaine maintained that only through case-by-case "reciprocal" negotiations could the United States expand overseas trade without making concessions on duties at home that might injure domestic producers.[10]

Blaine and President Benjamin Harrison agreed that the best way to open foreign markets to U.S. goods was through tactical bargaining with each country. Particularly concerned about the influx of products from Latin America on a duty-free basis, President Harrison wanted to maintain flexibility in his negotiations to persuade the governments of these neighbors to reduce duties on U.S. products. The rationale was that unless the United States retained some leverage, these countries would have no incentive to reduce trade restrictions.

The resulting congressional bill featured the following provisions. Certain items, including sugar, coffee, molasses, tea, and hides, would be put on the duty-free list. The president, however, had the authority to impose *retaliatory penalties* on these items "whenever he found that countries producing and exporting said articles to the United States imposed duties upon the products of the United States which, in view of the free introduction of such products into the United States, he deemed to be reciprocally unequal and unreasonable."[11] According to this provision, the president would proclaim that the other nation's policies were unequal and unreasonable. He would then insist on immediate suspension of duty-free access to the products listed above and authorize the duties levied according to a schedule prescribed by Congress.[12]

This method of reciprocal bargaining differed from that which the president hoped to employ and from that which was usually associated with substantive bilateralism. Instead of authorizing the president to negotiate tariff reductions abroad for the United

10. Ibid., 161–62, 164.
11. Ibid., 156.
12. Taussig, *Free Trade, the Tariff, and Reciprocity*, 120–21.

States through concessions of a similar nature, it autonomously determined the tariff and duty-free items and then empowered the president to revoke any unilateral concessions whenever a trading partner discriminated against the United States or failed to offer concessions in return.

The imposition of retaliatory punitive duties on items otherwise placed on the duty-free list, rather than the offer to reduce existing duties, secured a higher degree of U.S. autonomy and allowed the United States to retain its protectionist profile. No new penetration of the tariff was allowed, thus any changes resulting from the schedule of duties could be only more restrictive, not less so. Moreover, no new concessions on the part of the United States would occur as a result of bilateral negotiation. Unless Congress designed a new tariff policy, no nation could enter into tariff reduction negotiations. Congress had retained its position to set the tariff and the rules governing U. S. trade unilaterally. Significantly, Congress also provided for imposition of countervailing duties against subsidized imports whose purpose was to evade the tariff's exclusionary effect.[13]

The 1890 McKinley Tariff clearly demonstrates the clash between the desire for exports and the zealous commitment to protection from imports within the policy-making community. The debate leading to passage of this approach is convincing evidence of a shift in policymakers' attitudes about the U.S. position in international commerce. The United States was increasingly seen as an internationally interdependent economy, not simply in terms of vulnerability to competition from abroad but also in terms of desirability of markets beyond U.S. borders. Even protectionists such as Blaine realized that growth and prosperity at home were intrinsically linked to expanding markets, but they sought expansion in the purchasing potential of other countries even as they refused to allow influential domestic industries to suffer from competition.

---

13. Peter Buck Feller, "Mutiny against the Bounty: An Examination of Subsidies, Border Tax Adjustments, and the Resurgence of the Countervailing Duty Law," *Law and Policy in International Business* 1 (1969): 17–18.

Protectionists believed that the United States should compete outside its borders but that this could best be accomplished if the U.S. government secured for its manufacturers an umbrella of protective arrangements abroad while insulating them from competition at home. Blaine himself argued that *reciprocity* in international trade was the logical extension of *protective* policy when a country needed larger markets for its production. According to Blaine: "The enactment of reciprocity . . . is the safeguard of protection. The defeat of reciprocity is the opportunity of free trade."[14]

Under such a policy, every concession in a duty at the frontier, though unilaterally predetermined by Congress, paid in kind for an equivalent concession made elsewhere. Because U.S. commercial strategists carefully determined which items could be admitted duty-free under the watchful eye of Congress without harm to significant interest groups, reciprocal negotiations extended protection of U.S. industry exports abroad without placing U.S. industry in direct competition for its own home market. Even so, sufficient congressional members could not bring themselves to give the president authority to negotiate any new duty reductions. They recognized the need for expanded trade but rejected the method proposed by Blaine and Harrison for achieving such expansion. Despite Blaine's assurances, the die-hard traditionalists in Congress believed that the path of *reciprocity* actually risked closer ties to *freer trade* and to the loss of congressional autonomy. Their solution took the form of coercive retaliation written into the final version of the McKinley Bill.

This approach in the McKinley Tariff had mixed results. Because certain nations that had been asked by the United States to negotiate their tariffs—Colombia, Venezuela, and Haiti—had "failed to satisfactorily respond," the United States initiated penalty duties against their products. These retaliatory duties resulted in a marked decrease in imports from these countries, whereas imports from the reciprocity countries benefited. Moreover, "exports from the United States to the reciprocity states, favored by special reductions of duty, showed a substantial increase." Charges of unfairness were predictably leveled, however, the non-

14. Terrill, *Tariff*, 168.

reciprocating nations considered their punishment discriminatorily applied because "several other countries, producers of the specified articles, conspicuously the Argentine and Mexico, failed to conclude agreements, but the penalty duties were not imposed on them."[15] Inconsistency constituted the most troublesome flaw in even this limited plan for reciprocity, and the legislation's enforcement was undermined by its administration.

Rather than deal directly with the advantages and disadvantages of reciprocity under the McKinley Tariff, the new administration that was elected in 1892, again under the leadership of President Cleveland, chose to discard reciprocity altogether as a general approach to trade. According to Asher Isaacs, "The Democratic position was that the McKinley reciprocity policy was 'in intention and effect' not for reciprocity but for retaliation, [and] that it provoked ill feeling in countries discriminated against."[16] Under direction from the White House to revise the tariff downward, Congress passed the Wilson-Gorman Act of 1894, which modestly reduced the general level of duties to just less than 40 percent (from about 49.5 percent under the 1890 tariff). It also abrogated the McKinley Tariff reciprocity agreements, however, by unilaterally removing sugar from the duty-free list.[17]

Cleveland had wanted to keep sugar on the free list but to do away with the punitive nature of the reciprocal policy. Thus the Democratic administration could honor existing treaties but avoid the strict negative form of reciprocity that the Republicans advocated. Protectionist colleagues from across the aisle, however, joined with Republicans to thwart the liberal trade orientation of the Democratic administration. Immediate protests from abroad were issued against reimposition of the duty on sugar and its abrupt termination of the McKinley Tariff agreements. In 1919 the United States Tariff Commission study on reciprocity reported that "considerable resentment was shown, and measures of retal-

15. United States Tariff Commission, *Reciprocity*, 27–28.
16. Asher Isaacs, as quoted in Robert W. Barrie, *Congress and the Executive: The Making of United States Foreign Trade Policy, 1789–1968* (New York: Garland, 1987), 60.
17. Davis, *America's Trade Equality Policy*, 67.

iation followed in certain areas."[18] This ironic outcome of the president's intent—to draw the United States closer to freer trade—was a bitter blow for the Democrats. It undermined their credibility, even with former supporters. The Republicans had again won public opinion, and the man whose name evoked protectionism was elected president in 1896.

William McKinley had finally been convinced that reciprocity and protection could indeed go hand in hand. He had disapproved of the plan, developed under President Harrison by Secretary of State Blaine, that authorized executive prerogative in negotiations of reciprocal concessions. Largely due to his opposition, the McKinley Tariff of 1890 contained no such flexibility.[19] As president, however, McKinley's view shifted substantially, and he entered office intending to urge Congress to reinstate reciprocity as the foundation of trade policy. In a speech before the National Association of Manufacturers in Philadelphia, McKinley lauded reciprocity as the best avenue to achieve the most benefits for domestic industry.

McKinley explained that "the United States wanted to dominate its own market and export its agricultural and industrial surpluses without degrad[ing] our labor. . . . We want a reciprocity which will give us foreign markets for our surplus products and in turn that will open our markets to foreigners for those products *which they produce and we do not.*"[20] To achieve this protectionist goal for domestic exporters and at the same time ensure that U.S. industry in the home market would not be harmed by cheap imports, McKinley's government secured passage of the Dingley Tariff Bill in 1897.

As Lake has explained, the United States was free to pursue such protectionist policies alongside efforts to expand exports because the international system for trade was relatively open. Thus, the United States coerced Latin American nations and European powers on behalf of their colonies to offer market access in exchange for escaping specific penalty by U.S. import policies, all at

18. United States Tariff Commission, *Reciprocity*, 28.
19. Terrill, *Tariff*, 164.
20. Ibid., 199, emphasis added.

the expense of Britain, which had traditionally dominated these markets. Moreover, U.S. producers had for some time looked to the British home market for market access. Generally, though, "the continued openness of the British market created the opportunity for the United States, as a single opportunist, to free ride within the international economy. Although it could not do so with quite the impunity as before, the United States, could nonetheless maintain protection at home, thereby securing the benefits of its optimal tariff and subsidizing its increasing returns industries, and expand exports to Latin America, Asia, and other British trading preserves with little or no fear of retaliation from the hegemonic leader."[21]

The Dingley Tariff Act contained two distinct approaches to trade expansion without threat to domestic producers. The first empowered the president to reduce duties on a very limited list of articles, including wines, sugar, statuary, art, and certain liquors, "when coming from countries making equivalent concessions to the products of the United States."[22] The second involved a penalty provision, similar to that authorized by the 1890 McKinley Tariff Act, which altered the types of articles granted duty-free status. Hides were removed and replaced by vanilla beans and tonka, but the impact of the clause remained the same.[23] The major departure from past policy was the president's ability to initiate negotiations through concessions on items enumerated in the act. Accordingly, the president was not limited to retaliatory reimposition of duties against uncooperative nations but could encourage cooperation through overtures of duty reductions on these specific articles.

In the most obvious area of trade policy, the Dingley Tariff Act was more outwardly protectionist. It raised the general level of the tariff to 57 percent, "the highest point in the history of the nation."[24] Congress took this action autonomously without prior discussions with other nations and without considering their

21. Lake, *Power, Protection, and Free Trade*, 121.
22. United States Tariff Commission, *Reciprocity*, 28–30.
23. William S. Culbertson, *Reciprocity, a National Policy for Foreign Trade* (New York: McGraw-Hill, 1937), 156–57.
24. Davis, *America's Trade Equality Policy*, 67.

treatment of American goods. Although the reciprocity provision allowed ad hoc negotiations of certain duty reductions, the overall impact of the act actually raised the protective wall against foreign competition.

In one respect, however, the Dingley Tariff Act encouraged imports into the United States but in such a discriminatory manner as to draw widespread criticism within the United States. A feature inserted into the bill, known as the "Drawback Law," provided rebates to industries that used imported raw materials in products that they in turn exported. Section 30 of the tariff act stipulated that "when the imported materials on which duties have been paid are used in the manufacture of articles manufactured or produced in the United States, there shall be allowed on the exportation of such articles a drawback equal in amount to the duties paid on the materials used, less one percent of such duties; provided, that when the articles exported are made in part from domestic materials the imported materials, or the parts of the articles made from such materials, shall so appear in the completed articles that the quantity or measure thereof may be ascertained."[25]

Rather than remove or lower duties on imported raw materials, as President Cleveland had intended some years before, the act maintained them but offered substantial rebates to encourage reexportation of finished products. Through this measure, the important manufacturing sector conveyed its interests to the Republican administration and received the benefits of the cheapest raw materials for manufacturing processes in exchange for exporting the end product. This feature also indicated the shifting position of protectionists such as McKinley, who, Tom Terrill explains, increasingly "define[d] American prosperity in terms of foreign economic expansion and an interdependent world economy,"[26] yet their definition remained hamstrung by the commitment to protection. The limited reciprocity provisions and the Drawback Law together protected U.S. industry from competition by pro-

25. Richard Cleveland Baker, *The Tariff under Roosevelt and Taft* (Hastings, Neb.: Democrat Printing, 1941), 29–30.
26. Terrill, *Tariff*, 12–13.

35

ducers abroad while encouraging U.S. industrial competitiveness in foreign markets.

Weaker interest groups, such as farmers and consumers, were immediately antagonized by the Dingley Tariff Act, which fueled their demands for tariff reform, even though they had little impact on Republican trade policy. The tariff issue became so divisive that following President McKinley's assassination in 1901, no new legislation was seriously attempted. Although the new president, Theodore Roosevelt, meant to grapple with tariff reform, his advisers urged him away from such a politically volatile issue. Consequently, in May 1903 Roosevelt favored a "stable" tariff policy and argued that altering the existing duty structure would harm U.S. business.[27] Thus the 1897 Dingley Tariff guided U.S. commercial policy well beyond the death of its chief advocate, and the restrictionist policies of the McKinley administration continued under the Roosevelt administrations.

Worse yet, Congress refused to approve several treaties negotiated under the reciprocity provision of the 1897 act.[28] Although the act authorized the president to "transfer from the dutiable to the free list 'such goods, wares, and merchandise, being the natural products of such foreign country or countries and not of the United States'" and to "negotiate reciprocity treaties providing 'for the reduction . . . of the duties imposed by this Act,'" Congress maintained that the act would not allow duty concessions on competitive products.[29] Because of this highly protectionist point of view, Congress refused to ratify the treaties, and the U.S. government was forced to officially terminate them.[30] In the final analysis, the Dingley Tariff Act proved more restrictive and protectionist than did the McKinley Tariff. First, it increased the general tariff level. Second, except for the so-called argol agreements, which limited reductions for wine, liquor, sugar, and statuary specifically in exchange for equivalent concessions abroad, the act stipulated that Congress must approve all future reciprocal agree-

27. Baker, *Tariff under Roosevelt and Taft*, 37–38.
28. Culbertson, *Reciprocity*, 161–62.
29. Ibid., 165.
30. United States Tariff Commission, *Reciprocity*, 28–30.

ments, stripping the president of any real trade policy power. Third, initiation of the Drawback Law discriminated against goods produced for domestic consumption and left intact the notion that imports competing with domestic industry for consumers would not be tolerated. For the next twelve years, the Dingley Tariff continued to govern U.S. commercial policy.

William H. Taft's election as president in 1908 renewed enthusiasm for altering the tariff. Animosity against the discriminatory effects of the Dingley Tariff, along with its stimulation of retaliatory measures that affected U.S. farm exports, led farmers and farm exporters to pressure the new administration for lower tariffs on manufactured commodities.[31] Pressed by these demands for reform, Congress offered a different approach to commercial policy in the Payne-Aldrich Act of 1909. Introduced by Representative Payne, this bill reduced the general tariff level but levied a 20 percent retaliatory duty on the products of discriminatory countries. The bill left the Senate heavily laden with the protectionist amendments of Senator Aldrich, however, and it became much more exclusionary and failed to lower duties on manufactured goods.

Aldrich's amendments restored duties on several important items, including iron ore, hides, and coal, and increased duties on lumber, cotton textiles, and hosiery. In addition, the Senate bill raised the retaliatory duties to be imposed against discriminatory countries to 25 percent. To secure Republican support from agricultural states, Aldrich proposed to raise the duty on barley from twenty-four to thirty cents. With this bit of sweetening, he successfully deflected opposition to his version of the tariff reform bill, and the amended bill passed both houses. Paradoxically, President Taft, who had wanted some descrease in the tariff, signed the Aldrich-amended Payne bill so he would not alienate major Republican leaders in Congress.[32]

The Payne-Aldrich Act designated a two-tariff schedule for import duties—a minimum schedule and a maximum one. The minimum schedule, which listed duty-free goods and minimum rates

31. Baker, *Tariff under Roosevelt and Taft*, 74–75.
32. Ibid., 84, 100–101.

of duty for other goods, would be applied to those countries that did not discriminate against U.S. exports. The maximum schedule, derived from "adding to the minimum 25 percent of the values of the articles" listed, would be applied generally to all countries until the president determined that exceptions should be allowed for nondiscriminatory countries.[33]

Clearly, the burden of proof lay with the country doing business with the United States, which had to demonstrate eligibility for the lower duty schedule. As a result of this two-tiered tariff designation, the U.S. Tariff Board conducted investigations to determine which countries did in fact discriminate against U.S. products. Where they discovered several discriminations, they negotiated to achieve their removal. In 1919 the U.S. Tariff Commission reported that "in consequence of the negotiations, there were issued prior to April 1, 1911, proclamations applying the minimum rates to the countries comprising the entire commercial world; in no case was the maximum rate applied." In this report, the commission regarded the 1909 act as a major departure from the strict bilateral reciprocity of past tariffs; it noted that the United States had, through the two-tiered tariff in the Payne-Aldrich Act, applied reciprocally the principle of equal treatment for those countries that proved they did not discriminate against U.S. products.[34]

Even so, the Payne-Aldrich Act, overall, raised the general tariff level. Because the act did not stipulate that "minimum" rates had to be particularly *low* across the board, protectionism was not seriously limited by the two-tiered approach. Also, Congress had autonomously determined levels for the dual tariff schedules, so negotiations with foreign nations had no effect on previously set schedules, only on which level to apply.

The dust had barely settled on the negotiations to treat all nondiscriminating trade partners equally when a special strictly bilateral agreement with Canada was signed in 1911. In this new endeavor, Taft hoped to allay U.S. consumers' mounting suspicions that Republicans represented only the interests of domestic manufacturers by protecting higher-priced U.S. goods against lower-

33. United States Tariff Commission, *Reciprocity*, 31.
34. Ibid., 32, 268.

priced foreign imports. The Canadian–United States reciprocity agreement evidenced his good faith in this regard, but he went on the defensive within his own party for this action, which appeared more consumer-oriented and less protective of industry. Taft defended his policy by arguing that "no step could be taken more in the interest of a reasonable policy of protection than the approval of this [Canadian] treaty. The very existence of the policy depends on our abolition of the tariff where it is not really needed under the principle of the last Republican platform."[35]

Although the treaty aimed to obtain cheaper products for the U.S. consumer and provided free entry of raw materials, it still maintained protection for manufactured products. Consequently, as Richard Baker notes, Canadian agricultural "products which competed with those of the American farmer were permitted free access to this country, while manufactured goods, including those made from the farmer's own produce, were given considerable protection."[36] The arrangement so discriminated against the U.S. farmer that a great deal of opposition emerged from representatives of farm states, particularly those bordering Canada. Nevertheless, Congress ratified the reciprocal treaty that would have instituted the special bilateral duty structure, had the Canadian Parliament not rejected it.

Once again the most important interests determined where the tariff was retained. Farmers were not powerful enough to deflect the impact of the reciprocal agreement from falling so heavily on them, and consumers were not organized enough to demand more from the manufacturing sector. According to Terrill, Republicans had consistently maintained that protection was a "natural right," and the outcome of the reciprocity treaty in Congress appeared to confirm this view for American industry if not for American farmers.[37] Clearly, concessions would continue to be sought abroad for U.S. industry, but duties would be lowered only when goods in question did not compete with domestic manufacturers. Farmers were not well protected, but fortunately for

35. Taft, as quoted by Culbertson, *Reciprocity*, 153.
36. Baker, *Tariff under Roosevelt and Taft*, 50-51. The same was true of grains and cereal products; vegetables, fruits, and pickled or canned products as well as butter, milk, cheese, cream, eggs, and their derivatives.
37. See, for example, McKinley's statement in Terrill, *Tariff*, 199.

them, Ottawa overturned the treaty. Still, their discriminatory treatment at the hands of the Taft administration added new fuel to the persistently volatile tariff issue and benefited the opposition in the next election.

The Attempt for Liberal Reciprocity in the Underwood Tariff Act, 1913

In 1912 the Democrats captured the White House and both houses of Congress. On entering office in 1913, they immediately attempted to revise the tariff. Under the leadership of President Woodrow Wilson, as Raymond Leslie Buell observes, Congress passed the Underwood Tariff Bill, which drastically reduced duties on some nine hundred items, "especially food and clothing, and placed wool, iron ore, steel rails, coal and lumber on the free list. It lowered the sugar duty immediately and arranged for sugar to be put on the free list by 1916."[38] In addition, the act authorized the president to "negotiate reciprocity agreements with foreign countries, such agreements, however, to be submitted to congress for ratification or rejection."[39]

Unlike the Payne-Aldrich act, the 1913 act did not utilize a two-tiered tariff schedule of minimum and maximum rates. Underwood, the bill's sponsor, rejected the form of the 1909 act, which applied penalties only to secure more favorable tariff treatment rather than initiating new concessions to encourage duty reductions abroad.[40] Most significant, the 1913 bill retrieved the policy of reciprocity *and* offered the lowest tariff since before the Civil War.[41] This combination demonstrates that previous links between a restrictive tariff and reciprocal negotiations were consequences of protectionism, not necessary outcomes of reciprocity.

38. Raymond Leslie Buell, *The Hull Trade Program*, World Affairs Pamphlets (New York: Foreign Policy Association, 1939), 10.
39. United States Tariff Commission, *Reciprocity*, 32.
40. Ibid., 280.
41. Buell, *Hull Trade Program*, 10.

Moreover, as Lake has noted, President Wilson was aware of the changing global economy's character, that the United States should not only recognize its commercial opportunities but also the emerging constraints to the protectionist opportunism of U.S. trade policy. In particular, Wilson warned that the United States would have to reciprocate in liberalizing its own market for U.S. trade expansion to occur; otherwise, U.S. trading partners would retaliate in kind.[42] In Wilson's hands, reciprocity clearly took on liberal overtones by encompassing the genuine offer of concessions in exchange for market access abroad. Unfortunately, World War I sidetracked policymakers and overshadowed tariff issues for some time, stymying the new approach.

Earlier experiments with reciprocity and conditional most-favored-nation (mfn) treatment were plagued with inconsistency, narrowness, and an overwhelming protectionism. The desire for export markets for finished goods and imports of cheap raw materials did spur Congress to dabble with the notion of reciprocally negotiated trade agreements, but only the Underwood Bill genuinely sought to expand trade in a mutually beneficial way. Critics of free trade in this era of U.S. commercial history regard the halfhearted and often aborted attempts at a reciprocal trade policy as evidence that reciprocity was the culprit. This examination shows that the underlying protectionist sentiment as well as the actual protectionist limits on reciprocity experiments were the problem, not the reciprocity concept. Reciprocity achieved no liberalization of U.S. trade because it was never allowed to. This conclusion is supported even more dramatically by the policies and events of the 1920s and early 1930s, when the United States rejected reciprocal trade policies altogether and became even more protectionist.

Reciprocity Abandoned and Protectionism Retained, 1922–1933

In 1922, Congress enacted legislation that embodied the principle of equality of treatment as recommended by the Tariff Com-

---

42. Lake, *Power, Protection, and Free Trade*, 156–57.

mission in its 1919 report.[43] Secretary of State Charles Evans Hughes immediately used the equality-of-treatment clause in Section 317 of the new act to alter the posture of U.S. trade relations. In August 1923, Secretary Hughes notified U.S. diplomats that President Harding had "authorized the Secretary of State to negotiate commercial treaties with other countries by which the contracting parties will accord to each unconditional most-favored-nation treatment."[44] Clearly and unequivocally, the United States had embraced the principle of nondiscrimination in trade policy, and the secretary of state had high hopes for the effect on international relations. Writing to Henry Cabot Lodge in the spring of 1924, Hughes registered optimism for the far-reaching results of this new outlook.

> The time has come for demanding that conditions of commercial competition be placed upon a basis which will both assure our own interests and contribute to the peace of the world by eliminating unnecessary economic contentions. As we seek pledges from other foreign countries that they will refrain from practicing discrimination, we must be ready to give such pledges, and history has shown that these pledges can be made adequate only in terms of unconditional most-favored-nation treatment. We should seek simplicity and good will as the fundamental conditions of international commerce.[45]

Unfortunately, nondiscrimination was not enough to prevent conflict in international economic relations. Although it had opened the way for Secretary Hughes's application of the unconditional form of mfn treatment in U.S. policy, Congress at the same time *precluded any possibility of liberalizing the tariff*. By adhering religiously to past Republican attitudes that favored protection, the majority in Congress successfully passed the most effectively restrictive tariff in U.S. history. The 1922 Fordney-McCumber Tariff established a new general tariff that continued the

43. Davis, *America's Trade Equality Policy*, 103.
44. Confidential circular sent by Hughes to all American diplomats on 18 August 1923, as quoted in Culbertson, *Reciprocity*, 170.
45. Ibid., 102.

high level of protection initiated by the 1921 Emergency Tariff Act. The 1921 act had been passed in response to declining prices after the war for agricultural commodities. Fearful of a surplus that would send prices plunging even further, U.S. agricultural interests pleaded for tariff protection, and the more powerful manufacturing interests demanded similar assistance.[46]

Consequently, protectionist demands ran virtually unrestrained in Congress. The 1922 act, which went far beyond the tariffs of past Republican administrations, totally overturned liberalizing efforts made under Wilson in the Underwood Tariff. Overall, the bill raised the average tariff on dutiable goods to just over 38 percent and on all imports to an average of 13.9 percent.[47] This response to the postwar depression, a return to the "old time religion" of unilateral protectionism, seemed a safer refuge than did the less orthodox ideas of Wilsonian Democrats.

Although the Fordney-McCumber Act lowered the average duty rate below that of the Dingley Tariff, the impact on future rates was far more protective due to a provision that directed the president to raise or lower duties by up to 50 percent to equalize production costs between manufactures at home and those abroad.[48] Debate on this portion of the bill focused on the problem of dumping. Proponents of the measure wanted to ensure that U.S. producers would not be unfairly disadvantaged by higher costs in factors of production, including higher wages. The Fordney-McCumber Act buttressed the Anti-dumping Act of 1921, which declared unlawful the importation of goods at prices substantially less than market value with intent to destroy or injure U.S. industry, and excluded all products that held a price advantage over U.S.-produced goods.[49]

46. Buell, *Hull Trade Program*, 10–11.
47. Lake, *Power, Protection, and Free Trade*, 167.
48. Buell, *Hull Trade Program*, 11.
49. Fordney, explaining the bill before the House of Representatives, described the procedure: "The bill directs the Tariff Commission to find the difference between the cost of production in the United States and the landed cost of the imported article and to report the same to the President of the United States. The bill further directs the President to issue a proclamation at once raising or lowering the duty named to meet such difference, and the same shall become effective

This distinction altered the practical definition of dumping to include any products entering the United States at a price *below the U.S. cost of production*. With this provision, therefore, the 1922 tariff was for all intents and purposes exclusionary of all competing goods. Furthermore, the bill authorized the president to impose even higher retaliatory duties against goods imported as a result of "unfair competition."[50] This latter instrument enabled the president to remove from the most-favored-nation list any country that discriminated against U.S. products or dumped its goods on the U.S. market. This tariff law also added a serious punitive element to U.S. anti-dumping provisions by authorizing the Treasury Department to impose additional duties on specific items imported at prices lower than their cost of production in the exporting nation. The Fordney-McCumber Act, with its goal of cost equalization, included protection against all goods that entered the United States at a price lower than the U.S. cost of production. Administration of this new provision resembled the procedure embodied in the anti-dumping law, although it was far more exclusionary because no lower-cost product would be admitted without a duty that counteracted the price advantage. In addition, retaliatory penalties could be imposed against nations that had utilized unfair trade practices to penetrate the U.S. market, including dumping and subsidization to offset U.S. tariffs. Consequently, anti-dumping duties (or cost-of-production equalization duties, depending on the avenue chosen) would probably be followed with punitive duties, thus resulting in an effective nullification of mfn treatment in that particular bilateral relationship.

As Oscar Underwood notes, opponents of the Fordney-McCumber measure argued that "the new tariff has inaugurated at the custom house the highest system of taxation on competitive articles that has ever been written in the history of this country." The same critic went on to explain that this result gave "the

---

within 15 days from the date of the proclamation." 12 September 1922, *Congressional Record*, 67th Cong., 2d sess., 12508.

50. U.S. Congress, House Committee on Ways and Means, *Report to Accompany H.R. 8687 to Amend Tariff Act of 1930: Reciprocal Trade Agreements*, 73d Cong., 2d sess., 1934, Report no. 1000, 10–11. Hereafter cited as Ways and Means Report (1934).

American manufacturer a monopoly of the American market and to that extent prevented the European consumer of our products from sending to us the production of his labor in return for what we send abroad."[51] The majority in Congress, however, rejected this basic tenet of the workings of international commercial exchange—the necessity of a general reciprocity in sales and purchases. Despite impassioned arguments from certain members of Congress that the bill would likely contribute to the bankruptcy of Europe and result in retaliation against U.S. exports, the new tariff became law.[52] The era of peaceful commercial interaction promised by the equality-of-treatment principle was preempted by the protectionist thrust of the remaining legislation.

Thus, when the United States began to negotiate unconditional mfn agreements with trading partners, as Davis notes, the effort was undermined by punitive exceptions against nations that placed "the commerce of the United States at a disadvantage compared with the commerce of any foreign country."[53] Not only had the 1922 act set in motion a series of retaliatory responses to policies of other nations, but its very restrictive, single-column autonomous tariff also antagonized them at the outset.

Perhaps the most damaging aspect, according to D. J. M. Brown, was that "from 1920 to 1934 it was the firm policy of the United States government not to make the American tariff negotiable."[54] Congress set the rates of duty without considering the commercial interests of other nations. The administration could alter the duties, but only to equalize costs of production or to punish other nations for uncooperative acts. In the former instance, the duties would apply across the board to imports from all nations, regardless of their most-favored-nation status. In the latter case, punitive duties would apply as special cases against

51. Oscar Underwood, "The Tariff as a Factor in American Foreign Trade," *Foreign Affairs* 1 (Summer 1923): 26 and 31.

52. 13 September 1922, *Congressional Record*, 67th Cong., 2d sess., 12539.

53. Davis quoting Section 317 of the Fordney-McCumber Act, *America's Trade Equality Policy*, 103–4. See also 104–7 and 110–11 for discussion of the counterproductive nature of American retaliatory policy and mfn treatment.

54. D. J. M. Brown, *The United States and the Restoration of World Trade* (Washington, D.C.: Brookings Institution, 1950), 15.

nations that lost mfn status as a result of some practice the United States considered to be unfair or discriminatory. This alteration of the duty structure is worth explaining. Although the United States maintained an autonomous single-column tariff, rates could be altered for specific cases when retaliation warranted.[55] Simply put, the U.S. tariff was highly exclusionary to all import competition but, in addition, could be punitive if need be.

The deterioration of trade relations during the 1920s is well documented.[56] The U.S. insistence on pursuing an exclusionary trade policy, along with its refusal to discount more freely the loans resulting from the First World War, restricted international commerce and undermined international efforts to stabilize the world economy. Despite warnings by those who predicted such a policy would contract the world economy and stimulate retaliatory and protective reactions from other nations, the United States did not alter its position.[57]

While the United States held firmly to its protectionist position, international efforts were underway to solve the instability of the world economy. A series of conferences were called—most under the auspices of the League of Nations—to discuss proliferating trade restrictions and to advance viable solutions for their removal. As Percy Wells Bidwell suggests: "The recommendations of the conferences uniformly looked to the establishment of freer conditions of trade, but in the great majority of instances the recommendations were not carried out by national governments. They were either discarded or were applied on too small a scale

55. S. H. Bailey, "The Political Aspect of Discrimination in International Economic Relations," *Economica* 12 (February 1932): 105–6.

56. See, for example, League of Nations, *Trade Relations in the Interwar Period* (Geneva, 1941).

57. As early as 1923, Oscar Underwood, *Foreign Affairs* 1 (March 1923): 25–34, argued that there was a great need on the part of the world economy for the United States to act as creditor nation for the war-torn nations and to open its doors to European goods so that Europe would have some means of earning sufficient capital to pay its debts. He predicted that America's restrictive trade policy would be counterproductive and prevent postwar recovery. Charles P. Kindleberger develops this interpretation more elaborately in *The World in Depression, 1929–1939* (Berkeley: University of California Press, 1973).

or within too narrow an area to offset opposing trends."[58] The greatest obstacle to cooperation on reducing trade barriers, analysts generally agree, was the U.S. refusal to participate by negotiating its tariff.[59]

With trade restrictions on the rise, tariffs were increasingly supplemented by quotas to restrict importation of foreign goods, and the United States was at the forefront in their use.[60] This form of protection, which was wholly in conflict with the principle of unconditional most-favored-nation treatment, increasingly undermined its application in U.S. trade relations. The incompatibility arose because quotas were variously applied. According to Jacob Viner, "If import quotas are allotted by countries . . . there is not much choice except between more or less arbitrary allotment and deliberately discriminatory allotment."[61]

Some analysts have taken the position that the United States moved closer to liberal trade because of the inclusion of the unconditional most-favored-nation clause in commercial relations after 1922.[62] The retaliatory provision in the Fordney-McCumber

58. Percy Wells Bidwell, *A Commercial Policy for the United Nations* (New York: Committee on International Economic Policy in Cooperation with the Carnegie Endowment for International Peace, 1945), 12.

59. Analysts who reviewed American economic policy by and large agreed that America's leadership in trade and financial liberalization was vital to world recovery. See, for example, Buell, *Hull Trade Program*; Herbert Feis, *The Changing Pattern of International Economic Affairs* (New York: Harper and Bros., 1940), *The Sinews of Peace* (New York: Harper and Bros., 1944), and *1933: Characters in Crisis* (Boston: Little, Brown, 1966); Cordell Hull, *International Trade and Domestic Prosperity* (Washington, D.C.: U.S. Government Printing Office, 1934), and *Memoirs of Cordell Hull* (London: Hodder and Stoughton, 1948); and Tasca, *Reciprocal Trade Policy*.

60. S. H. Bailey, "Reciprocity and the Most-Favored-Nation Clause," *Economica* 13 (November 1933): 437.

61. Jacob Viner, "Conflicts of Principle in Drafting a Trade Charter," *Foreign Affairs* 25 (July 1947): 618.

62. David Lake has argued that "in conjunction with the flexible tariff provision of the Fordney-McCumber Tariff, this shift in policy illustrates the desire of the United States to play a greater and more liberal role within the international economy." Lake, "International Economic Structures and American Foreign Economic Policy," *World Politics* 35 (July 1983): 535. This may have been true for elements in the executive branch, but the coauthor of the bill certainly did not see

Act, its general exclusionary intent, the autonomous tariff, and the increased application of quotas make this conclusion inappropriate, however. U.S. policy throughout the 1920s was dominated by protectionist actions, despite the best intentions of Secretary Hughes in the early period for equality of treatment as a step toward international economic tranquility. Commitment to protection was clear, whether reciprocity or equal treatment were present. Moreover, America's refusal to negotiate tariffs and quotas with other nations far more damningly indicated the country's uncooperativeness than did the tenuous reciprocal negotiation efforts of the pre-1922 period.

The replacement of "conditional" with "unconditional" in most-favored-nation treatment, therefore, was not the breakthrough in development of U.S. commercial policy that liberal reformers envisioned. Combined with a negotiable tariff, this change might have transformed the previous policy of coercive and restrictive reciprocity to balanced treatment and mutual benefit (as hoped for in the Underwood Act) to reward trading partners and expand trade. The U.S. policy of maintaining a nonnegotiable tariff, however, prevented this liberalizing function of the unconditional mfn principle and, in fact, reduced the principle to a very narrow and negative concept.

Congress passed a new tariff in 1930 that dealt a debilitating blow to the world economy with even more protective measures. Finally going too far, the Hawley-Smoot Act was a turning point in the U.S. attitude toward, and experience with, protectionism in trade.

National governments, including that of the United States, already pursued policies to insulate domestic economies from uncertainties of international conditions; but the sudden onslaught of the Great Depression brought cries for government protection to such a pitch that Congress intervened against imports to address falling prices. As Buell states, the resultant tariff of 1930, which increased the average rate of duties from 38.5 percent (the

---

freer trade as its purpose. See the debate in the House of Representatives, August 29–September 22, 1922, *Congressional Record*, 67th Cong., 2d sess., in particular, 12506–8.

level in 1922) to 52.6 percent, was the "highest tariff in the whole history of the United States."[63] Not only did the tariff retain the exclusionary language of the 1922 act against goods competing with U.S. products, but it also raised to an alarming rate duties on other goods as well. In addition, the 1930 act once again allowed the executive branch to impose retaliatory duties on imports from countries that practiced trade "unfairly."

According to Elmer Schattschneider's analysis, the public interest, which would have been better served by a lower, more sensible tariff on many import items and one that did not stimulate retaliations, was sacrificed to a multitude of private interests that demanded individual protection. Once Congress awarded new levels of protection to one sector, there was no rationale for not protecting others. This scramble for protection meant that every interest got something in the way of higher duties from Congress. In the final analysis, however, everyone suffered.[64]

As J. B. Condliffe observes, the new U.S. tariff dealt "a fatal blow to any remaining hope of international economic equilibrium,"[65] not only by restricting trade with the United States but also by engendering a series of retaliations and defensive actions by its trading partners that worsened relations and constricted the world economy even further. In most cases, these countries attempted to cushion themselves from the loss of this important export market, and in many there was an obvious "reprisal motive."[66]

Joseph M. Jones, who chronicled protective reactions in his studies of Spain, Italy, Switzerland, France, Canada, and Great Britain, demonstrated that protective steps taken by these governments following passage of the Hawley-Smoot Tariff were retaliatory. In fact, Canada's retaliatory tariff bill, passed in May 1930, established "automatic reciprocal duties" against the new U.S.

63. Buell, *Hull Trade Program*, 12.
64. Elmer Eric Schattschneider, *Politics, Pressures, and the Tariff: A Study of Free Private Enterprise in Pressure Politics, as Shown in the 1929–1930 Revision of the Tariff* (New York: Prentice-Hall, 1935).
65. J. B. Condliffe, *The Reconstruction of World Trade: A Survey of International Economic Relations* (London: Allen and Unwin, 1941), 184.
66. Ibid.

tariffs on agricultural products.[67] Secretary of State Hull, upon entering office, found in the State Department files "no fewer than thirty-four formal and emphatic diplomatic protests from as many nations" that objected to the 1930 tariff.[68] Furthermore, "adoption of a general system of protection by Great Britain and the complementary extension of imperial preference during 1931 and 1932 may be regarded as two of the most important developments of the depression period . . . [and] as far as America's two greatest markets, Great Britain and Canada, were concerned, no amount of rationalization can quite conceal the fact that their chief object at Ottawa was mutually to divert as great an amount as possible of the purchases previously made in the United States."[69]

It is by no means conclusive that the reversal of British commercial policy during these two years resulted solely from the Hawley-Smoot Tariff (as pressure had been building for some time), but Condliffe suggests that most observers agreed that the tariff "facilitated both the adoption of protective tariffs in Great Britain and the negotiation at Ottawa of preferential agreements within the British Empire."[70] This result was primarily due to the fact that the 1930 protectionist act "precipitated a series of tariff reprisals in many countries, the ultimate result of which was a canalizing of world export surpluses upon the few remaining free trade markets."[71] The flood of goods was far too threatening to be ignored and the demands for protection far too insistent to be left unanswered.

Protective reactions and retaliations rippled through the world economy, building destructive force as together they contributed to the worsening depression and to the heightening of international tension. Those who had kowtowed to demands made in Congress for protection in 1930 failed to recognize the fundamental truth that they had clung to over the years in their attempt to

67. Joseph M. Jones, Jr., *Tariff Retaliation Repercussions of the Hawley-Smoot Bill* (Philadelphia: University of Pennsylvania Press, 1934), 178.
68. Hull, *Memoirs*, 353.
69. Jones, *Tariff Retaliation Repercussions*, 211–12.
70. Condliffe, *Reconstruction of World Trade*, 185–86.
71. Ibid.

secure markets abroad for U.S. products. Again and again, they had proclaimed the desirability of reciprocity before abandoning it in 1922. If the United States could not obtain specific equivalent concessions for its goods in other countries, then those countries would not have access to its market, even if access were limited to noncompetitive imports. These protectionists sought to reserve both foreign and domestic markets for U.S. industry, yet they failed to see that other nations sought similar goals.

The more moderate officials had recognized the larger meaning of reciprocity: that to buy U.S. goods, other nations must sell their own goods on the world market. The process was complementary, and U.S. participation as an importer would go a long way toward keeping that market open. Even so, their voices were few and unheeded. Not until America's trading partners began to restrict their markets severely to American goods and to utilize other devices to enhance their own exports to the detriment of American producers was it realized that reciprocity could work against the United States as well as for it. Other nations, moved by the tariff to retaliate against the United States, convinced U.S. policymakers that America was vulnerable to their reactions.

The so-called tariff reformers, who had insisted on a higher, more protective tariff in 1930, failed to realize that commercial policy could no longer be treated as an independent domestic issue. The U.S. economy was far too intertwined with economies of other nations for such an extreme protective action not to sound a reverberating effect elsewhere, especially in the midst of widespread economic difficulty. Interdependence, coupled with the serious nature of the world depression, made institution of such a restrictive tariff incredibly irresponsible.[72] The reciprocal defensive actions and reprisals that followed the U.S. tariff demonstrated

---

72. Although Helen Milner does not look directly at the links between interdependence and retaliatory activity in this period, she argues convincingly that trade interdependence places certain constraints on the protectionist impulses of firms, in part for fear of retaliation. This argument lends support to the idea that retaliation can serve a useful enforcement purpose. Milner, *Resisting Protectionism: Global Industries and the Politics of International Trade* (Princeton: Princeton University Press, 1988), 23.

the interdependence of the world economy and became proof that retaliation could inflict serious damage.

Conclusion

This historical analysis of U.S. trade policy between 1880 and 1933 demonstrates the lack of factual basis for the liberal myth that assumes bilateral reciprocity in trade will inherently engender conflict and cause trade to contract. Evidence indicates that U.S. experiences with reciprocal trade negotiations were severely limited, both in duration and in scope. Also, they were nearly always distorted by overriding protectionist norms, thus taking on the character and outlook of protectionism. Reciprocity was never used in any serious way to expand trade, and in fact, the history of this period reminds us that dubbing a policy reciprocal does not necessarily make it so.

Classical liberal economists have categorized reciprocity as illiberal and counterproductive based on these earlier protectionist examples; their analysis, however, ignores the fact that all politically acceptable trade policies of this period were illiberal, regardless of strategy. In fact, the years between 1922 and 1934 formed the most protectionist period in U.S. history, even when the United States abandoned reciprocity in favor of unconditional most-favored-nation treatment.

Only when the costs of autonomous protectionism became intolerably high did policymakers become convinced that insularity was no longer a viable option and that a new, more liberal orientation was in the best interests of the United States. Ironically, the retaliations of the 1930s, though dramatically trade restrictive, proved valuable catalysts to American cooperation in future international trade negotiations.

3

The Reciprocal Trade Act
and the Origin of the GATT

The retaliatory trade wars that erupted in reaction to the Hawley-Smoot Tariff deepened the Great Depression and sharpened nationalistic antagonisms; yet they also moved American policymakers and member of Congress to reconsider their notions of insularity and their adherence to autarky. Under the leadership of Cordell Hull, Franklin Roosevelt's secretary of state, the United States shifted away from its costly protectionist orientation toward liberalism and a recognition of the interdependent nature of the global economy.

Three major factors facilitated this change of direction. First, the immediate trauma of retaliation, trade contraction, and depression called into question old patterns in U.S. trade policy and opened the way politically for departure from years of extreme protectionism. Second, Hull and others retrieved the reciprocity principle and fashioned a liberal trade policy that recognized the political desirability of mutually advantageous trade arrangements. Third, the Roosevelt administration used the first two factors to convince Congress to transfer some authority over commercial affairs to the executive, which could then negotiate effective trade agreements with foreign governments.[1] Embodied

---

1. I agree with most analysts who identify the shift of trade policy power from Congress to the executive branch as the single most important change in the institutional history of U.S. trade policy. I contend, however, that this transfer of

in the Reciprocal Trade Agreements Act of 1934, these factors shaped U.S. efforts to expand trade and eventually to create a multilateral framework for trade cooperation after World War II.

This chapter examines the normative and practical underpinnings of U.S. reciprocal trade policy from passage of the Reciprocal Trade Agreements Act until negotiation of the General Agreement on Tariffs and Trade in 1948. During this pivotal period in U.S. commercial history, policymakers from the executive branch were allowed to acquire successfully from Congress the political power to set and maintain the foreign trade agenda. A hybrid trade policy resulted, which was based on bilateral reciprocal negotiations to reduce trade barriers and enforce rules of fair trade on the one hand and the institution of unconditional most-favored-nation treatment for multilateralization of agreements on the other. This combination, a highly successful strategy for liberalizing trade between the United States and participating nations, became the blueprint for international trade cooperation under the GATT.

The Effect of Global Retaliation: Change in U.S. Trade Policy

The grave state of the international economy by 1932 had sensitized all nations to the restrictive policies of others, and America's blatant disregard for the effect of the Hawley-Smoot Tariff made retaliation an important matter of principle as well as a defensive reaction.[2] Cordell Hull carried this lesson with him in his quest for a different approach to world trade. Speaking before

---

authority would not have occurred without a preceding shift in normative views about trade or without the practical reassurance of the reciprocity principle. For an excellent treatment of the domestic structural shift in trade policy and negotiation authority, see in particular Stephan Haggard, "The Institutional Foundations of Hegemony: Explaining the Reciprocal Trade Agreements Act of 1934," in G. John Ikenberry et al., eds., *The State and American Foreign Economic Policy* (Ithaca: Cornell University Press, 1988), 91–119.

2. League of Nations, *World Economic Survey, 1931–32* (Geneva, 1932), 281.

the National Foreign Trade Council in New York City in November 1934, Hull reviewed the counterproductivity of the 1930 act.

> The appalling repercussions of the 1930 tariff act upon our own domestic prosperity bring home the lesson that in this day and age the tariff is no longer a purely domestic issue. We learned that a prohibitive tariff is a gun that recoils upon ourselves. The time was when we could fix the tariff to suit ourselves without serious injury to our exports, then consisting largely of raw materials of which we were the chief source of supply. That day is gone. We now face vigorous world competition in both our agricultural and our industrial products. Slamming the door shut against foreign products, we have found the door shut against our own products. Other countries were forced to raise their tariffs as a means of protection in retaliation for our own exclusive attitude.[3]

Armed with evidence of recent retaliatory activity, Hull and his advisers constructed a new trade program that considered interdependence of the U.S. economy with the rest of the world. The crucial objective—to remove international trade barriers—would encourage a flourishing international trade that was increasingly vital to domestic prosperity. Hull's trade program blended past practices with a new approach. Basically, he sought to secure authority for the executive to negotiate reciprocal tariff reductions on the basis of unconditional mfn treatment. Reciprocal negotiation was not a new concept, but the narrowly limited form previously used by Congress was intended to protect the domestic market rather than liberalize trade.

Hull hoped to alter the *intent* as well as the form of reciprocal negotiations. Recent experience had shown expanding U.S. exports to be incompatible with reducing U.S. imports. To enhance the U.S. position in foreign markets, international trade in general had to be encouraged, a step that would be impossible without firm U.S. commitment to lower trade barriers. When he retrieved the concept of reciprocity to renew U.S. commercial relations, Hull also firmly renounced the previous philosophy. Hoping to

3. Cordell Hull, *International Trade and Domestic Prosperity*, U.S. Dept. of State Commercial Policy Series no. 3 (Washington, D.C., 1934), 5.

liberalize international trade in general, he intended first to ease U.S. policy as the catalyst to similar action elsewhere. Under this view, he argued that only if the United States took the lead in conciliatory offers to reduce its tariff would trading partners be willing to lower theirs. Genuine concessions in the U.S. duty rate would be available to nations who offered concessions in return. Moreover, the same concessions would be granted to all nations that had been granted mfn status by the United States. That status would generally be determined by the other nation's commitment not to discriminate against U.S. exports. For the first time, equality of treatment *and* a negotiable tariff would unite as fundamental components of U.S. trade policy.[4]

Earlier reciprocal policy had failed to effectively expand trade. Congress restricted what items were negotiable, what reductions were possible, and whether concessions would be allowed. Relying on congressional approval for concessions meant that nearly every instance that required ratification received none.[5] Therefore, the limited purpose of reciprocal agreements was in reality even more restricted due to Congress's failure to ratify. When the principle of unconditional mfn treatment was adopted in 1923, the same congressional stubbornness prevented this new approach from having any impact. From instigation of the new tariff in 1922 to passage of Hull's trade program in 1934, the nonnegotiable tariff was based on one highly restrictive duty schedule. Although the United States espoused a new policy of unconditional mfn treatment, the U.S. continued a protective, autonomous course that rendered the new interpretation meaningless in practice.

To effectively expand trade, the new program would have to incorporate lessons learned from previous policy failures. Therefore, reciprocity must be based on principles of liberalism and a negotiable tariff. If Congress flatly set duty rates, a reciprocal policy would be impossible; if it continued to specify negotiable

---

4. Henry J. Tasca, *The Reciprocal Trade Policy of the United States* (Philadelphia: University of Philadelphia Press, 1938), 21–22.

5. The United States–Canada Reciprocal Trade Act of 1911 was ratified by Congress but was overturned by the Canadian Parliament. Only ten short-lived agreements resulted from reciprocal negotiations between 1880 and 1920. See Chapter 2.

items and to limit concessions for each, its practice would be severely restricted. If every agreement were subject to congressional approval, there would be little success. History had already demonstrated this reality. The solution, according to Hull, was to combine reciprocity with equality of treatment in U.S. commercial policy under a new program that ensured a negotiable tariff. He would achieve this through congressional approval for a bill to grant the executive authority to negotiate reciprocal tariff reductions with the nation's trading partners, which would include congressional recognition that any such agreement had a binding effect on the U.S. government without its ratification.

For the most practical reasons, the Hull plan relied on bilateral reciprocity as the means to carry out tariff reductions. Agreements could be defended domestically by guaranteeing that U.S. concessions would be granted conditional to the receipt of equivalent reciprocal concessions from the trading partner in the bilateral negotiation. This useful strategy assuaged congressional fears that the executive branch might grant unilateral concessions without bargaining for reciprocity. In order to liberalize global trade significantly, however, Hull incorporated the principle of equality of treatment to multilateralize the results of bilateral agreements.

After some persuasion by Hull, President Roosevelt approached Congress with this plan for U.S. and world trade expansion by first recalling to American people's minds the connection between the policies of the past administration and the depression. Pointing to the Hawley-Smoot Tariff of 1930, which raised import duties to such a high level that other nations reacted in kind, he charged that the plague besetting international trade and preventing economic recovery was caused by such protectionism. In a message to the public on 28 February 1934, the president noted that U.S. exports in 1933 had fallen to 52 percent of the 1929 volume and to 23 percent of the 1929 value. Furthermore, he argued: "Full and permanent domestic recovery depends in part upon a revived and strengthened international trade. . . . American exports cannot be permanently increased without a corresponding increase in imports."[6]

---

6. Franklin Roosevelt, as quoted in Cordell Hull, *The Memoirs of Cordell Hull* (London: Hodder and Stoughton, 1948), 357.

Reciprocity, U.S. Trade Policy, and the GATT Regime

On 2 March 1934, President Roosevelt sent Congress his appeal for a new approach to commercial policy based on the recommendations of Secretary Hull and the State Department. In a carefully phrased message, he wrote:

> I am requesting the Congress to authorize the Executive to enter into executive commercial agreements with foreign nations; and in pursuance thereof within carefully guarded limits to modify existing duties and import restrictions in such a way as will benefit American agriculture and industry. . . . If the American Government is not in a position to make fair offers for fair opportunities, its trade will be superseded. If it is not in a position at any given moment rapidly to alter the terms on which it is willing to deal with other countries, it cannot adequately protect its trade against discriminations and against bargains injurious to its interests. Furthermore, a promise to which prompt effect cannot be given is not an inducement which can pass current at par in commercial negotiations.[7]

During the next several months, members of Congress debated their willingness to grant future presidents the right to bind the United States to treaties not ratified by the legislative branch of government. The process was arduous, and arguments were heated.

Focusing on the importance to U.S. recovery of markets abroad for surplus production, the Roosevelt administration stressed the trade-expanding advantages of this program. More aggressively than either Blaine or McKinley, New Deal officials broadened the protective concept to include protection for exporters, as well as for domestic-oriented industry, and tied price stabilization to maintenance of foreign commerce. The House Ways and Means Committee Report of 17 March 1934 recognized the general belief that protection of U.S. industry was necessary to prevent injury from cheap imports but also that export markets were vital to industry survival in many cases. "If protection is necessary for these," the report argued, "it is all the more compellingly necessary for agricultural and industrial pursuits involving millions of farmers and working men who would normally be engaged in

---

7. Franklin Roosevelt, as quoted in Tasca, *Reciprocal Trade Policy*, 31.

agriculture and industry to produce goods for our foreign trade."
Rhetorically, it asked, "Can a policy be called protection in any
true sense which does not protect such farmers and working men
also?"[8]

Although Hull and Roosevelt had both publicly stated that concessions abroad could best be exchanged for concessions in the
U.S. tariff and that freer trade would improve world economic
conditions, they played down these liberal aspects before Congress. Moreover, punitive duties applicable against goods imported under unfair trade practices were retained from the 1930 act,
and no changes were made in the Anti-dumping Act, which had
been carried over from the 1921 version by the Hawley-Smoot
Tariff and retained in the same form by the Roosevelt administration. Congress, which persisted in a strong protectionist bias, was
wary of Hull's program. The Republican side of the aisle voiced
adamant rejection of any change in policy that might subject U.S.
industry to import competition, particularly if it were unfairly
generated. Repudiating the notion that export trade was as vital
to the economy as was domestically geared industry, Representative Dirksen argued that passage of the bill would "invite [other
nations] to send manufactured goods into our market and further
aggravate conditions. It will retard instead of aid recovery."[9] Even
supporters such as Representative Kopplemann insisted that the
president not allow duties to be lowered on "import-vulnerable"
industries, only on those industries with strong export capabilities.[10]

Given such attitudes, the administration had to walk a fine line
in both policy formulation and presentation. Speakers emphasized
overall continuity with past policy. In testimony, administration
officials cited precedents for reciprocal tariff negotiation under
Republican administrations, arguing that the only major changes

8. Ways and Means Report (1934), 13.
9. Representative Dirksen (Illinois), 29 March 1934, *Congressional Record*,
73d Cong., 2d sess., 78, pt. 6: 5765.
10. See the statement made by Representative Kopplemann (Connecticut),
ibid., 5786.

combined reciprocity with unconditional mfn treatment and presidential power to rapidly and effectively negotiate reductions.[11]

Although consistency with past commercial policy was exaggerated to persuade Republican support, precedents existed for nearly every new aspect. Crucial differences resulted from packaging together for the first time certain past policies and rejecting others. If the opposition saw the value of discarding congressional control over an autonomous tariff and of moderating the tariff level as a bargaining device to secure reciprocal concessions, then major hurdles to the bill's passage could be overcome. At the same time that continuity with past practice was cited as evidence that no one contemplated a revolution in U.S. trade policy, supporters of the Hull program had to convince a majority that the American economy would be better served by modification.

Henry Grady, who advocated a reduction of the tariff, argued that the last tariff "had gone far beyond the bounds of legitimate protection. It [had] given rise to retaliatory measures . . . which [had] greatly injured our trade." In fact, he went on to point out the conservative nature of the 1934 act, which would provide legitimate protection without the excesses of the last tariff but was hardly revolutionary. Addressing those who thought otherwise, he reassured them that "the trade agreements program is not in any sense a free trade program. It is merely an attempt to remove the causes of retaliation and to restore thereby to American enterprise its natural markets abroad and to retain at the same time reasonable protection for domestic industry."[12]

This moderate protectionist outlook characterized support for the Reciprocal Trade Agreements Act. There was no general rejection of tariff protection. Many recognized that the high tariff rate had been counterproductive; they supported reduction but not as a unilateral action. Bilateral negotiation would make certain that the United States—and more specifically various congressional constituencies—would receive something in return for something offered. No serious attempt was made to liberalize U.S. trade pol-

11. Ways and Means Report (1934), 7–11.
12. Henry Grady, "The New Trade Policy of the United States," *Foreign Affairs* 14 (Spring 1936): 295.

icy radically, and congressional proceedings clearly show that such attempts would have been doomed.[13] Although protection remained a sacred cow, the concept had a broader content and meaning, defining not only defense from injurious foreign competition but also shelter from injurious retaliation that prevented sales abroad, which meant moderation and genuine reciprocity. Further deterioration of the international trading situation had to be prevented, which required Americans purchase foreign goods to stimulate other nations to purchase U.S. goods. Only reduced import barriers could make possible such exchanges.

That the bill finally passed both houses of Congress and went to the president for his signature signaled cautious support for this goal. The version that was signed into law authorized the president to negotiate trade agreements with foreign countries to reduce American duties by not more than 50 percent in exchange for equivalent concessions. But the president was given no authority to alter items on the duty-free list, a right that Congress retained for itself. Moreover, the president's power to conclude tariff reduction treaties was granted for a three-year period, to be renewed only by congressional action. The bill also revitalized the principle of unconditional mfn treatment by pledging to most-favored nations the concessions granted in any subsequent negotiation. Finally, it retained the provision under Section 338 of the Hawley-Smoot Act for application of penalty duties, in addition to the penalty of nongeneralization for nations committing unfair trade acts.[14]

The history of the marriage of reciprocity with the unconditional mfn principle explains why proponents considered the bill so important. Not until the disastrous trade contractions of the early 1930s did attitudes toward the use of reciprocity as a policy instrument begin to change. Retaliations against the U.S. tariff finally brought home to the United States that it had *interdependent* commercial relations that made reciprocity a two-edged sword.

13. See generally the debate recorded in 29 March–17 April 1934, *Congressional Record*, 5765–811.
14. Hull, *Memoirs*, 358–59.

The Reciprocal Trade Program

Although the president was authorized by the 1934 Reciprocal Trade Agreements Act to negotiate reduced trade barriers with foreign governments, this power was proscribed within the framework defined by Congress. For example, as W. A. Brown notes, the president could not commit the United States to any trade agreement until he had obtained "information and advice with respect thereto from the United States Tariff Commission, the departments of State, Agriculture, and Commerce and from such other sources as he [might] deem appropriate and in each case to give reasonable notice of intention to negotiate so that any interested person might have opportunity to present his views."[15]

To facilitate this process and to further aid the president, the Interdepartmental Trade Agreements Committee was created in 1934 to prepare technical studies on trade questions and to develop negotiation proposals. In turn, this committee received detailed reports from the Committee for Reciprocity Information, which conducted hearings and accepted written briefs from interested parties before each proposed negotiation. The purpose of these committees was twofold: to ascertain which duty reductions abroad would expand U.S. exports and to determine which duties on imported goods could be reduced without injury to domestic industry. The process was inherently conservative. According to the act, the president had the burden of proof to show that his proposals for tariff reductions were necessary because certain enumerated duties were "unduly burdening and restricting the foreign trade of the United States."[16] Moreover, he could not reduce duties that would put domestic industries at a competitive disadvantage.

Even so, the bilateral trade negotiations process initiated by the 1934 act produced positive consequences that lowered barriers and expanded trade. More important, this bill was a significant

15. The 1934 Reciprocal Trade Agreements Act, as quoted by W. A. Brown, *The United States and the Restoration of World Trade* (Washington, D.C.: Brookings Institution, 1950), 17.
16. Ibid.

departure from past policy, demonstrating to the world the United States' new approach to international trade. For the first time, the U.S. government had firmly established a progressive, trade expansion–oriented reciprocal policy.[17] The partnership between reciprocal trade negotiations and unconditional mfn treatment proved crucial to the normative shift in U.S. commercial policy. The generalization of reciprocal concessions via the principle of equality of treatment meant that individual tariff reduction negotiations were conducted bilaterally but that they would be multilaterally applied to all other nondiscriminatory nations. At the time the 1934 act was passed, the United States had mfn treaties from past administrations with forty-eight other nations which made the immediate effect of any new bilateral negotiation substantial.[18]

This two-tiered reciprocal policy proved successful in reducing barriers and expanding overall trade. According to Hull, the first two years of the trade agreements program saw the value of U.S. imports from third countries—those who benefited indirectly from reduced duties as a result of unconditional mfn treatment— amount to $30 million. Significantly, exports from the United States, which also benefited from reciprocal equality of treatment, amounted to $265 million, making the "ratio of benefit in [favor of the United States] nine to one."[19] The United States' direct gain from the administration's new trade policy contributed to congressional willingness to renew the president's negotiating authority for additional three-year periods.[20]

Program experience also reinforced the commitment to reciprocity. Many nations were pursuing restrictive bilateral arrangements; without modification, these arrangements proved serious

17. Tasca, *Reciprocal Trade Policy*, 5–6. He noted that "bilateral action appears most feasible under existing conditions. It permits a full frontal attack upon trade barriers in foreign countries as well as a revision of the American tariff. . . . Moreover, bilateral action avoids to a great extent the political implications of an autonomous downward tariff revision in the United States."
18. Ways and Means Report (1934), 15.
19. Hull, *Memoirs*, 362.
20. J. B. Condliffe, *The Reconstruction of World Trade: A Survey of International Economic Relations* (London: Allen and Unwin, 1941), 205.

obstacles to any effort at expanding trade. Unless nations were willing to reject their own restrictive policies, the United States would not offer concessions for fear of encouraging free-riding. The U.S. pledge of reciprocity in negotiating tariff reductions carried the reservation that agreements were possible only if negotiating parties agreed to be bound by the same generalizing principle of equality of treatment.[21]

A case in point emerged within one year of the enactment of the reciprocal trade policy. Germany, hoping for a better trading relationship with the United States, sent a note to the U.S. government on 24 May 1935 "expressing a desire to enter into reciprocal trade relations." On 28 June 1935 the State Department declared willingness to negotiate with any country "provided that its commercial policies do not in fact impose discriminatory or inequitable conditions upon American commerce and do not arbitrarily divert its trade from this country to other countries."[22] As long as Germany retained discriminatory policies, the United States refused participation in reciprocal negotiations. The State Department, however, was explicitly willing to act in a reciprocally cooperative manner if the German government rejected those policies and favored equal treatment.

Even so, this condition was rather loosely applied. For example, Canada retained its position in the Imperial Preference arrangement made with Britain. In negotiations completed during 1935, according to R. L. Buell, the United States undertook duty reductions "on about sixty percent of the dutiable imports of which Canada was the principal source of supply in 1929. In re-

---

21. "The program emphatically rejects substantive bilateralism in favor of formal. It envisages U.S. negotiation of commercial agreements with individual nations, providing for mutual grants of specific concessions and a mutual pledge of unconditional most-favored-nation treatment or its equivalent. This pledge means that any concession accorded in the future by either signatory to any third country will be extended, automatically and without compensation, to the other signatory. As an indispensable corollary of such a pledge, two countries must adopt, as a matter of general policy, the rule of generalizing the concession granted in bilateral agreements to other nations as well." Leo Pasvolsky, "Bilateralism in International Commercial Relations," *Harvard Business Review* 14 (Spring 1936): 287.

22. Tasca, *Reciprocal Trade Policy*, 81–82.

turn, Canada made direct tariff reductions on almost one-third of the dutiable imports from the United States . . . and it extended most-favored-nation treatment to the United States for all its imports, as a result of which duties were lowered on 767 Canadian tariff items."[23] With such incremental steps, the new trade program began to penetrate the exclusive, discriminatory commercial pacts that had proliferated in recent years. Within five years, the United States had negotiated twenty-one reciprocal agreements that not only reduced barriers abroad but also reduced the high duty levels of the U.S. tariff set in 1930.[24]

For the initial expansion of U.S. trade, this significant achievement marked a turning point in the direction of U.S. reciprocal negotiations. Unlike the limited efforts of the pre-1922 period, which were reciprocal in name but generally extortionary in reality, the post-1934 negotiations included genuine (though carefully considered) concessions on the part of the United States. Moreover, the removal of case-by-case congressional approval made possible agreements that endured long enough to establish credibility for the new policy with U.S. trading partners, as well as legitimacy at home.

The Origins of Reciprocity and Unconditional MFN Treatment in the GATT

As time and experience bolstered the optimism of U.S. policymakers, their efforts to expand world trade became more internationally oriented. More and more, activity in the State Department mirrored the original wishes of Secretary Hull that U.S. leadership create a new, vital economic order. In a confidential memorandum to Undersecretary of State Sumner Welles dated 10 November 1937, Leo Pasvolsky echoed clearly and precisely the principles he had supported earlier.[25] This time, however, he was not writing to a public audience about the value of formal bilat-

---

23. R. L. Buell, *The Hull Trade Program* (New York: Foreign Policy Association, 1939), 34.
24. Condliffe, *Reconstruction of World Trade*, 205.
25. Pasvolsky, "Bilateralism," 287.

eralism in the Hull trade program. He was giving one of the country's key policymakers his recommendations for U.S. action in founding a new international economic regime, and his memorandum contained specific proposals for such an endeavor. Prefacing these suggestions with his belief that the time was ripe for international financial and commercial reform, he enumerated three "imperative" courses of action.

First, Pasvolsky argued for "repairment and normalization of the mechanism of international commerce through a gradual relaxation and eventual abandonment of such extraordinary barriers to trade as quotas, other forms of quantitative restriction, and exchange control, with a view to reestablishing customs duties as the predominant means of regulating international commerce." Second, he proposed a "downward adjustment of unreasonably high tariff rates" and, third, the "firm reestablishment of the most-favored-nation principle, in its unconditional and unrestricted form, as the basis of commercial treatment." Moreover, he continued, international agreement should be secured on four specific practices to achieve these important goals:

1. Reestablishment of monetary relations based on stable foreign exchanges;
2. Reexamination and, if necessary, adjustment of existing international debt obligations;
3. Resumption of international lending, more particularly in the field of short-term commercial credit but to some extent also in the field of long-term investment and in that of financial arrangements designed to facilitate abandonment of exchange controls and reorganization of monetary systems;
4. Creation of safeguards against dumping and other unfair trade practices.[26]

26. Leo Pasvolsky, "Memorandum from the Special Assistant to the Secretary of State to Sumner Welles, November 10, 1937, on Possibilities of Action in International Economic Field," Papers of Leo Pasvolsky, 1937–1953 (File no. 1, Subject File International Economic Relations, 1937), Library of Congress Manuscript Division, Washington, D.C. Hereafter cited as Pasvolsky, "Memorandum."

Not surprisingly, Pasvolsky's recommendations closely reflected existing U.S. policies, although they were much more far-reaching than anything yet established by Congress. These proposals remained firmly founded on current practice and they were modified by the normative view from the State Department that a multilateral means for liberalizing trade and regulating monetary and credit policies should be pursued. U.S. concepts about fair trade and equality of treatment were retained as guidelines for any new approach to the international economy.

As policymakers ruminated about the need for U.S. leadership in this effort, the political dimension of nondiscrimination in commercial relations, along with freer intercourse in general, received more attention. S. H. Bailey, an often-quoted liberal analyst, targeted commercial discrimination as a cause of international tension and conflict. He concluded that "the intervention of government has resulted very largely in the superposition of the artificial system of discriminations upon natural economic inequalities already existing. This struggle for wealth and power has led not only to competitive rivalry but to friction." Bailey's rationale was based on his observation of a "psychological reaction of states to the general instability and uneasiness which the existence of the practice [of discrimination] itself engenders. The fear that economic sovereignty may be used ruthlessly against any one state, is sufficient to alarm all. Discrimination, then, is always a potential source of international friction, while the fear and jealousy to which it gives rise in turn drive states to its practice."[27] With the outbreak of World War II, this analysis became popular as observers attempted to pinpoint its origins. More and more, policymakers argued a connection between the emergence of aggressive dictatorships and the exclusive, discriminatory economic policies that had proliferated during the 1930s. Bailey's conclusion seemed prophetic in light of contemporary experience.

Recalling this important evolutionary period in U.S. foreign trade policy after the war, Hull reaffirmed his belief that international economic discord and competition rendered political coop-

27. S. H. Bailey, "The Political Aspect of Discrimination in International Economic Relations," *Economica* 12 (February 1932): 96.

eration improbable. He wrote: "Over and above the economic side of our foreign policy, but closely tied with it, I believed, hung the political side. . . . To me it seemed virtually impossible to develop friendly relations with other nations in the political sphere so long as we provoked their animosity in the economic sphere. How could we promote peace with them while waging war on them commercially?"[28] Events leading up to World War II seemed to corroborate this viewpoint, and contemporary analysts who delved into its contributing factors found economic relations increasingly significant.[29]

The connection between economic relations and political cooperation was not lost on the president or his advisers, as evidenced by postwar planning that became preoccupied with international economic matters. Furthermore, once the United States entered the war, the president was at pains to make certain that the country did not repeat the mistakes of isolationism that followed World War I. Realizing the vast importance of U.S. leadership to establish and promote a postwar world order, Roosevelt encouraged congressional participation, along with that of the departments of State and Treasury, in plans and negotiations for political and commercial cooperation. As Robert Pastor put it, "All too aware of the rise of isolationism after World War I and the rejection of the League of Nations by the Senate, Roosevelt was determined to keep history from repeating."[30]

The lessons of history weighed heavily on important figures throughout the ranks of the American foreign policy bureaucracy, and efforts aimed at directing postwar policy were generally couched in terms of past experience and the vital need for U.S. leadership in building a new cooperative framework that avoided past problems. As Richard Gardner observes, differences in out-

28. Hull, *Memoirs*, 353.
29. See, for example, Albert O. Hirschman, *National Power and the Structure of Foreign Trade* (1945; reprint, Berkeley: University of California Press, 1980). Hirschman analyzed the trade policy of Nazi Germany and determined that the country had deliberately used trade relations to enhance political and strategic dominance, particularly with regard to the Balkan nations.
30. Robert A. Pastor, *Congress and the Politics of United States Foreign Economic Policy, 1929–1976* (Berkeley: University of California Press, 1980), 94.

look existed among the various responsible groups, but individuals "were all deeply influenced by the 'lessons' drawn from the unsuccessful efforts at peacemaking that followed the First World War." These included a resolve to ensure coordinated planning for the postwar era and active U.S. participation in this planning. Because it was also "recognized that a major reason for the breakdown of the last peace settlement lay in the inadequate handling of economic problems," these policymakers "placed great emphasis on economics in drawing blue-prints for a better world."[31] In addressing this particular aspect of the deterioration of relations between nations, officials identified two major contributing and interrelated factors: the competitive devaluations of currency to which nations had resorted in order to make their exports more attractive abroad and the complementary practice of imposing import barriers to discourage purchase of foreign goods. At the same time, various governments used such practices to advance their own positions at the expense of everyone else and often with the clear purpose of establishing economic and political dominance.

As Hirschman wrote in 1945, the spiral of "economic nationalism, more restriction, and more discrimination" that characterized the period following World War I had proved disastrous to peace because "restrictionism and discrimination undoubtedly sharpen national antagonisms. They provide also excellent opportunities for nationalist leaders to arouse popular resentment. And if these leaders, once in power, should feel the slightest doubt concerning the best policy to adopt, they will be much encouraged in their aggressive intentions by realizing that international economic relations provide them with an excellent instrument to achieve their ends."[32] This analysis was mirrored in the attitudes of foreign policy planners, who believed that cooperation to prevent the recurrence of these nationalistic, self-defeating practices was necessary to enduring peace. Plans began to form for interna-

---

31. Richard N. Gardner, *Sterling-Dollar Diplomacy: The Origins and the Prospects of Our International Economic Order*, 2d ed. (New York: McGraw-Hill, 1969), 4.

32. Hirschman, *Structure of Foreign Trade*, 72–73.

tional organizations to resolve financial and commercial disputes between nations. By incorporating the lessons of the past and anticipating future national objections to international governance, wartime planners tried to amend what they considered to be the previous mistakes of extreme protectionism and discrimination.

Officials sought ways to achieve freer flows of trade and to control fluctuations in currency values without toppling domestic economic policies developed during the 1930s. In the United States, New Deal economic planners certainly did not advocate laissez faire; as we have already seen, reform of U.S. tariff policy in 1934 was hardly revolutionary. For both political and practical reasons, protection of U.S. industry was not repudiated, nor was the principle of reciprocity.

Consequently, the new U.S. blueprint for postwar economic order combined seemingly contradictory principles. At once a reaction to the autarky of both the 1920s and the 1930s, it was also a product of New Deal commitments to governmental intervention and past assurances to U.S. industry that it would not be exposed to "unfair" competition from other countries, even if that competition resulted from previous mfn pledges. Policymakers knew that offering an open-ended promise of liberal trade would be futile, given congressional power to authorize each round of presidential tariff negotiations. The Roosevelt administration, though desirous of lower trade barriers and equality of treatment, did not want to forfeit governmental management of financial policy and fair trade practices.[33] Accordingly, the new commercial order was to be designed to encourage freer trade on the basis of equality of treatment and on *fair* methods of exchange as defined by the United States. It would also incorporate enough flexibility to allow escape from injurious agreements on specific duty reductions. In general, the United States remained seriously committed to the process of reciprocity for mutual reduction of trade barriers and for maintenance of fair trade, despite its nondiscrimination pledge.

---

33. Gardner, *Sterling-Dollar Diplomacy*, 76; and Pasvolsky, "Memorandum," 2–3.

American Proposals and ITO/GATT Negotiations

U.S. reciprocal trade policy, combined with a new commitment to leadership in world affairs, guided policymakers toward a new international economic order. Hopeful that they could reverse the trend of protectionism that had plagued the commercial world between the wars, they sought to establish a new cooperative framework that was to be molded from existing U.S. policy and in reaction to past U.S. experience. In normative terms, as well as in legal terms, this was a product of the recently revised commercial orientation of the United States.

Although Britain and the United States had implicitly considered commerce in economic discussions during the war, no formal negotiations took place until 1945, after its end. Beginning in September, the United States presented its position to the British for discussion, and *Proposals for the Expansion of World Trade and Employment* was published.[34] These proposals closely followed Pasvolsky's points in his 1937 memorandum to the undersecretary of state, but they also reflected the compromises from negotiations with Britain. Whereas the State Department had wanted an international effort to eliminate quantitative barriers to trade because such instruments were inherently discriminatory, the British adamantly refused to completely abolish them, and existing U.S. policies made their abandonment unlikely for the United States as well.

Britain feared that postwar economic conditions would place its debt-bound nation in a very disadvantageous position. The freedom to impose import quotas to control the outflow of British pounds was considered vital to stabilizing the balance of payments. Therefore, the compromise recognized that quantitative restrictions should be prohibited in principle but that an exception would be made in case of problems with the balance of payments. They were also to be permitted only during a temporary period of transition (the duration of which was left unspecified) to allow recovery from the war. A second exception was granted for quan-

---

34. United States Department of State, *Proposals for the Expansion of World Trade and Employment* (Washington, D.C., 1945).

titative restrictions in agricultural commodities, to which both nations readily agreed because of the expansion of agricultural production during the war. This exception was particularly important for the United States, whose current administration had created support programs for agricultural commodities to stabilize domestic prices. As Gardner notes, on U.S. Department of Agriculture insistence, quotas would be allowed when they were "necessary to the enforcement of national price-support schemes."[35]

In each case, discriminatory policies were sanctioned in the name of domestic policy flexibility. The State Department had desired a postwar economic order in which such tactics would be shunned, but its first official proposals supported their perpetuation. Pasvolsky's original recommendation, that all quantitative restrictions be abandoned in favor of tariffs as the only means of commercial regulation, had been significantly modified. Tariffs would play the dominant role in regulating trade, but not the only role. The ideal—that equality of treatment could be achieved in the postwar economy—was seriously damaged even before multilateral negotiations took place.

Quotas are by their very nature discriminatory; even if a formula were devised to grant all importers an equal quota, the amounts would not reflect the importer's productive capabilities and relative efficiency. Moreover, quotas set by legislative or bureaucratic designs are quite inflexible; thus, changes in product origin, efficiency, and prices cannot be reflected immediately in any scheme aimed at offering quotas as rewards for efficiency. Economists argue that tariffs, on the other hand, are the least discriminatory and most efficient means of regulating imports. Easily monitored, tariffs are the best trade barrier from the standpoint of international supervision. Despite exceptions allowed for quantitative restrictions, the proposals to which Britain and the United States agreed emphasized the value of tariffs as the least problematical form of protection under the principle of equality of treatment. Where trade barriers had to exist, it was maintained, tariffs constituted the least damaging form.

35. Gardner, *Sterling-Dollar Diplomacy*, 148–50.

Still, the postwar economic planners proposed to lower all barriers to trade, including tariffs. The U.S. experience with the Hawley-Smoot Tariff of 1930, as well as the subsequent defensive and retaliatory actions on the part of U.S. trading partners, had taught them that nondiscrimination in the face of protectionism was not adequate to encourage trade and cooperation. In the short period between implementation of the 1934 Reciprocal Trade Agreements Act and America's entry into World War II, U.S. policymakers had witnessed a significant reversal of trade restrictions as a direct consequence of reciprocal trade negotiations. Consequently, they were convinced that freer exchange of goods as a result of mutually beneficial agreements would be a vital component of any meaningful plan for trade expansion and international accord.

In its negotiations with Britain, the U.S. government proposed to retain the procedure established by the 1934 Reciprocal Trade Agreements Act. In this way Congress would be assured of reciprocity in each and every concession offered by the United States. The bureaucratic mechanisms were already in place for such a plan, and it had proven popular enough for renewal by Congress. To multiply the effects of the trade negotiations, however, U.S. policymakers decided to alter the approach in one important way. As Gardner notes:

> Instead of entering into bilateral negotiations separately with a number of countries, the American Government was prepared to negotiate for tariff reductions at a large conference in which many pairs of bilateral negotiations could be carried on simultaneously. This multilateral-bilateral method of negotiation would enable participating countries to make reductions, not just on the basis of concessions offered to them directly, but on the basis of concessions gained indirectly through the operation of the unconditional most-favored-nation clause.[36]

When the proposals were issued in 1945, the U.S. government included these negotiations for mutually reciprocal tariff reduction, which were drawn directly from existing U.S. policy but

36. Ibid., 151.

modified by the multilateral process of bringing interested nations together to achieve more immediate international results. This procedure would reduce tariffs of all participating countries through a mutually acceptable process of reciprocal concessions. Each country would target the crucial import restrictions for its products, yet the simultaneous negotiations would, via the principle of equality of treatment, have a multilateral effect.

In other important areas of reciprocal treatment, the proposals mirrored U.S. legal practice and earlier State Department wishes. Pasvolsky had specified that the new international economic order encompass rules governing the "fair" practice of international trade, and he specifically identified dumping as an activity that required regulation. The 1945 proposals contained provisions that defined and specified how governments should respond to such unfair practices, and in virtually every respect they adopted existing U.S. practice. Anti-dumping duties were to be allowed for any government that ascertained injury to a domestic industry by the importer's dumping practices. Countervailing duties were also to be given international approval. Interestingly, justification for the latter was couched in the liberal normative view that private economic activities were to be favored over state trading practices, not in the protection of the American tariff from penetration, as had been the law's original intent. And reference was made to other unfair trade methods that would be discouraged by inclusion of an escape clause through which signatories could seek protection from imports entering their market via unfair practices.

Finally, the United States insisted on a general escape clause like that which had appeared in its reciprocal trade negotiations since 1934.[37] Any concession made as a consequence of negotiations on reciprocal tariff reduction that resulted in injury to a domestic industry could thus be legally nullified by temporary ef-

---

37. See, for example, clause 17 of the Mexican Agreement of 1942, as quoted by W. A. Brown: "An escape clause in the event of injury to the producers of particular products made subject to concessions." Brown, *Restoration of World Trade*, 21.

forts to "prevent sudden and widespread injury to the producers concerned."[38] Granting reciprocal concessions could then be effectively revoked by one party if escape were necessary, even if its trading partner maintained the original duty reduction. Problems that the escape clause created for maintenance of reciprocity would seriously occupy international negotiators in the future.[39]

Countries entering the negotiation for the International Trade Organization (ITO) from 1946 to 1948 generally accepted the proposals from the 1945 American and British deliberations. Trade arrangements were to be made on a basis of unconditional mfn treatment. Tariffs would be lowered through reciprocal and mutually advantageous bilateral agreements. Quantitative restrictions would be discouraged, except under specified circumstances. Certain unfair trade practices would be regulated by individual retaliatory action and escape allowed when they threatened domestic industry.

The GATT, drawn directly from the ITO provisions, was largely a U.S. creation and, in fact, replaced the ITO in practice when congressional resistance jeopardized the proposed trade organization. Although modified by other states' input, the U.S. normative view was effectively adopted by delegates to conferences in London, Geneva, and Havana; moreover, the codification of international trading rules in the first General Agreement reflected U.S. trade policy and commitment to "fair" trade practices. This outlook was molded not only by inherited institutions and the events of the 1920s and 1930s but also by a new adherence to liberal trade and reciprocity.[40]

Most analysts agree that "free trade" in 1945 meant something quite different from the laissez-faire concept of the nineteenth century. As Karin Kock maintained, "Today a free trader is an individual who believes that tariff protection is sufficient and that duties should be fairly stable and should be subject to the most-

38. United States Department of State, *Proposals*, Chap. 3, Sec. B.
39. The Tokyo Round of trade negotiations on proposals for a safeguard code spent a good deal of time on this issue.
40. Judith Goldstein, "Ideas, Institutions, and American Trade Policy," in Ikenberry et al., eds., *American Foreign Economic Policy*, 179–217.

favored-nation principle, i.e., should be non-discriminatory."[41] Despite missing the point about multilateral tariff reductions, this view does suggest that the liberal order envisioned at the end of World War II was liberal only within certain recognized constraints, in other words, a framework for liberalism that would allow national maneuverability in economic planning, protection for import-sensitive industries, and protection against unfair trade practices. The starting place would be negotiations for 50 percent tariff reductions on a reciprocal mfn basis, not total abolition of barriers.

Caution ruled, due not only to Congress's fear of abandoning protection but also to world apprehension about free trade. Therefore, according to John Ruggie:

> The task of postwar institutional reconstruction . . . was to maneuver between these two extremes [of unimpeded multilateralism and nationalist isolationism] and to devise a framework which would safeguard and even aid the quest for domestic stability without, at the same time, triggering the mutually destructive external consequences that had plagued the interwar period. This was the essence of the embedded liberalism compromise: unlike the economic nationalism of the thirties, it would be multilateral in character; unlike the liberalism of the gold standard and free trade, its multilateralism would be predicated upon domestic interventionism.[42]

The paradox, of course, is that this new order was founded on contradictory policies—liberal trade and also the recognition that some state economic planning and protection was necessary, not simply for recovery, but also for preservation of fair trade in the new liberal order.[43] Extremist behavior of any kind would be avoided, and this policy of moderation, self-contradictory though it was, appeared in the GATT provisions as well. As Ruggie notes, "The principles of multilateralism and tariff reduction were

---

41. Karin Kock, *International Trade Policy and the GATT, 1947–1967* (Stockholm: Almqvist and Wiksell, 1969), 7.

42. John Gerard Ruggie, "International Regimes, Transactions, and Change: Embedded Liberalism in the Postwar Economic Order," in Stephen D. Krasner, ed., *International Regimes* (Ithaca: Cornell University Press, 1983), 209.

43. Kock, *International Trade Policy*, 8.

affirmed, but so were safeguards, exemptions, exceptions, and restrictions, all designed to protect the balance of payments and a variety of domestic social policies."[44]

U.S. Leadership and the New GATT Regime

Because the world's major trading nations emerged from war with highly protected economies, the first multilateral negotiations required something from everyone, and U.S. leadership played an important role by encouraging cooperation. From the U.S. point of view, one of the most obvious lessons of its 1934 attempt to initiate a unilaterally conceived but bilaterally negotiated policy of reciprocity was that this plan was instituted without benefit of other truly complementary policies. Though individual negotiations were pursued under the policy, a *regime* was not created under which the same rules and general expectations governed actors' behaviors.[45]

To multilateralize trade liberalization, the United States insisted on the principle of unconditional mfn treatment between the GATT contracting parties but also upheld reciprocity as the most efficacious means to cooperation. Knowing well that the U.S. tariff had deterred cooperation between partners, the United States offered a substantial tariff reduction if equivalent offers were reciprocated.[46] Because of its hegemonic position following World War II, this country could liberalize its vast market at little political cost and great economic benefit at home.

At the same time, the international setting was ripe for the success of U.S. leadership. Although its trading partners wanted proof that the United States would shoulder its responsibilities as the world's healthiest economy, they were also highly amenable

44. Ruggie, "International Regimes," 209.
45. I am utilizing the well-known definition advanced by Stephen D. Krasner, "Structural Causes and Regime Consequences: Regimes as Intervening Variables," in Krasner, ed., *International Regimes*, 2.
46. Gloria Waldron and Norman S. Buchanan, *America's Stake in World Trade* (New York: Twentieth Century Fund Public Affairs Pamphlet 130, 1947), 23; and, generally, Gardner, *Sterling-Dollar Diplomacy*.

to a cooperative stance toward U.S. ideas. The trauma of devastating war on the heels of the disastrous 1930s world economy convinced victors in the West of their interdependent concerns. A certain momentum of perceived mutual interest resulted in cooperation,[47] and the development of international economic linkages and mutual recognition of a normative and legal framework to govern them characterized the immediate postwar period.

47. Robert Jervis, "From Balance to Concert: A Study of International Security Cooperation," in Kenneth A. Oye, ed., *Cooperation under Anarchy* (Princeton: Princeton University Press, 1986), 58–79, argues that during traumatic periods, a "stag hunt" may be more typical than a prisoner's dilemma, where the incentive to cooperate outweighs the incentive to defect, making concert possible, if tenuous. Though he applies this notion to the security dilemma, it may be equally analogous to the economic sphere following the depression and World War II.

4

GATT Norms, Retaliation, and Dispute Settlement

The GATT embodied the hybrid character of trade policy, which placed principles of nondiscrimination and liberalism alongside reciprocity and fair trade. Grafted upon a multilateral design for trade cooperation and dispute settlement, these principles underpinned the evolving international trade regime after 1948. Expectations about cooperative and uncooperative behavior, trade openness and protectionism, and dispute resolution within the GATT framework have been influenced by these original principles as well as by transnational trade interactions, domestic and international politics and international bargaining.

Consequently, as it was established, the GATT regime consists of "norms, rules, and decision-making procedures"[1] that reflect and enforce principles of multilateralism and liberal trade along with principles of equal treatment, compensation, and national sovereignty. Inherently contradictory, the GATT regime has nonetheless been remarkably adaptable and resilient, primarily because neither of the two dominant regime principles—nondiscrimination and reciprocity—have been rigidly or exclusively enforced. Parties have generally respected nondiscrimination but have allowed exceptions for purposes of fair trade enforcement and com-

---

1. Stephen Krasner, "Structural Causes and Regime Consequences: Regimes as Intervening Variables," in Stephen Krasner, ed., *International Regimes* (Ithaca: Cornell University Press, 1983), 2.

pensation. The latter principle has also been flexibly applied since 1948 in a liberal context so that the coercive and narrowly limited reciprocity of the early 1900s has been avoided.

The contradictory nature of these two fundamental principles, inherent in the philosophical and legal origins of the GATT, has created ambiguity in expectation convergence among the GATT member nations, which, paradoxically, has also balanced international goals of open trade with national means of settling disputes when those goals are not attained. Nowhere is the reciprocity dilemma more evident than in the General Agreement, which provides that multilateral trade openness and nondiscrimination will be enforced by discriminatory retaliations and bilateral resolutions.

The GATT Norms

Overarching the multilateral trade agreement are four norms of behavior that enhance international trade and encourage cooperation between trading partners. Contractual in nature, each nation's accession to the GATT signals commitment to these principles.

1. Nondiscrimination. All countries accept unconditional most-favored-nation treatment for all contracting parties, which establishes the expectation that individual trading nations will not discriminate in dealings with other trading nations except as allowed by the agreement in specific circumstances.

2. Transparency. The GATT contracting parties commit themselves to openness in trading practices. Regulations, international arrangements, tariff schedules, and quotas are transparent so that trading partners are not tricked, surprised, or discriminated against by hidden domestic rules and procedures or secret international agreements. One of the most important GATT provisions requires that individual members report to the GATT their trade policies. As John Jackson has emphasized, "One of the most significant functions that the GATT has filled during the last several decades is that of gathering and collecting |with the

aid of the GATT Secretariat in Geneva] information about international trade policy so that governments can act more intelligently."[2]

3. Consultation and dispute settlement. Contracting parties commit to negotiate trade practices and to consult with one another when conflict arises. This principle also implies willingness to engage in good-faith efforts to reach a mutually acceptable arrangement.

4. Reciprocity. All GATT members enter the agreement with the understanding that commercial treatment between members should be balanced. As clearly stated in the preamble, the objectives of higher living standards, increased trade volume, and expanded employment will be served "by entering into reciprocal and mutually advantageous arrangements directed to the substantial reduction of tariffs and other barriers to trade and to the elimination of discriminatory treatment in international commerce."[3]

The concept of balance in international trading relations is particularly important because it indicates that reciprocity between GATT trading partners will be expected and granted; if this fails, however, then compensation can be taken. In a sense, this important normative principle provides the incentive and inducement for compliance with other GATT norms, while it is a significant end itself.

Therefore, reciprocity—where trade concessions are mutually beneficial and trade restrictions are mutually injurious—becomes not only a guiding principle but also the means that the GATT provides to achieve and maintain such balanced treatment. This practical consequence of demands by sovereign nations to retain some leverage over others ensures that no significant market liberalization will be required without their receiving similar access elsewhere.

The coincidence of unconditional mfn treatment and reciproc-

2. John H. Jackson, *World Trade and the Law of GATT* (New York: Bobbs-Merrill, 1969), 124.

3. GATT, Preamble, *Basic Instruments and Selected Documents*, vol. 3 (Geneva, 1958), 3, hereinafter cited as GATT, *BISD*.

ity, however, has created tension within the GATT. For example, disparties in liberalization can develop over time between member nations, leading to conflicts and individual demands for balance. Rule violation and even legal trade restrictions may result in removal of concessions that injure another nation. Therefore, the principle of reciprocity implies that injured nations impose some equivalent injury against the offender or seek some other form of compensation. In either example, the mfn principle may be violated in favor of reciprocity.

Cooperative Reciprocity

At the most fundamental level, reciprocity in the GATT includes mutual extension of unconditional mfn treatment by contracting parties to all other contracting parties. Reciprocity in this sense is contractual where member nations reward other members for committing themselves to cooperation. Each member must agree to adhere to the principle that every other member be guaranteed the same treatment as that granted to its mfn trading partner in any existing or future trade compact. When the contracting party accedes to the GATT, all forthcoming trade relations are guided by the unconditionality of mfn treatment, and initial acceptance of Article 1 guarantees such treatment to all other signatories in exchange for receiving this status.

Reciprocal Acceptance of Unconditional MFN Treatment

In reality, however, the process is not so sweeping or clear cut. As Gerard Curzon observes, new members of the GATT are "expected to enter into tariff negotiations with existing contraction parties. The acceding government thus 'pays' an entrance fee in exchange for all the benefits and concessions which have already been negotiated in the past, making balanced treatment the contractual goal." The immediate initial benefits, therefore, go to the "newcomer," whereas tariff reductions are contingent on successful negotiations. Reciprocity is not sacrificed in the interests of new membership, however, because Article 35 stipulates that the agreement "would not apply as between any two contracting parties which had not entered into tariff negotiations with each other, either of which, at the time either became a contracting party, did not consent to such application."[4]

If existing members fear one-sidedness in granting mfn status to a new contracting party, they may invoke Article 35 to delay immediate and unconditional mfn treatment, a provision used by several GATT members against Japan during its first several years of membership. These members reacted to Japan's unwillingness to negotiate what were considered serious impediments to trade with that country.[5] This example shows how the principle of reciprocity, though embodied in the initial mutual guarantee of unconditional mfn treatment, may actually contradict such treatment when perceived imbalances emerge in subsequent trade relations.

Even so, GATT reciprocity should not be confused with the conditional mfn form that the United States practiced before 1922, which made each and every trade agreement inherently conditional on the trading partner's meeting terms of trade equal to those secured in a previous agreement. In contrast to conditional mfn treatment, reciprocity indicates that once the contracting party to the GATT accepts the contractual provisions, it cannot legally place conditions on maintenance of mfn status for other GATT members except when *specifically* allowed. Much like Thomas Hobbes's social contract, accession to the GATT involves an initial one-time-only compact between sovereign entities, a process that is not reintroduced for each new trade arrangement. Consequently, all subsequent trade relations are theoretically conducted on the basis of unconditional mfn treatment so that negotiated concessions are extended multilaterally to all members. Unlike Hobbes's social contract of course, international relations—trade or otherwise—require no transferal of power with the contractual agreement. Although nations pledge

---

4. Gerard Curzon, *Multilateral Commercial Diplomacy: The General Agreement on Tariffs and Trade and Its Impact on National Commercial Policies and Techniques* (London: Michael Joseph, 1965), 35 and 37.

5. Ibid., 37.

to adhere to the principle of unconditional mfn treatment and to the other GATT norms, individual national sovereignty is not superseded.

The early U.S. effort to make the GATT an exclusive international club failed because of the sovereignty issue. The United States had proposed that binding every member to a restrictive agreement that granted unconditional mfn status to *other members only* would strengthen the enforcement aspect of the GATT because only members would benefit from the multilateral negotiation process. This exclusivity would also encourage other nations to join the GATT, the U.S. delegation at Geneva argued in 1947, because they would have to sign in order to secure the benefits of mfn treatment from all original signatories. This position was opposed, however, because it would interfere with the sovereign rights of members to trade with nonmembers.[6] To maintain the integrity of the GATT effort and at the same time ensure sovereign latitude, the negotiators in Geneva compromised. Any member nation could voluntarily grant equality of treatment to nonmember nations on the basis of the unconditional mfn principle.[7]

Therefore, nonmembers have been able to free-ride on the collective effort of the GATT multilateral trade negotiations by securing mfn treatment from one contracting party. For example, Mexico, whose major trading partner is the United States, benefited for nearly three decades from the GATT negotiations that produced lower U.S. barriers to trade because of its mfn status with the United States.[8] Although the traditionally accepted definition of the GATT is not a pure collective good in game theoretic terms because actors can be excluded from benefits, the treaty does have the characteristic that non-cost-absorbing actors, in this

6. Clair Wilcox, *Report on ITO*, Transcript of Proceedings, 1 October 1947, Files of the Department of State, Record Group 560, AL/10–147, National Archives, Washington, D.C.

7. Khurshid Hyder, *Equality of Treatment and Trade Discrimination in International Law* (The Hague: Martinus Mijhoff, 1968), 76–78.

8. Sidney Weintraub, *Free Trade between Mexico and the United States?* (Washington, D.C.: Brookings Institution, 1984), 40. Mexico joined the GATT in 1986.

case those uncommitted to the multilateral concession process, can obtain collective benefits if any contracting party elects not to exclude them.

More important, once unconditional mfn status has been obtained, members themselves may free-ride. The principle of reciprocity cannot guarantee that all countries will continue to pay participation costs because mfn treatment guarantees security of concessions multilaterally. For example, Australia and Canada have often been chided within GATT delegation circles for such behavior, that is, participating in relatively few bargains but enjoying others' results.[9]

As we shall see, the GATT's dichotomous nature creates contradictory pressures within the regime. Although unconditional mfn is originally granted on a contractual basis, as discussed above, it subsequently takes the form of nearly open-ended security (except for delineated temporary departures). During periods when free ridership is not perceived as a problem, tension between reciprocity and mfn treatment does not mount; when surplus capacity makes nations sensitive to the trading behavior of others, however, reciprocity, not unconditional mfn, has become the more important principle.

Procedural Reciprocity

Hand in hand with the mfn provision in Article 1 goes contractual acceptance on accession to the GATT of the rules and procedures prescribed by contracting parties. In a sense, all signatories agree to be reciprocally guided by principles of liberal trade, transparency of commercial regulations, and commitment to negotiate trade barriers. A legal point of view deems the GATT a constitutional document by which national trade policies are to be guided and in reference to which international disputes are settled.[10] This element of reciprocity is characterized by the will-

9. Frieder Roessler, GATT Legal Division, GATT Secretariat, interviewed by author, Geneva, 23 November 1984.

10. John Jackson, "Dispute Settlement Techniques between Nations Concerning Economic Relations—with Special Emphasis on GATT," in Thomas E. Car-

ingness of nations to adhere to the provisions of the GATT, in terms of both commercial actions and international conciliation when practices or policies cause concern. National treatment, mutual recognition of trade law, and national application of international codes and procedures all fall under this general categorization.

Reciprocity in Trade Negotiations

The negotiation process, which was designed to reduce barriers to trade around the world, employs the principle of reciprocity. GATT negotiations, as we have seen, were modeled on the bilateral trade agreements that resulted from the 1934 United States Reciprocal Trade Agreements Act. Although they occur in a multilateral setting and extend to all contracting parties, the actual tariff reductions are settled in bilateral discussions. This approach was taken because of the realization that principal suppliers of the product under discussion could deal directly with delegates of importing nations whose tariffs and other barriers impeded importation. It was also taken partly because of the belief that trade barriers would be reduced as a result of "reciprocal and mutually advantageous arrangements."[11] The bilateral setting for specific tariff negotiations has lent itself more readily to the culmination of mutually satisfactory agreements. As Robert Hudec explains:

> The dominant purpose of a trade agreement was the exchange of tariff reductions. The concept of a balanced exchange was central. The appearance of a sound bargain was usually regarded as essential to the political support of such agreements, and trade policy officials were not opposed to the idea, for they saw that their own tariff reductions would contribute most to general trade liberalization if they were used to pry similar concessions from others. The word for the idea of balanced exchange was "reciprocity."[12]

bonneau, ed., *Resolving Transnational Disputes through International Arbitration* (Charlottesville: University Press of Virginia, 1984), 39–72.

11. GATT, Preamble, *BISD*, 3.

12. Robert Hudec, *The GATT Legal System and World Trade Diplomacy* (New York: Praeger, 1975), 19–20.

Politically, the concept of reciprocity of trade barrier reductions has been crucial. Unconditional mfn treatment guarantees non-discrimination and accelerates the trade liberalization process, whereas reciprocity encourages trading partners to participate. If they are to benefit from reductions of barriers, then they are expected to offer something equivalent in return.

During negotiations, if one country fails to meet a reduction offer with what its trading partner considers an equivalent offer, then no agreement occurs because the original offer will be withdrawn. This bargaining dynamic appropriately describes negotiations that took place on an item-by-item basis before the Kennedy Round that began in 1964. Still, the description continued to be meaningful with adoption of linear, or across-the-board, tariff cuts during this round as the major participants refused to forgo reciprocity as a basis for negotiation. When the GATT ministers agreed to the "linear approach to tariff reduction," as Evans notes,

> It was with the provision that reciprocity be achieved. Exceptions lists were to be subject to negotiation "for reciprocity." The E.E.C rejected tariff reductions of equal percentage because it would not give them reciprocity. Furthermore, all the participants have made it clear that if their partners will not accord them reciprocity by improving their offers, they will seize it by withdrawing some of the reductions in their own tariffs which they had been prepared to grant.[13]

Even in the Tokyo Round, during which Swiss participants devised a formula for downward harmonization of tariffs, reciprocity continued to play a role because delegations were willing to put certain product categories on the negotiating table because of offers made by others.[14] Therefore, the formula reduction ap-

13. John W. Evans, *United States Trade Policy: New Legislation for the Kennedy Round* (New York: Harper and Row, 1967), 29–30.
14. The Swiss formula of $Z = AX$ was "generally accepted by the main industrialized countries as a working hypothesis; . . . [however], there were considerable variations in its application. The European Economic Community and the Nordic Countries—followed later by Australia—used the coefficient 16, whereas

proach eliminated neither the inclination nor the ability of the negotiators to wrangle deals for particular products to be included in the overall package of tariff cuts.[15] Moreover, the Tokyo Round had been launched at the end of the ministerial meeting held in Tokyo in September 1973, in which it was declared that "the negotiations shall be conducted on the basis of the principles of mutual advantage, mutual commitment and overall reciprocity."[16] The U.S. delegation was also legally bound to be guided in negotiations by reciprocity. According to the 1979 U.S. Trade Agreements Act, "No agreement accepted by the President . . . shall apply between the United States and any other country unless the President determines that such country (1) has accepted the obligations of the agreement with respect to the U.S., and (2) should not be denied the benefits because it has not accorded adequate *reciprocity* to the commerce of the United States, required from other industrial countries by Section 126 (c) of the 1974 Trade Act."[17]

Not only were the rounds of negotiation to be guided by reciprocity, but the 1974 act also mandated that the U.S. delegation adhere to its reciprocity provisions; if it did not do so in the eyes of the administration (watched carefully by Congress), the 1979 act would require nullification of the delegation's offers. Such domestic constraints not only kept considerations of reciprocity at the forefront of the bargaining process but also created some interesting problems for the principle of unconditional mfn treatment with regard to the Tokyo Round code negotiations.

As for the economic validity of reciprocity in tariff reduction negotiations, many economists maintain that the concept is vac-

---

the coefficient 14 was used by the United States, Japan and Switzerland. Canada employed its own formula. These variations were designed to yield an approximately equal average cut in each country's overall tariff. Certain other countries, New Zealand for example, resorted to the item-by-item technique." GATT, *The Tokyo Round of Multilateral Trade Negotiations* (Geneva, April 1979), 46–47.

15. Frieder Roessler, interviewed by author, Geneva, 23 November 1984.

16. GATT, "The Tokyo Declaration," *GATT Activities in 1972* (Geneva, 1973), 7.

17. John H. Jackson, Jean-Victor Louis, and Mitsuo Matsushita, "Implementing the Tokyo Round: Legal Aspects of Changing Economic Rules," *Michigan Law Review* 81 (December 1982): 364.

uous, and some even indict reciprocity as the main villain to trade liberalization. This point of view seems well worth discussing to clarify why the dynamic of reciprocity is more important as a *political* process than as an economic one. According to the classical school of free trade, any trade barrier will result in inefficiency and a net cost to the country imposing it. Following this logic, therefore, reductions in trade barriers should benefit the country as a whole, and a government guided by rational calculation of costs and benefits would opt for unilateral abolition of such barriers.[18] Reciprocity finds no logical place in this construction because it assumes that tariff reduction is a concession to be painfully surrendered only if an equivalent concession is made in compensation. The classical economist asks, Why is a tariff reduction viewed as a concession to importers when in reality it increases the overall wealth of the importing society?

This same economist finds no value in the notion of reciprocity other than the use it might have in convincing domestic pressure groups that injury to certain import-competing industries by lower tariffs will not only be compensated by cheaper imports for consumers but will also be softened by stimulation of export industries when tariff reductions are reciprocated abroad.[19] As Frieder Roessler argues, governments are in reality "not guided by economic theories aiming at the maximization of efficiency and national welfare. Instead they act in response to the various pressures to which they are subjected thus maximizing the interests of the strongest pressure groups. Given the predominance of producer interests in political life, governments can liberalize trade only if they gain their support. The insistence on counter-conces-

---

18. Gerard Curzon and Victoria Curzon, "The Management of Trade Relations in the GATT," in Andrew Shonfield, ed., *International Economic Relations of the Western World, 1959–1971* (Oxford: Oxford University Press, 1976), 156–57. Classical economists recognize two exceptions: infant industry and optimum tariffs.

19. Harry G. Johnson, "Trade Negotiations and the New International Monetary System" (Paper prepared for a series of Conferences on the Multilateral Trade Negotiations of the GATT, sponsored by the Graduate Institute of International Studies, Geneva, and the Trade Policy Research Centre, London, 11 March 1976), 9–10.

sions benefiting producers serves to create such support."[20] Even grudging acceptance of this political necessity has generally caused free trade economists to support the GATT negotiation process that for over forty years has been predicated upon reciprocity.[21]

The debate over the economic efficacy of reciprocity is important because it reveals the vagueness and uncertainty in which "reciprocal concessions" are made. If reciprocity has uncertain economic meaning in the first place, then quantifying the equivalence of concessions is impossible. Consequently, reciprocal concession becomes a highly subjective concept based more on national negotiators' perceptions than on some universally agreed formula,[22] hence the reluctance of Tokyo Round participants to accept unconditionally the Swiss formula for across-the-board tariff cuts for all product categories.

Even so, not all economists take the strict classical view. Debates over optimal tariffs have for some time focused on the practical benefits of certain degrees of protection under certain circumstances.[23] Beth Yarborough and Robert Yarborough's contributions to international trade theory indicate that reciprocity in fact facilitates "the successful negotiation of trade agreements which would otherwise be impossible."[24]

National governments may be pressured to respond in like manner to trade liberalization policies of other nations in recipro-

20. Frieder Roessler, "The Rationale for Reciprocity in Trade Negotiations under Floating Currencies," *Kyklos* 31 (1976): 264.

21. See, for example, Richard Blackhurst, "Reciprocity in Trade Negotiations under Flexible Exchange Rates," in J. P. Martin and A. Smith, eds., *Trade and Payments Adjustment under Flexible Exchange Rates* (London: Macmillan, Trade Policy Research Centre, 1979), 212–44, especially 230, for a critique of the argument that concessions or promises are actually linked to support by export industries.

22. Jan Tumlir, director, GATT Economic Research Division, GATT Secretariat, interviewed by author, Geneva, 22 January 1985.

23. John Whalley, *Trade Liberalization among Major World Trading Areas* (Cambridge: MIT Press, 1985), 234–37, especially his discussion of the historical argument on optimal tariffs and retaliation.

24. Beth V. Yarborough and Robert M. Yarborough, "Reciprocity, Bilateralism, and Economic 'Hostages': Self-enforcing Agreements in International Trade," *International Studies Quarterly* 30 (March 1986): 8.

cal negotiations, whereas they might never consider doing so unilaterally. The U.S. historical experience supports this. With one eye on the advantages of an open trading order and one on immediate negotiations, a government may consider the effect that uncooperative behavior could have on relations with its trading partner, as well as assess the domestic political consequences of its position.

An action that spurs its trading partner to retaliate by withdrawing an earlier concession would have a deleterious impact on both the export industry in the domestic economy of the first country and on the broader liberalization process in which it participates. Three different dynamics are at work in such a case: first, the government contemplating an uncooperative action must consider the benefits to be gained at home if such action is carried out; second, it must calculate the costs that such action might impose on its relationship with the other nation; and finally, it must judge how its actions might undermine the larger cooperative framework within which these relationships exist. Robert Keohane has described this latter consideration. To understand how nations make such choices involves understanding actors' expectations about future patterns of interaction, their assumptions about the proper nature of economic arrangements, and the kinds of political activities they regard as legitimate. As Keohane observes: "Each act of cooperation or discord affects the beliefs, rules, and practices that form the context for future actions. Each act must, therefore, be interpreted as embedded within a chain of such acts and their successive cognitive and institutional residues."[25]

As long as an individual member of the GATT intends to maintain the liberal trading order, then its calculation of interests must include the potential effect that actions may have on encouraging counterrestrictive measures that could be immediately costly or ultimately lead to destruction of trade openness. Reciprocity, therefore, immediately reminds others that trade restriction may be matched by trade restriction and trade liberalization by trade

---

25. Robert O. Keohane, *After Hegemony: Cooperation and Discord in the World Political Economy* (Princeton: Princeton University Press, 1984), 56.

liberalization. As free trade economists have generally demonstrated why reducing trade barriers remains in the global interest, a political dynamic that maintains relative openness may be a small price to pay, even if it at times constitutes very "uneconomic" notions about fairness and equivalence.

Reciprocal trade negotiations in the GATT also include nontariff barriers (NTBs), which may be even more cumbersome than tariffs for establishing reciprocity. Reciprocity could be assessed by simply logging which nations signed a particular code, but this system does not identify how a specific agreement affects one nation more than another, how the exact wording of the arrangement reflects the interests of the concerned parties, or what bargains were struck. As such problems plague analysts, they are also likely to plague negotiators, who are responsible for assuring their governments that they have reached an equitable arrangement based on reciprocal concessions. Increasingly, nontariff barriers rather than tariffs concern international trade analysts.[26] Quotas, export subsidies, orderly marketing arrangements, government procurement practices, and other trade restrictions have replaced tariffs as the main sources of protection for most nations. Reciprocally acceptable agreements that are multilateral in scope may create new challenges for their signatories.

The behavior codes negotiated during the Tokyo Round have demonstrated that reciprocity, rather than mfn, has increasingly become the most important guiding principle for contracting parties. For example, the United States, in accordance with the 1979 Trade Act, has made application of the various codes (government procurement, subsidy and countervailing duties, customs valuation, technical barriers to trade, import licensing, and civil aircraft) conditional on the trading partner being a signatory to the code and demonstrating a good-faith effort to meet the code's terms.[27] This application of the policy of strict reciprocity directly violates Article 1 of the GATT, yet the unconditional mfn principle upholds the original GATT negotiating tradition that the

26. United States Senate Committee on Finance, *MTN Studies* (Washington, D.C., 1979).
27. Jackson, Louis, and Matsushita, "Implementing the Tokyo Round," 363–64.

agreement itself be accepted contractually and that balanced treatment be maintained over time. This dichotomy is yet another example of the general tension that exists between unconditional mfn treatment as a general principle of behavior and reciprocity as the practical means to achievement.

Reciprocity within the GATT framework, therefore, consists in large part of all contracting parties' willingness to adhere to the argument's rules and to submit trade policies to negotiation; in return, fellow members promise each nation the same. Reciprocity in this sense is generally concessionary in character with "positive" connotations. W. A. Brown, an early observer of the GATT, has noted that its "achievements are not only the speeding up and broadening of the process of tariff negotiation through the multilateral-bilateral technique, but the creation of an *esprit de corps* and a sense of mutual respect and trust among the contracting parties in meeting many common problems."[28]

Although concessions may be withdrawn during negotiation in direct retaliation against perceived uncooperativeness on the part of one's trading partner, the overall achievement has historically been constructive. Reciprocity has consisted of offers made, counteroffers assessed, and final positions taken in light of those assessments. Forward movement occurs, although there might be specific bargaining setbacks. The process consists of rewards that generally match the cooperation, nondiscrimination, and rule adherence of trading partners with equivalent responses, at the same time as they take into account the cooperative momentum from the multilateral trade negotiations. Implicit in each cooperative encounter, however, is the threat that retaliation may be imposed as a form of leverage.

Retaliation

Unlike cooperative reciprocity, which consists largely of rule observance and contractual good faith within the GATT and which generally rewards cooperative behavior with cooperative

28. W. A. Brown, *The United States and the Restoration of World Trade* (Washington, D.C.: Brookings Institution, 1950), 378.

behavior, retaliation forms the complementary side of commercial interactions where harmful acts are matched with punishment in the form of compensation. When analyzing reciprocal behavior in regard to the GATT regime, legalized retaliations must not be confused with retaliatory behavior that lies outside the regime. To clarify this distinction, I will explain legal and illegal actions and then assess their respective impact on GATT norms.

GATT-Legalized Retaliations

Concession withdrawals during negotiations. I have already discussed how national delegations may use withdrawal of concessions during multilateral trade negotiations or the threat thereof, as leverage on trading partners. Although no set of rules governs the bargaining process, the principle of "mutual advantage" as laid down in the preamble to the GATT guides bilateral negotiations. Implicit in this principle is the freedom of nations to induce other nations to make acceptable offers. The bargaining dynamic that ensues from such bilateral efforts often involves retaliation as well as cooperative reciprocity.[29]

Because offer withdrawals during negotiations are part of concessionary reciprocity, they are implicitly sanctioned as acceptable practices under the GATT framework. Therefore, if a national government announces termination of an earlier offer while negotiations are in progress, if no new arrangements have been signed, and if this termination constitutes retaliatory action against the behavior of the trading partner involved, such a retaliation is perfectly legal. Such actions thus make very effective leverage in the negotiation process.

Article 23 nullification and impairment. Concessionary withdrawals during trade negotiations are predicated on a delegation's belief that its trading partner has not given equivalent concessions

---

29. See, for example, Curzon and Curzon, "Management of Trade Relations," 187–88, for a discussion of tariff bargaining during the Kennedy Round, in which concessions, withdrawals, and counterwithdrawals characterized a dispute between the European Economic Community (EEC) and the United States, the Nordic countries, and Switzerland.

in return. A similar rationale lies behind some of the major provisions of the GATT that authorize retaliation or compensatory action, although they are primarily motivated by efforts to maintain the existing order under standing rules, not by the hope of new concessions. The key GATT provision that allows retaliation is Article 23, which may be invoked

> if any contracting party should consider that any benefit accruing to it directly or indirectly under this Agreement is being nullified or impaired or that the attainment of any objective of the Agreement is being impeded as the result of (a) the failure of another contracting party to carry out its obligations under this Agreement, or (b) the application by another contracting party of any measure, whether or not it conflicts with the provisions of this Agreement, or (c) the existence of any other situation.

Retaliation in this case means withdrawal of "such concessions or other obligations as [the contracting parties] determine to be appropriate in the circumstances."[30] Furthermore, retaliation under Article 23 can legally result only from the dispute settlement procedure of the GATT, after all efforts to reach a bilateral settlement have failed. Thus, Article 23 retaliation is not the prerogative of the injured state but must be authorized by contracting parties to the GATT to be strictly legal. Since 1948, only once has retaliation against violation nullification and impairment been formally authorized by the contracting parties in a 1952 authorization for the Netherlands to take protective action in response to a confessed U.S. legal violation.[31]

Another case brought to the GATT under Article 23 was a complaint by the United States that the French had illegally retained several quantitative restrictions from the years following World War II, when balance-of-payments difficulties had forced that country to impose quotas. According to Robert Hudec, the GATT panel ruled that the "French restrictions had caused 'nulli-

---

30. GATT, *BISD*, vol. 1, Article 23, 51.
31. Robert Hudec, "Retaliation against 'Unreasonable' Foreign Trade Practices: The New Section 301 and GATT Nullification and Impairment," *Minnesota Law Review* 59 (1975): 505.

fication or impairment of benefits to which the United States is entitled under the General Agreement.' The results of the case arrived in 'two installments.' Shortly after the decision, the French agreed to remove some of the quotas and to liberalize others. Nothing further happened until 1972 when the United States renewed demands to completely eliminate the remaining quotas. After the U.S. formal request for authority to retaliate beyond its compensatory actions, the French government agreed to remove all but one of the remaining restrictions."[32] This case illustrates how the threat of authorized retaliation may have induced France to cooperate; as the contracting parties had not formally ruled that the French violated the GATT, even though the GATT panel ruled that nullification or impairment of U.S. benefits resulted from French actions, quite possibly authorization for retaliation would not have been forthcoming. In fact, the doctrine of nonviolation nullification and impairment has never been used to authorize retaliation by contracting parties as a whole.

Article 19 escape clause nullification and impairment. Other GATT provisions allow governments to withdraw concessions that have already been made "unilaterally and without prior authorization, as a means of restoring the balance of reciprocity with another member which has taken advantage of an escape provision."[33] The most notable is the Article 19 provision for emergency action, which authorizes exporting nations adversely affected by the escape action of an importing nation to take compensatory or retaliatory measures.

Escape action can be taken in the first place when "any product is being imported into the territory of that contracting party in such increased quantities and under such conditions as to cause or threaten serious injury to domestic producers in that territory of like or directly competitive products, the contracting party shall be free . . . as may be necessary to prevent or remedy such injury, to suspend the obligation [incurred as a member of GATT] in

32. Ibid., 496.
33. Ibid., 507.

96

whole or in part or to withdraw or modify the concession."[34] Because such emergency action may nullify or impair the benefits that the importing nation previously conceded to the exporting nation, the latter may be free to take retaliatory protective action, both as compensation and as leverage to make escape action an unattractive last-resort option.[35]

Article 28 nullification and impairment. Working much the same way as the escape provision of Article 19, GATT Article 28 allows national governments "to cancel tariff concessions in periodic 'open seasons' (such as for the purpose of customs union harmonization)."[36] Consequently, nations whose trade is adversely affected by such cancellations have benefits previously granted to them withdrawn, and the nullification and impairment provision applies here also.

The most famous invocation of Article 28 occurred in 1963 as part of the so-called chicken war between the United States and the European Economic Community (EEC). As Hudec notes: "During the formation of the E.E.C common external tariff the E.E.C had 'unbound' a number of member country tariff concessions under Article 28. The unbinding itself had been perfectly legal, and the United States had acquired compensation rights as a matter of course. The E.E.C then chose to replace the bound tariffs with the infamous variable levy, a device which guaranteed that imported products would always be priced higher than domestic support prices." When its poultry exports were affected by the new variable levy, the United States considered the new protectionist provision unreasonable, following as it did cancellation of EEC member states' earlier concessions. Instead of being content with the original compensatory measures, the United States decided to retaliate further.

Technically, U.S. escalation of the trade dispute was illegal under the GATT because it went beyond compensation. Even though Article 28 justified the original demand for compensation,

---

34. GATT, *BISD*, vol. 1, Article 19, 47.
35. Hudec, "Retaliation," 507.
36. Ibid., 509–10.

retaliation was initiated on the basis of U.S. domestic law that had been designed to punish "unreasonable foreign trade restrictions, citing the variable levy as the justification for the action [Section 252 (c) of the Trade Expansion Act of 1962]."[37] The "chicken war" was eventually settled through GATT conciliation efforts to provide the United States with greater compensation.

In the end the U.S. loss was put at $26 million because of the Common Market's increased poultry levies, and the U.S. government took reciprocal compensation by raising tariffs on certain items of importance to the EEC. Although the GATT settlement proved acceptable, this should not be construed to imply that the United States had strictly followed GATT rules. The initial retaliation was taken within GATT rules, but the second round of retaliations was taken outside them. The dispute settlement procedures of the GATT led to arbitration of the issue, but only after Article 28 compensation procedures had failed.

Article 6 anti-dumping and countervailing duties. Unlike the nullification and impairment provisions of the GATT, which aim to compensate a contracting party for export losses due to the withdrawal of previous concessions (or other actions that have the same effect), anti-dumping and countervailing duties are imposed unilaterally by the importing nation against imports coming from another contracting party. In this case the domestic rather than the foreign market is being protected.

Dumping has long been considered an unfair trade practice that puts domestic producers at a disadvantage that is not due to lack of competitiveness. Echoing U.S. commercial law very closely on this point, GATT Article 6 states that "the contracting parties recognize that dumping, by which products of one country are introduced into the commerce of another country at less than the normal value of the products, is to be condemned if it causes or threatens material injury to an established industry in the territory of a contracting party or materially retards the establishment of a domestic industry."

To "offset or prevent dumping," a contracting party may levy

37. Ibid.

an anti-dumping duty "not greater in amount than the margin of dumping" for the product in question. This applies to goods dumped by private industries and to government-subsidized goods. Anti-dumping duties are applied in reaction to the former, and countervailing duties are applied against the latter. In the second case, "no countervailing duty shall be levied on any products of the territory of any contracting party imported into the territory of another contracting party in excess of an amount equal to the estimated bounty or subsidy determined to have been granted, directly, or indirectly, on the manufacture, production or export of such product in the country of origin or exportation."[38]

In principle, therefore, anti-dumping duties cannot exceed the price difference between the imported good and that same good's price in the exporter's home market and cannot be levied at all unless material injury is threatened or has already occurred. Similarly, countervailing duties, which offset artificial price advantages bestowed on a product through subsidization, are applied only if injury is threatened or proven. Basically, these provisions provide importers with legal means to counter predatory price cutting and unfair state trading practices, as Clair Wilcox says, not to prevent "normal competition in international trade."[39]

In this case the initial uncooperative action is dumping or subsidizing, and the reciprocal response is the anti-dumping or countervailing duty. Retaliation in these instances conforms to the rules and norms of the GATT, or that is how it looks at face value. The anti-dumping and countervailing duty provisions in the GATT, however, along with Article 16 (the instrument dealing more specifically with subsidies), have been the subject of considerable debate among contracting parties.

During the Tokyo Round, varying interpretations led to negotiation of a new code on countervailing duties, but persistent con-

38. GATT, *BISD*, vol. 1, Article 6, 22.
39. Clair Wilcox, *A Charter for World Trade* (New York: Arno Press, 1949), 79. The injury provision for countervailing duties was avoided by the United States until 1979 because of a grandfather clause exception for nations with existing countervailing duty (CVD) laws not requiring such a condition. On signing the Subsidy–CVD Code, the United States accepted GATT terms but applied them only to other code signatories. See the discussion below.

fusion and discord in this area indicate that this code has not settled the matter. Consequently, problems of interpretation, as well as problems accruing from administration of anti-dumping and countervailing duties, make it very difficult to determine exactly which action is initially uncooperative, the alleged dumping or the charge that dumping has occurred. The anti-dumping or countervailing duty procedure itself may possibly be protectionist and, therefore, uncooperative. In fact, many exporters have taken this position when charged with dumping or subsidization.

In particular, exporters to the United States have long viewed the U.S. countervailing duty law as unfair, cumbersome, and unpredictable, making that market very uncertain and thus impeding trade.[40] With regard to reciprocity, the anti-dumping and countervailing duty codes are also problematic because they make exceptions for products from lesser-developed countries in an effort to recognize the incomparable nature of markets in the importing and exporting nations.[41]

In an effort to standardize anti-dumping and countervailing duty procedures, individual codes of conduct have been negotiated, but with various degrees of acceptance by contracting parties. Because formal amendments to the GATT require the consent of two-thirds of the contracting parties, separate codes of behavior were considered the best means of "increasing the level of obligations of those contracting parties that were willing to assume further legal commitments," without risking complete rejection by a vote.[42] Consequently, many GATT members either

40. John Jackson, "Anti-dumping Law," in Steven M. Harris, ed., *Anti-dumping Law: Policy and Implementation*, vol. 1 of the Michigan Yearbook of International Legal Studies (Ann Arbor: University of Michigan Press, 1979), 5.

41. The revised anti-dumping code, which took effect on 1 January 1980, "recognizes that, as special economic conditions in developing countries affect prices in the domestic market, these prices do not provide a commercially realistic basis for dumping calculations; and the fact that a developing country's export price is lower than the comparable domestic price shall not in itself justify an investigation or the determination of dumping." GATT, *GATT Activities in 1978* (Geneva, 1979), 26. A similar exception is made in the 1979 Code on Subsidies and Countervailing Duties, which recognizes the use of subsidies by lesser-developed countries to promote new industries. See GATT, *BISD*, Code on Subsidies and Countervailing Duties, pt. 3, Article 14, "Developing Countries."

42. Frieder Roessler, "The Scope, Limits, and Function of the GATT Legal System" (unpublished paper, GATT Secretariat, 1985), 4.

have not signed the codes and are not legally bound by the provisions or have made application conditional on the reciprocal application of other members.

Although contracting parties pledged that the codes would in no way interfere with the basic principle of mfn treatment, the United States, for example, made application of the injury requirement of the countervailing duty code conditional on the trading partner having also signed and implemented the code in its domestic law. In dealings between the United States and a nonsignatory, therefore, the principle of unconditional mfn is superseded by the principle of reciprocity. The American position is supported by a reservation from the countervailing duty code, although the only case referred to the GATT that might have drawn an opinion was resolved bilaterally before the GATT panel convened.[43]

The Gray Areas in and out of GATT

Article 19 escape clause action. Although the GATT helps define acceptable norms of behavior and enumerates rules and procedures to govern that behavior, many of the rules contradict the norms in certain cases. For example, Article 19 escape clause rules cannot prevent initiation of unnecessary (and, therefore, technically illegal) escapes; thus consultations and subsequent GATT investigations may reverse the original Article 19 action, but a lag in time occurs in the meanwhile. During this period, the importer is injured by de facto protection that is already in place. Even if it

---

43. The wording of the Code on Subsidies and Countervailing Duties, pt. 7, Article 19, Section 9 (GATT, *BISD*)—"this Agreement shall not apply as between any two signatories if either of the signatories, at the time either accepts or accedes to this Agreement, does not consent to such application"—does not sanction across-the-board conditional application. The United States, however, has used this section to delay application when the acceding nation fails to meet what is believed to be the criteria of the code. This use led to a dispute between the United States and India when the United States refused to apply the new code's injury requirement on the grounds that India had not yet conformed to the subsidies portion of the code. The dispute was resolved bilaterally after a GATT panel of conciliation had been appointed, although it never met. Gary Clyde Hufbauer and Joanna Shelton Erb, *Subsidies in International Trade* (Washington, D.C.: Institute for International Economics, 1984), 122.

withdraws certain concessions in retaliation, the exporting nation still experiences restricted export prospects for which retaliation is no real compensation.[44]

GATT rule waivers. Because contracting parties can make or break rules by consensus, the constraints of the formal agreement have occasionally been circumvented by special waivers in which contracting parties agree to allow a particular behavior under supervision and within time limits, even though it violates the GATT. These range from waivers granted upon accession to the GATT as a provision of that accession to special waivers for separate bilateral trade agreements, such as the Canadian-American arrangement for automobile manufacture and sale. The Canadian–United States "Autopact" violates Article I by discriminating against other contracting parties and fails to conform to requirements for a customs union or an area of free trade as specified in Article 24. Even so, this agreement received legal status in the GATT through a special contracting party waiver.[45]

Generalized System of Preferences. Probably the greatest single departure from the original legal norms of the GATT has been the Generalized System of Preferences (GSP), which has removed requirements of nondiscrimination and reciprocity in commercial relations between the industrialized countries (ICs) and the lesser-developed countries (LDCs). A special provision concerning the GATT role of LDCs was put into force in 1957. Embodied in Article 28 and codified in Part 4, this section introduced special preferential duty rates for products imported into ICs from LDCs. This process established a different concept of reciprocity between ICs and LDCs in which concessions depend on their *reciprocal impact*, not on some arbitrary notion of fungible equivalence, so that concessions may be offered to LDCs that are not offered equally to other contracting parties.

The process of negotiating preferential treatment is purely vol-

44. Kenneth W. Dam, *The GATT Law and International Economic Organization* (Chicago: University of Chicago Press, 1970), 356–57.
45. GATT, *Analytical Index* (Geneva, 1970), 160.

untary. An LDC nominates itself as such, and it is up to the IC to accept that condition and negotiate accordingly. During tariff negotiations, basic efforts were made to "reduce barriers to exports of the less-developed countries but . . . developed countries [could not] expect to receive reciprocity from the less-developed countries." The Tokyo Round adopted a provision that gave "a permanent legal basis with the GATT for preferential trade treatment on behalf of, and between, developing countries."[46]

The GSP, however, has several drawbacks for LDCs. First and foremost, the system is individually and voluntarily applied, which means that each IC maintains a list of duty preferences for LDCs as a group, although the group may differ from one GSP-granting country to another. Because the system violates unconditional mfn treatment, countries on the list are not assured such treatment in relation to each other. Therefore, duty rates may vary from importer to importer, even though all are classified as LDCs.

Second, the GSP can hardly be described as generalized in another way. The product categories of most importance to the LDCs—and of most threat to the ICs—have been dealt with in other ways, such as the orderly marketing arrangement for textiles, that do not guarantee preference. Despite GSP goals to treat LDC products even more favorably than those of other ICs, the reality in the most crucial sectors has been that protectionism undermines the comparatively weak efforts made elsewhere. This fact explains why the LDCs remain discontented with results of the Tokyo Round, which did little to break down nontariff barriers to trade. Over the years, LDCs might have been more willing to accept reciprocity had it not been that the developed countries have refused to grant reciprocal benefits in the sectors most important to the expert interests of LDCs.

Consequently, for analytical purposes, it is difficult to examine relations between the ICs and the LDCs on the basis of the rules governing GATT reciprocity. Exceptions to the principles of nondiscrimination and mutually advantageous negotiations put LDCs on a completely different legal footing than are the ICs, which

46. GATT, *GATT Activities in 1978* (Geneva, 1979), 16–17.

makes measuring reciprocity between the two groups within the GATT regime problematic.

Orderly marketing arrangements and voluntary export restraints. Another development that creates analytical difficulties concerning legal and illegal behavior has been the creation of orderly marketing arrangements (OMAs). By regulating imports into the ICs through special agreements between the governments of importing and exporting countries, these arrangements have contravened the principle of nondiscrimination. They set quantitative limits on imports that are selectively restrictive, thus favoring some producers or nations over others, not always the same ones each time. Favored producers who are in a good position to continue accommodating protective interests in the importing countries avoid the risk of all-out protectionism and maintain their own market share where restriction of supply in turn stabilizes prices.[47] Less-favored producers must lobby for access and quota reallocations. Reciprocity according to the legal norms of the GATT does not explain OMAs such as the internationally negotiated textile and apparel Multifiber Agreement, as import restrictions are theoretically retaliated against only through the various legal mechanisms outlined above, not agreed to and institutionalized.

Voluntary export restraints (VERs), which are analytically very similar to OMAs, involve the exporter's decision to restrain exports to countries that have pressured for such a decision. Unlike the Multifiber Agreement, however, VERs result from a bilateral ad hoc collusion between the importing government and the exporting one. Technically, the importing government does not actually enter into a formal agreement with the exporting government; on the face of it, the exporter unilaterally imposes limits on its exports, but this is only part of the story.[48] Often negotiations

47. David B. Yoffie, *Power and Protectionism* (New York: Columbia University Press, 1983), 19–21.

48. The United States maintains the outward pretense that VERs are purely voluntary policies on the part of the exporting nation; analysts and the evidence dispute this, however. See, for example, Kent Jones, "The Political Economy of Voluntary Export Restraint Agreements," *Kyklos* 37 (1984): 83.

take place between the nations at the insistence of the importing government, and the resulting voluntary export restraint avoids the problem of the exporter's complaint to the GATT or of politically difficult policies such as unilaterally imposed import quotas.[49]

Thus VERs have become the most effective method to achieve some degree of protection and to maintain bilaterally acceptable trade flows. Because no formal agreement is signed, no particular individuals or bureaucracies can be "blamed" for negative results, and they can readily claim protective effects when politically expedient. Consumers who wish to pursue legal means of redress have no standing in a domestic court because the decision is officially taken outside the country. Due process does not exist either in the policy formation phase or in the policy review phase, even though negotiations between the two governments are common knowledge and VERs resulted from those negotiations.[50]

With regard to the GATT regime, both the VER and the OMA technically violate Article II, which prohibits export as well as import restrictions. Collusion, although a happy enough affair between the two countries involved, runs contrary to the broader meaning of cooperation in the trade order as originally conceived simply because it discriminates. Nevertheless, GATT members increasingly accept this practice and, just as OMAs have been negotiated under the auspices of the GATT, VERs are gaining legitimacy as well.

Unnoticed at the time by the GATT Secretariat, for example, the Tokyo Round subsidies and countervailing duty code legal-

49. See, for example, the discussion of the Japanese government's decision to take measures to limit automobile export to the United States in Mitsuo Matsushita and Lawrence Repeta, "Restricting the Supply of Japanese Automobiles: Sovereign Compulsion or Sovereign Collusion?" *Case Western Reserve Journal of International Law* 14 (1982): 49–50.

50. In a letter to the ambassador of Japan on 7 May 1981, Attorney General William French Smith stated that "we believe that the Japanese automobile companies' compliance with export limitations directed by MITI would properly be viewed as having been compelled by the Japanese government, acting within its sovereign powers. The Department of Justice is of the view the implementation of such an export restraint by the Government of Japan, including the division among the companies by MITI of the maximum exportable number of units, and compliance with the program by Japanese automobile companies, would not give rise to violations of United States antitrust laws." Quoted in ibid., 81.

ized bilaterally negotiated VERs.[51] Article 4 Section 5 stipulates that a possible alternative to countervailing duties exists "if undertakings are accepted under which . . . the government of the exporting country agrees to eliminate or limit the subsidy or take other measures concerning its effects."[52] Many have interpreted "other measures" to mean quantitative restrictions, as specified, for example, in the implementing legislation of both the United States and the European Community.[53] The code, in fact, specifies that the importing country must find acceptable "undertakings" that relieve the effects of the subsidized trade and even authorizes the importing country to play a role in suggesting the type of undertakings that the exporting country consider.[54] This development has, in effect, legalized export restraint agreements as an alternative to the imposition of countervailing duties, even though it runs counter to the principle of nondiscrimination. Whatever quota is set has the potential for limiting market access for other suppliers or for that supplier relative to newcomers. Moreover, the straightforward procedure of matching subsidies with countervailing duties to punish and thereby discourage those "unfair" trade practices has been augmented by an alternative arrangement that provides import protection but allows continuing subsidies.

Homemade retaliation outside GATT authorization. What Hudec has dubbed "homemade retaliation" has chiefly enforced agreements from the various rounds of trade negotiations, including but not confined to anti-dumping and countervailing duties, which are legalized measures of retaliation.[55] More far-reaching and technically illegal are unilateral retaliations involving tacit invocation of the Article 23 Nullification and Impairment Clause to charge that a contracting party has, through some action, nulli-

51. Jan Tumlir, director, GATT Economic Research Division, GATT Secretariat, interviewed by author, Geneva, 22 January 1985.

52. GATT, *BISD*, Code on Subsidies and Countervailing Duties, Article 4, Section 5.

53. Hufbauer and Shelton Erb, *Subsidies*, 113.

54. GATT, *BISD*, Code on Subsidies, Article 4, Section 5 (c).

55. Robert E. Hudec, "Retaliation against 'Unreasonable' Trade Practices: The New Section 301 and GATT Nullification and Impairment," *Minnesota Law Review* 59 (1975): 497–510.

fied or impaired benefits it had previously granted in trade negotiations. Legally, such a reference requires collective approval of
the contracting parties. Individual nations, however, knowing the
difficulties of obtaining multilateral authorization, have resorted
to unilateral retaliation.

Because the GATT has always encouraged bilateral dispute settlements over the multilateral dispute settlement machinery, contracting parties do not recognize such unilateral retaliations unless
the victim files a complaint. Because individual contracting parties
usually prefer to settle disagreements bilaterally, without publicity
and the possible unfavorable legal precedents that GATT involvement might entail, most unilateral retaliations lead to bilateral
bargaining, not referrals to GATT. Even when disputes are referred, the GATT facilitates bilateral settlement rather than the
multilateral forum.

Therefore, GATT norms embody a "self-help" system of bilateral negotiation, with the GATT dispute settlement process an
alternative of last resort. Retaliations and counterretaliations
come to the attention of contracting parties only if one of the
nations or an adversely affected third party elect to officially con-
front the issue. Thus, underlying the principles of mfn treatment
and nondiscrimination reside not only the delineated uses of reciprocity but also the bilateral dispute process that often includes
retaliation and threats of retaliation to achieve mutually acceptable bargains. These interpretive and procedural problems plague
virtually every commercial interaction covered by the GATT. To
establish the facts of specific conflicts so that a mutually acceptable accord may be reached, the GATT provides investigative and
interpretive efforts in the interests of dispute settlement (see Table
3 for an overview of GATT organizational structure for dispute
settlement).

Dispute Settlement, Reciprocity, and the GATT

The actual dispute settlement process within the GATT regime
can take many forms: In virtually every case, however, pressure
for balanced treatment between trading partners is the motivating

Table 3. GATT organizational structure for dispute settlement and negotiations

Contracting parties (collective)

- Collective representation of individual member nations by delegations in Geneva.
- Have full power to oversee the GATT Council and approve or disapprove council decisions and working party or panel reports.
- May review trading practices of member nations.
- May request reports.
- May make recommendations for dispute settlement, including authorization by two-thirds vote (though consensus is the preferred procedure) for joint retaliation against errant nation.
- May waive obligations under the GATT by two-thirds majority vote (consensus again preferred).

Contracting party (individual)

- Each contracting party may withdraw from the GATT with short notice if it objects strongly to joint action; thus, state sovereignty is recognized as supreme.

GATT Council

- Established in 1959 by the contracting parties to provide continuous attention to GATT matters (arising between contracting party sessions).
- Authorized to make decisions approving or disapproving certain contracting party actions or compensation offers.
- May request reports.
- Authorized to initiate discussions on particular trade barriers and sponsor negotiations between concerned contracting parties.
- May appoint committees, special panels, and working parties and assign investigations and reporting responsibilities.

Committees (standing)

- Established to consider disputes, provide a forum for consultations, and assign and administer panel investigations in specified areas of trade relations.

Committees (special)

- Established temporarily at the behest of the council or contracting parties to consider disputes, provide a forum for consultations, and assign and administer panel investigations.

Panels

- Specially selected panel of experts in a particular area of trade.
- Authorized by the council or a committee to review particular contracting party practices and issue recommendations (generally resulting from a complaint and request for panel report by another contracting party).

Working parties

- Group of representatives from contracting parties interested in the interpretation or settlement of a particular issue meeting to consider same.

108

- Authorized by the council or a committee to review particular contracting party practices and issue recommendations (generally resulting from a complaint and request for a working party by one of the concerned parties).

Director general and the GATT Secretariat

- Administrative support.
- Collection of information at request of contracting parties, the council, committees, panels, and working parties.
- HAS NO AUTHORITY TO INTERPRET GATT MATTERS ON ITS OWN.

factor, and threat of retaliation—implicit or explicit—is often an important catalyst for negotiation. Generally speaking, the GATT encourages dispute settlement at any point in a conflict, favoring bilateral conciliation over formal GATT intervention and making the latter a mere facilitator of the process when one or more of the interested contracting parties consider it necessary (see Table 4). This point is crucial. While casual perusal of GATT actions would reveal only the one authorized retaliation mentioned above, a more careful inspection unearths many cases where conciliation has been achieved with GATT assistance long before the dispute reaches full contracting party consideration.

Jackson has discovered that in only 8 of the 159 formal disputes filed with the GATT up until 1984 has a party in the dispute refused to comply with the dispute settlement procedure;[56] in addition, countless numbers of successful dispute settlements take place before the GATT intervenes. Measuring such frequencies becomes difficult because no central mechanism exists for recording those disputes dealt with solely on a bilateral basis where no complaint was filed with the GATT. Jackson has noted, however, that about half of the 159 disputes were settled before a panel report was issued.[57] The following tour through the GATT dispute settlement process will illustrate the tendency toward bilateral conciliation rather than reliance on GATT institutional intervention.

When a trading partner perceives that uncooperative behavior

56. Jackson, "Dispute Settlement Techniques," 56.
57. Jackson, *World Trade*, 160.

Table 4. Trade conflict and likely sequence of dispute settlement procedures under the GATT regime

Sequence if full GATT dispute mechanisms utilized	*Bilateral settlement possibilities encouraged by the GATT*
(1) Uncooperative behavior by nation A (as perceived by nation B)	
(2) Protest by nation B to nation A	Outcome: nation A revises behavior to satisfaction of nation B
(3) Persistence of A's behavior	
(4) Threat by nation B to retaliate against nation A	Outcome: nation A revises behavior to satisfaction of nation B
(5) Nation A threatens counterretaliation	Outcome: nation B withdraws protest and accepts A's behavior
(6) Bilateral consultations (whether GATT officially notified or not)	Outcome: consultations result in mutually acceptable settlement
(7) Complaint to GATT Council if no settlement forthcoming bilaterally	Bilateral consultation continues
(8) GATT working party or panel authorized to review dispute	Bilateral consultation continues; outcome: settlement possible without GATT report
(9) Working party or panel reports recommendation for settlement to the contracting parties	Outcome: Bilateral acceptance of GATT recommendation
(10) If *no* settlement forthcoming, contracting parties may approve recommendation and possibly authorize retaliation by 2/3 vote (in reality consensus), but improbable	Outcome: Acceptance and *revision of behavior* (if necessary) based on recommendation or nonacceptance and *stalemate*

has occurred, that country will likely protest the action, possibly threaten retaliation, and request consultations. Even at this early stage, the perpetrator's negotiations or clarification of the action could result in resolution, and the matter would go no further: If bilateral consultations do not prove fruitful and the dissatisfied state remains unhappy with the situation, however, it might file a formal complaint with the GATT. This action serves two purposes. First, it raises the problem's visibility as complaints are made public and other interested parties are implicitly invited to take part in discussions, thus putting the alleged noncooperator on the defensive. Second, the formal complaint initiates GATT involvement, setting into motion mechanisms for facilitating conciliation.

At this point, either party may request a working party or panel review of the case. In the former instance, official representatives from nations interested in the case (including the disputants) consult and review both the complaint and the alleged injurious behavior. This option is the most likely if several interested nations desire clarification of the acceptability of a particular behavior. By "working out" the dispute in mediation, controversial matters can be reconciled. In the event that a party requests panel review, experts who are not officially attached to any national delegation convene to review the facts and render an opinion on the legality and injurious effect of the behavior in question. This option is most attractive when one or more of the disputants desire adjudication by a neutral body. Should the subject fall within the purview of one of the standing committees, such as the Subsidy Committee, then the panel would be requested and assigned under that authority.

In either approach, ongoing bilateral negotiations between disputing parties are encouraged. If a mutually amicable settlement can be reached at any point in the process, the matter is dropped from the GATT agenda and the working party or panel dissolved.[58] No institutional prerogative exists to pursue a case when a contracting party withdraws its complaint. Although working party and panel decisions influence future interpretation of GATT principles and rules, the GATT facilitates such conciliations between members without creating a body of law.[59] As the record demonstrates, cases that reach the stage where working party or panel reports are completed and recommendations or interpretations issued are highly likely to culminate in acceptance by disputing parties. If one disputant refuses to accept the determination, the case may then be considered by the body of contracting parties.

Except concerning waivers, member accession, customs unions,

---

58. For example, the dispute between the United States and India concerning U.S. application of the subsidies code was settled bilaterally in 1981 before the panel of experts could render a decision. Hufbauer and Shelton Erb, *Subsidies*, 122–23; and Gerard Curzon, panel expert for the case, interviewed by author, Geneva, 19 April 1985.

59. Corroborated by Jan Tumlir, Richard Blackhurst, and Claude Mercier, GATT Secretariat, interviewed by author, 19 April 1985 and 3 May 1985.

and amendments, which all require at least a two-thirds majority vote, contracting party decisions theoretically may be taken on a simple majority. In reality, however, *consensus* is usually expected, especially if a major trading power dissents, and rigorous negotiations take place off the floor to achieve consensus before a vote.[60] This process puts a good deal of pressure on the dissenting delegation to accept the determination; but unless the contracting parties decide to vote without consensus and authorize retaliation (which has happened only once in GATT history), the GATT has no actual enforcement power over the nation in question. Therefore, this action is less important to evaluating the success of dispute settlement than are the earlier stages where conciliation often occurs.

Conclusion

Because the GATT agreement provides various means for ensuring reciprocity between trading partners—from anti-dumping duties to Article 23 nullification and impairment compensation—GATT members utilize its provisions to secure compensation or apply retaliatory leverage to restore balance in their relationships. Such action may violate the principle of unconditional mfn treatment, but this contradiction is inherent in the agreement and unavoidable in enforcement.

Retaliatory actions taken outside specific provisions of the GATT, such as might occur during bilateral negotiations of an unfiled dispute with the trade organization, must be considered in a similar light. Because the GATT always encourages bilateral dispute settlement as the first and best solution of conflict, unilateral efforts to restore balance, which result in either the partner's acceptance of the restoration or in consultation and mediation, remain an integral component of the dispute settlement process.

Individual members who choose this "homemade" option do not necessarily depart from GATT norms; on the contrary, reci-

60. Jackson, *World Trade*, 128; and Claude Mercier, GATT Secretariat, interviewed by author, 3 May 1985.

procity both motivates cooperation and enforces most practical and compensatory mechanisms available to members. That this action often violates the principle of unconditional mfn treatment happens naturally because of the juxtaposition of these two principles as governing norms. The case studies that follow allow us to examine the uses and effect of reciprocity and retaliation in dispute settlements involving the United States and its three largest trading partners. The context of the GATT regime is crucial to defining cooperative and retaliatory behavior, facilitating dispute settlement, and influencing these actors to contain conflicts within flexible interpretations of GATT governing norms.

5

U.S. Trade Relations
in Steel

One of the most difficult tasks in analyzing the role played by reciprocity in U.S. trade relations is discerning between domestically motivated unilateral protectionism and reciprocal actions that redress domestically perceived violations of fair trade. Although the former violates the mfn as well as the mutual benefit norms of the GATT regime, the latter reinforces principles of balanced treatment and fair trade while it contradicts the principles of nondiscrimination and free trade.

Whether reciprocity or unilateral protectionism characterized a particular case in U.S. steel trade relations, which involved both types of actions, is difficult to determine. This ambiguity is largely due to the fact that domestic producers have often perceived unfairness that has not been clearly established and also to the reality that, regardless of the issue of fairness, domestic producers desired protection when import competition became uncomfortable. The world steel market became very complex in the 1970s. New competitors challenged old producers who attempted to retain traditional market shares, which made the steel sector particularly vulnerable to mixing protectionist demands with fairness issues. Plagued by surplus capacity and the need to restructure, the U.S. steel industry became very sensitive to foreign trading practices. These included alleged supply diversions that resulted from bilateral restraint agreements abroad as well as price advantages gained through government subsidization of restructuralization efforts in other countries.

114

Between 1968 and 1985, the period of study, steel imports were subjected to numerous U.S. industry efforts to secure protection and target "unfair" practices such as dumping and subsidization. The dispute settlement efforts between the United States and two of its largest steel importers, Japan and the European Community, illustrate how the United States used both protectionist policies and retaliatory responses to leverage cooperation.[1] They also demonstrate how differences in market interdependency between the United States and these respective trading partners, as well as the reactions of the latter, affected outcomes. Although Japan, whose asymmetrical dependence on the U.S. market share was much greater than that of the European Community, continually pursued an accommodative strategy toward U.S. pressures for protection, the European Community often pursued a reciprocal strategy of counterpressure and threatened retaliation. The European Community's ability to press the United States into negotiated settlements, in comparison with Japan's inability to do so, distinguished transatlantic relations from transpacific relations in this sector. The fact that the European Community credibly threatened U.S. commercial interests with retaliation altered U.S. calculations of self-interest, at times giving the European Community preferential treatment over that afforded Japan.

U.S. steel import policy after 1968 involved four distinct approaches: (1) unilateral congressionally mandated quotas, (2) escape clause action under GATT Article 19 and Section 201 of U.S. trade law to secure temporary relief from imports, (3) antidumping and countervailing duties to deflect unfair trading practices, and (4) voluntary export restraint agreements to secure bilateral compromises.[2]

---

1. Canada generally avoided bilateral disputes with the United States during this period. In 1981, Canada was the subject of an anti-dumping proceeding under the U.S. Treasury Trigger Price Mechanism that culminated in a suspension agreement in 1982. Otherwise, Canadian exports were adversely affected only when Article 19 nondiscriminatory escape clause actions were taken.

2. Although eighteen Section 301 petitions were filed between 1975 and 1979 against the alleged unfair trading practices of foreign nations, none resulted in the U.S. executive taking retaliatory action. Consequently, these cases are not included unless they overlap with other, more effective avenues.

115

As we have seen, Congress has historically defended the interests of domestic producers against foreign competition. After the Roosevelt administration effectively wrested away from Congress much of its prerogative for trade negotiations, Congress generally deferred to the executive in this area. When protectionist appeals and charges of unfair foreign trading practices became too strong to ignore, however, Congress threatened a political remedy outside the legally established guidelines for import relief under the GATT. Such intervention, which was clearly a case of unilateral protectionism, responded to domestic political pressure without regard for regime rules governing trade. When unilateral protection was threatened against established liberal trade, with the purpose of leveraging trading partners to modify their export practices, then congressional action took on a coercive character. In the steel sector, such coercive protectionism provided political pressure to urge the executive to leverage bilaterally negotiated restraint arrangements.

Escape clause action clearly exemplifies unilateral protectionism, although it may also be used to coerce alternative import protection. Although trading partners do not like escape clause action, the GATT does provide for its nondiscriminatory use when importing nations find it necessary for domestic restructuring efforts. Because trading partners prefer bilaterally negotiated arrangements that allow some continued control of market share, the threat of escape clause action has served effectively as a coercive tool to secure a more acceptable bilateral alternative. When this has occurred, nations have colluded against GATT provisions to compromise on a relief arrangement that continued to allow bilaterally managed trade flows.

Anti-dumping and countervailing duty suits, as we have seen in Chapter 4, are even more ambiguous due to the institutional process of fair trade enforcement. When U.S. domestic producers have filed petitions against the alleged unfair importing practices of competitors, disputes have arisen over whether pricing practices actually constituted dumping or subsidization. Since 1974, domestic producers have found it easy to cry foul, file suit, and force the investigation process when their motivation was merely import protection, not fair trade enforcement. Importers have felt a great deal of uncertainty, even though an administrative investigation may, in the end, reveal that they have committed no violation. On the other hand, when domestic producers were motivated by fair trade enforcement, the anti-dumping and countervailing duty remedies have had the potential to force the violator to import according to established rules of fairness. The analytical question arises over whether a particular U.S. action has constituted fair trade—motivated reciprocity or blatant protectionism. Context of the action helps discern the differences, but a definitive interpretation may be elusive when the two motivations have clearly overlapped. Moreover, as we shall see below, domestic steel producers, which often sought fair trade remedies, suspended those remedies in dispute settlements and replaced them with voluntary export restraint agreements.

Voluntary export restraint agreements (VRAs) constituted the major departure from free trade in the 1970s. VRAs have appealed to both importing nations and exporting nations as solutions to bilateral trade disputes. When domestic producers press for protection, yet the international relationship and larger national interest require consideration of foreign commitments and economic efficiency, bilaterally negotiated arrangements offer attractive compromises for the importing nation. On the other side, exporting nations that face restrictions on their producers' exports but do not want to lose total control of the foreign market find ways to secure some predictability for their exports. VRAs allow them to retain a degree of their traditional market share and enable their producers to obtain the quota rent that supply limits may generate. VRAs in steel were rarely introduced at the outset of a dispute; instead, they arose as bilaterally negotiated alternatives to U.S. unilateral protection or fair trade retaliation.

The nature of the bilateral relationships that evolved from these four different approaches and their outcomes provide a number of cases involving protectionism, coercive protectionism, and reciprocity. These cases indicate that the first three approaches—congressionally initiated protection, escape clause action, and fair trade enforcement—have been used by the United States to coerce the trade-restricting cooperation of Japan and the European Community. In steel, this leverage has tended to produce bilaterally negotiated voluntary export restraint agreements.

Reciprocal strategies were distinguishable from unilateral protectionist actions in their legitimate use as enforcement instruments of the GATT regime. When GATT norms guided execution of U.S. anti-dumping duty and countervailing duty law, the latter reinforced the principles of fair trade as well as mutual benefit. When the United States suspended legal procedures in favor of diplomatically negotiated settlements, however, GATT fair trade enforcement was sacrificed to the principle of mutual benefit. In the steel sector, bilaterally managed trade was often the preferred alternative to strict enforcement of fair trade rules. Consequently, reciprocal policies, as well as U.S. protectionist actions, catalyzed foreign responses that aimed at retaining market shares through voluntary export restraint, and the U.S. government often pursued this avenue of protection for domestic producers rather than the originally threatened action. This pattern demonstrated that actors expected trade management rather than a free market in steel, and the particular strategies of U.S. producers had little differential effect on outcomes given these preferences.

The First Japanese and E.C. VRAs, 1968

By the end of the 1960s, steel imports had so penetrated the U.S. market—16.7 percent of the U.S. steel supply in 1968—that industry and labor leaders began to pressure the government for protection.[3] Arguing that steel was being unfairly imported into the United States at unrealistically low prices, lobbyists set on Congress in full force. By 1967, demands had made such an impression that a bill was introduced that provided for mandatory import quotas.

While debate over the issue raged during 1968, two of the most significant exporters of steel to the United States—Japan and Germany—proposed directly to the heads of the House Committee on Ways and Means and the Senate Finance Committee an alternative to a mandatory quota. Their proposal consisted of an offer to voluntarily restrain exports of steel to the United States if a bargain could be struck with Congress to shelve the steel quota

3. Craig R. MacPhee, *Restrictions on International Trade in Steel* (Toronto: D.C. Heath, 1974), 49, 52, 54–55.

legislation. A series of discussions resulted in the agreement of Japan and the European Coal and Steel Community (ECSC) to restrict imports into the United States to fourteen million tons.[4] This bold preemptive offer had the desired effect. Congress dropped the quota bill, and voluntary export restraints governed steel imports for the next three years.

ECSC and Japanese conciliatory maneuvers were accommodative responses to the imminent threat of U.S. protection. Their preemptive restraint offer allowed them to retain control over their exports to the United States and provided their industries with a level of market certainty. From their point of view, measures pending in Congress were uncooperative acts, but they did not consider retaliation to be in their best interests, given their important share of the U.S. steel market.

Voluntary export restraints logically resulted from Japanese and ECSC calculations that ending the quota bill and continuing access to the U.S. market were worth the costs of restricting exports. Although total volume of imports into the United States from 1968 to 1970 resulted in a 25 percent decline, the import value remained roughly the same.[5] Decreased volume of imports gave the exporters the chance to sell steel at somewhat higher prices without threatening demand.[6] In addition, imports increased substantially for higher-priced fabricated structural steel and cold-finished bars, even though the VRAs stipulated that exporters fill quotas with a product mix that approximated past sales.[7] This strategy by Japan and the ECSC worked rather handily. The VERs gave them a high degree of marketing flexibility, a

4. Letters from Yoshihiro Inayama and from the Club des Siderurgistes to Dean Rusk, secretary of state, 13 December 1968, and Secretary Rusk's communication to Wilbur Mills, 14 January 1969, as recorded in ibid., 55–57.

5. A. W. Harris, *U.S. Trade Problems in Steel: Japan, West Germany, and Italy* (New York: Praeger, 1983), 34–35.

6. This price increase follows the general pattern that economists have identified for import prices of products on which VERs have been imposed. For a discussion of the phenomenon, see Philip Turner and Jean-Pierre Tuveri, "Some Effects of Export Restraints on Japanese Trading Behavior," *OECD Economic Studies* (Spring 1984): 96–99.

7. Harris, *U.S. Trade Problems*, 35. This increase was partly due to the fact that Japan and the ECSC did not consider these steel categories as part of the VER arrangement.

substantial share of their original market at strong prices, and defused protectionist demands in the U.S. Congress. For two years, this situation persisted, but two events in 1971 threatened the arrangement.

The Second VRA, 1972

In August 1971, President Nixon announced his decision to unilaterally impose a 10 percent surcharge on all imports into the United States, an action that America's trading partners viewed as a nationalistic, protectionist effort to pass the costs of economic adjustment to others in the international trading system.[8] In particular, Japanese and ECSC steel exporters to the United States charged that this action violated the understanding on which the VERs were based, namely, that the United States would not raise barriers against steel for the arrangement's duration. At the same time, imports of steel into the United States had increased substantially. As Craig MacPhee notes: "By the end of 1971, a record 18,303,959 tons of steel products had been imported. This was approximately 2.7 million tons above the voluntary restraint agreement level."[9] In reaction, domestic producers threatened new protective action.

Clearly, blame for deterioration of the VER agreement lay on both sides. Although finger-pointing delayed negotiations somewhat, renewal of the arrangement came in May 1972. The new bargain held more protection for the U.S. domestic industry, including limitations on specialty steels. It also included an arrangement with the United Kingdom, whose export share increased the E.C. quota substantially. For both Japan and the European Community, the quotas for 1972 through 1974 were somewhat higher than before.[10] All evidence indicates that steel imports were ex-

8. Robert A. Pastor, *Congress and the Politics of U.S. Foreign Economic Policy, 1929–1976* (Berkeley: University of California Press, 1980), 131.
9. MacPhee, *Restrictions on International Trade in Steel*, 60–61.
10. Ibid., 60–64. As it was finally signed, the agreement differed substantially from the 1968 version. The United Kingdom was included among the European countries, and a number of stipulations on the tonnage of specialty steels were

ceeding quota levels before President Nixon's action. Changes in the product mix, including increases in specialty steels, affected this, but even without counting these it appears that restraints were not being followed. Both Japan and the ECSC were culpable on this count, and the U.S. government, acting on behalf of the steel industry, took the view that these exporters had reneged on the arrangement and that these actions, not the surcharge announced well after violations were detected, rendered the arrangement null and void.

The approaching end of the VRA period undoubtedly brought with it incentives to take advantage of the deteriorating situation and allow an export surge before the negotiation of a new agreement. Even so, the conflict over Nixon's surcharge and the higher import levels gave each side bargaining leverage. The resulting agreement, signed in 1972, set new quotas for the European Community and Japan, established definite limits on specialty steels, but expanded general import levels. This second VRA governed steel imports into the United States until May 1975,[11] during which time no significant steel trade disputes emerged.

Following renewal of the steel restraint agreement in 1972, write Hugh Patrick and Hideo Sato, the Consumers Union of the United States filed a suit against the State Department, the domestic steel industry, and foreign steel producers, "charging they had violated the Sherman Act by conspiring to restrain foreign commerce."[12] Although the courts ruled that the "executive branch could make agreements or diplomatic arrangements with private foreign steel firms as long as these arrangements did not violate existing legislation regulating foreign commerce," writes A. W.

---

spelled out. "The European version states that total shipments in 1973 would be 1 percent higher than the 8,013,794 net tons to be shipped in 1972. In 1974, total exports from the E.C. and the United Kingdom, which will be part of the community at that time, will not exceed the 1973 shipments by more than 2.5 percent. . . . The Japanese letter of agreement stated that they would not exceed 6,498,059 net tons in 1972, which would increase by 2.5 percent for both 1973 and 1974" (64).

11. Harris, *U.S Trade Problems*, 35–36.
12. Hugh Patrick and Hideo Sato, "The Political Economy of United States–Japan Trade in Steel," Kozo Yamamura, ed., *Policy and Trade Issues of the Japanese Economy* (Seattle: University of Washington Press, 1982), 200.

Harris, they also "held that the executive branch had no authority under the Constitution or acts of Congress to exempt the VRAs on steel from the antitrust provisions of the Sherman Antitrust Act."[13] The latter opinion made the executive wary of entanglement in future arrangements that the courts could find in violation of the country's antitrust laws. This created some concern about whether VRAs offered viable sources of protection, and along with important changes in U.S. trade law, encouraged domestic steel interests to seek relief through other mechanisms.

The most important changes in commercial policy concerned anti-dumping provisions. In 1972 the Treasury Department took steps to make anti-dumping and countervailing duty provisions more effective by no longer allowing importers to voluntarily assure the government that they would cease dumping on their own.[14] Significantly, Congress passed the Trade Act of 1974, which streamlined anti-dumping procedures, made them easier to impose, and beefed up the policy options available against other unfair trade practices. The change of greatest consequence was introduction of a new method for determining fair prices. As John Barcello observes:

> Dumping refers to the practice of selling goods in an export market at prices below those prevailing in the home market. It is a form of international price discrimination. . . . The nations of the Western trading world and Japan have all enacted anti-dumping laws which assess a special duty against dumped goods. The duty is generally designed to raise the dumping price to the level of home market sales and is imposed in addition to regular tariffs.[15]

13. Harris, *U.S. Trade Problem*, 36. Note that the Consumers Union did drop "its allegation that the VRA violated U.S. antitrust law"; the U.S. District Court, however, chose to address the issue anyway. Michael K. Levine, *Inside International Trade Policy Formulation: A History of the 1982 U.S.-E.C. Steel Arrangements* (New York: Praeger, 1985), 6–7.

14. *National Journal*, 24 July 1971, 1547.

15. John J. Barcelo III, "Anti-dumping Laws as Barriers to Trade—The United States and the International Anti-dumping Code," *Cornell Law Review* 57 (1972): 494. Up to this point, the Japanese government had never issued an anti-dumping duty order, largely because it used other import controls instead and Japanese industry in product areas that might be dumped had been "suffi-

Previously, the U.S. anti-dumping law had determined "fair price" by comparing the product export price with a "constructed value" based on the costs of production, a 10 percent overhead allowance, and a certain profit margin. As Patrick and Sato note, the new criteria required measuring

> average production cost in making the comparison with export prices. It made anti-dumping suits more attractive since the constructed-value criterion for determining less than fair value could be applied. In recessions, producers in industries with high fixed costs will sell at prices below average cost because small losses are preferable to large. Now they run the risk of anti-dumping suits if they practice this in pricing exports to the United States.[16]

The 1974 changes in U.S. foreign trade law not only facilitated anti-dumping suits but also included other avenues for protection against "unfair trade practices." Sections 201 and 301 of the act improved opportunities for domestic industries to obtain protection. Section 201, which is the domestic legislation implementing Article 19 of the GATT, gave the executive the prerogative to determine the appropriate measure of import relief once the International Trade Commission (ITC) found that imports had not injured a domestic industry; as Pastor notes, however, Congress retained the authority "to override a Presidential determination."[17]

In Section 301, write Hufbauer and Shelton Erb, "the U.S. Congress attempted to improve the ability of the United States to

---

ciently competitive" not to be injured by imports. Mitsuo Matsushita in John H. Jackson, Jean-Victor Louis, and Mitsuo Matsushita, eds., "Implementing the Tokyo Round: Legal Aspects of Changing Economic Rules," *Michigan Law Review* 81 (1982): 322–23.

16. Patrick and Sato, "United States–Japan Trade in Steel," 199.

17. Pastor, *Politics of U.S. Foreign Economic Policy*, 171. The relevant provision of Section 201 of the Trade Reform Act of 1974 states: "Upon the request of the president or the Special Representative for Trade Negotiations, upon resolution of either the Committee on Finance of the Senate, upon its own motion or upon the filing of a petition under subsection (a) (1), the Commission shall promptly make an investigation to determine whether an article is being imported into the United States in such increased quantities as to be a substantial cause of serious injury, or the threat thereof, to the domestic industry producing an article like or directly competitive with the imported article."

respond to certain 'unfair' trade practices" whether or not injury occurred as a result.[18] This provision also empowered the executive to choose countermeasures against foreign trade partners that utilized unfair trade methods to the detriment of U.S. interests. All these measures allowed domestic interests to initiate charges against foreign practices, giving them much more power to ensure that the government would investigate. These were significant developments given that the renewed VRA on steel expired in 1975 and that new avenues for protection were being considered. At the beginning of that year, as Michael Borrus observes, "United States Steel filed seven countervailing duty petitions with the Treasury Department against six E.E.C. producers and Austria. U.S. Steel argued that rebates of value-added taxes on steel exports were subsidies subject to countervailing duties under U.S. law."[19] The Treasury Department dismissed the petitions a few months later, but this move deflected actions against pricing policies of foreign competitors only temporarily.

Section 201 Relief for Specialty Steel, 1976

In the meantime, the specialty steel industry, which was quite distinct from the mainstream carbon steel industry, petitioned in July 1975 for relief from imports of specialty steel under Section 201 of the 1974 act. In January 1976, the ITC determined injury to the domestic industry by foreign competition and recom-

18. "In the Trade Act of 1974, the US Congress attempted to improve the ability of the United States to respond to certain 'unfair' trade practices. Section 301 of that act permits presidential retaliation against 'unreasonable' and 'unjustified' foreign import restrictions, export subsidies, or other practices that 'burden, restrict or discriminate against United States commerce' either in the home market or in third-country markets. . . . In short, Section 301 codifies latent US executive branch powers to impose economic countermeasures against foreign countries." Gary Clyde Hufbauer and Joanna Shelton Erb, *Subsidies in International Trade* (Washington, D.C.: Institute for International Economics, 1984), 114–15.

19. Michael Borrus, "The Politics of Competitive Erosion in the U.S. Steel Industry," in Laura Tyson and John Zysman, eds., *American Industry in International Competition* (Ithaca: Cornell University Press, 1983), 87.

mended that import quotas be imposed for five years.[20] President Gerald Ford refused the recommendation, hoping instead to negotiate VRAs with governments of the major importers, thus avoiding the antitrust problem and possibly deflecting foreign antagonism. Only Japan was willing to cooperate, however; both the European Community and Sweden, the other major suppliers of specialty steel, refused to accept an orderly marketing arrangement. Political considerations forced President Ford to act when voluntary restraints were not forthcoming.[21] Although specialty steel constituted only 5 percent of U.S. steel imports in value and 1 percent in tonnage, most of the industry was located in Pennsylvania, which was to hold its presidential primary in April.[22] Needless to say, the time was politically ripe for announcement of positive action.

In June 1976 the president officially set import quotas on specialty steel, in accordance with Article 19 of the GATT.[23] Austria, Canada, the European Community, and Japan formally "expressed their concern and dissatisfaction over the measure at the [GATT] Council meeting that month [June]. They repeated the view expressed by Japan at a Council meeting earlier in the year that the difficulties of the United States specialty steel industry were mainly brought about by the recession in the United States." Further, they would analyze the effects of the quotas on trade with the United States, reserving their right, under GATT, to retaliate.[24] The United States in turn reassured the council delegates that it had considered ramifications on the trade of other nations, which was why the quota would be set for three years rather than

---

20. Patrick and Sato, "United States–Japan Trade in Steel," 200.

21. Under Section 201 of the 1974 act, "the President still retained the authority to reject the recommendations of the Commission if he found a rejection to be in the national economic interest, but the Congress gave itself the power to override a Presidential determination," thus forcing the president to find some kind of acceptable remedy if the VERs were not forthcoming. Pastor, *Politics of U.S. Foreign Economic Policy*, 171.

22. *Economist*, 20 March 1976, 82.

23. GATT, *Activities in 1976* (Geneva, 1977), 74. As a result of its willingness to comply with the president's request for voluntary restraints, Japan was given a more lenient quota than were the others. Harris, *U.S. Trade Problems*, 37.

24. GATT, *Activities in 1976*, 74.

for five years as recommended by the ITC. In the wake of U.S. reassurances, the GATT received no retaliatory notifications.

A truce on this particular aspect of the steel issue, however, did not carry over into carbon steel, which constituted the bulk of steel imports into the United States. No longer protected by the VRA, which expired in 1975, U.S. producers were sensitive to any development that might increase imports. With considerable unease, therefore, domestic steel producers observed conclusion of an orderly marketing arrangement between the European Community and Japan in October 1976. They immediately filed a Section 301 complaint with the U.S. trade representative (USTR) to seek retaliatory action against what they viewed as an unfair arrangement that diverted exports headed for the European Community from Japan to the U.S. market.[25] The USTR investigated to determine whether the E.C.-Japanese arrangement had produced such a diversion. Japanese exports to the United States had indeed risen during this period but whether this was coincidental or a result of the E.C.-Japan deal could not be determined.[26] When no link could be made between the E.C.-Japan agreement and U.S. imports, the investigation appeared to satisfy the president that the petitioners' claim was not warranted, and the case was dropped.[27]

When Section 301 relief could not be secured, the U.S. steel industry continued to press for quotas but also turned to another avenue for stemming the flood of cheaper imports. Facilitated by the legal changes described above, their efforts now focused on anti-dumping suits.[28] Evidence supported claims of U.S. steel producers that imports were at less than fair value and that this price undercutting was injuring U.S. industry. For Japanese imports, the price difference "appeared to be on the order of $25 per net

25. Patrick and Sato, "United States–Japan Trade in Steel," 200–201.
26. *Economist*, 25 December 1976, 71.
27. Harris, *U.S. Trade Problems*, 47.
28. The steel industry had been pressuring the Carter administration to pursue separate sectoral steel negotiations in the new round of trade negotiations in Tokyo to address the fair trade issue; Robert Strauss, U.S. trade representative, refused this, however, and "instead advised big steel to seek relief under the anti-dumping laws." Borrus, "Politics of Competitive Erosion," 88.

ton in 1976."[29] For the European Community, Borrus writes, the difference was even greater, reportedly averaging "$50 per net ton below cost and profit during the first nine months of 1977."[30]

Trigger Price Mechanism, 1978

Such evidence was by no means definitive, however, and the Federal Trade Commission (FTC) and the Council on Wage and Price Stability launched a study to determine the accuracy of industry claims. Meanwhile, a rash of anti-dumping suits were being prepared against Japanese steel companies in conjunction with the concern over diversion of Japanese exports to the U.S. market.[31] Although the study indicated that much of the price advantage held by Japanese imports was due to greater productive efficiency, a test anti-dumping case took a different view. At the end of September, the Treasury Department issued a preliminary ruling on a suit filed by Gilmore Steel, finding that Japanese carbon steel was being dumped in the U.S. market. As Borrus notes, this suit encouraged numerous others, "mostly against the E.E.C. and Japan," and "the E.E.C. began to threaten retaliation in anticipation of the additional antidumping filings."[32]

To deal with mounting domestic pressure for comprehensive protection, President Carter met with representatives of the steel industry and steel workers to declare that he considered quantitative restrictions on carbon steel to be an unacceptable policy option. Instead, he argued, U.S. producers should be protected only against unfair trade practices such as dumping. As Matthew Marks notes, the president "condemned foreign dumping practices and declared that he would, in the future, ensure more vigorous enforcement of American anti-dumping laws. He even went so far as to charge the Treasury Department with a 'derogation of

29. Ibid., 16.
30. Ibid., 17. Canadian steel was not a target of U.S. anti-dumping suits during this period.
31. Patrick and Sato, "Political Economy," 210.
32. Borrus, "Politics of Competitive Erosion," 91.

duty' over the enforcement of the Anti-dumping Act."[33] At the same time, the president launched a special interagency task force under the direction of Anthony Solomon, treasury undersecretary for monetary affairs, to determine how best to achieve such enforcement.[34]

The shift in U.S. attention from quotas as a protective means to anti-dumping suits had support in both the GATT and in The Organization for Economic Cooperation and Development (OECD). The GATT, of course, allows nations subjected to dumping to initiate anti-dumping duties following an affirmative finding,[35] a product, as we have seen, of the original U.S. normative view that dominated negotiations creating the GATT. As Frank Benyon and Jacques Bourgeois state, the U.S. position was buttressed by a 1977 OECD report on the steel crisis, which concluded that "to absorb for long periods substantial imports at unjustifiably low prices to the detriment of its own production" was not the importing nation's responsibility.[36] Both Japan and the European Community, however, argued that the fairness issue was two-sided. According to Borrus, they charged that the U.S. anti-dumping law violated the GATT anti-dumping code "by enabling retaliation even where substantial injury was not proved."[37] This was particularly problematic given the fact that the Carter administration did not want Tokyo Round negotiations derailed by deepening conflict over the steel dumping issue. Even so, the doubling of E.C. steel exports to the United States during 1977 made administration efforts to downplay the dumping charges impossible.[38]

33. Matthew Marks, "Remedies to 'Unfair' Trade: American Action against Steel Imports," *World Economy* 1 (January 1978): 223–29.

34. Steven J. Warnecke, "The American Steel Industry," in Susan Strange and Roger Tooze, eds., *The International Politics of Surplus Capacity: Competition for Market Shares in the World Recession* (London: Allen and Unwin, 1981), 142–43.

35. GATT, *Basic Instruments and Selected Documents* (Geneva, 1958), Article 6.

36. Frank Benyon and Jacques Bourgeois, "The European Community— United States Steel Arrangement," *Common Market Law Review* 21 (June 1984): 317.

37. Borrus, "Politics of Competitive Erosion," 92.

38. During 1975, exports to the United States accounted for 3.2 million metric

The Solomon Report, announced in December 1977, proposed that the old method—relying on formal complaints before anti-dumping could be initiated—be replaced by an administrative mechanism that would allow the Commerce Department to investigate on its own initiative.[39] This idea offered the president an alternative to quantitative restrictions that ran counter to GATT obligations and to executing the spate of anti-dumping investigations that so worried Japan and the European Community. At the same time, the plan assured the steel industry that something positive was being done on its behalf.

The trigger for dumping investigations would be a reference price under which importers could not sell without automatically setting in motion the anti-dumping procedure. The so-called Trigger Price Mechanism (TPM) would use a reference price based on Japan's cost of producing the most efficient source of imports, thus lending credence to Japan's claim and to the evidence of the FTC–Council on Wages and Price Control study that Japan was generally not dumping. Even so, the trigger price would prevent Japanese dumping if it occurred and would reflect the most efficient of Japan's industries.[40] Harris notes that officials undertook updates of the data along with on-site inspections of Japanese mills to "revise the trigger prices quarterly." The TPM went into effect in May 1978 with the understanding that domestic steel industries would not initiate anti-dumping suits. Legally, the U.S. government could not stop them from doing so, but the Carter administration bargained for no anti-dumping suits to be filed independently; otherwise, the TPM would be revoked.[41] This understanding was particularly important, given that E.C. and Japanese officials had been pressing the administration to convince U.S. steel producers to drop their anti-dumping suits.[42] European and Japanese producers, who would then know what prices were acceptable, could operate in a more secure marketing environment.

---

tons; in 1976, 2.4 million metric tons; in 1977, 5.5 million metric tons; and in 1978, 6.2 million metric tons.

39. Warnecke, "American Steel Industry," 142–43.
40. Harris, U.S. Trade Problems, 87.
41. Patrick and Sato, "United States–Japan Trade in Steel," 212.
42. Borrus, "Politics of Competitive Erosion," 93.

Although the TPM seemed a more efficient method to detect and prosecute importers in violation of the anti-dumping law, the plan had certain drawbacks according to both steel exporters and domestic producers. Basing the TPM on an average of the most efficient Japanese production made it difficult for Japanese firms to take temporary profit losses by selling below cost when recessionary pressures made such an option attractive to maintain capacity. This kept even temporary dumping to an absolute minimum. On the other hand, the European Community, which heavily subsidized much of its steel production and operated far less efficiently than the Japanese, was given a "license" to dump. Europeans could sell at any price at or above the trigger price and not be charged with dumping, even though this was heavy dumping in relation to its own cost of production.[43] The Japanese, who were very displeased with the arrangement, saw themselves paying for the "free ridership" of the European Community and being unfairly targeted. They also resented the absence of gratitude for Japan's efforts to unofficially and voluntarily restrain exports to the United States.[44] Japan took no formal action against U.S. policy, however.

Harris says that E.C. criticism was muted because the community realized the benefits of the TPM to their policy of "maintaining artificially high domestic steel prices."[45] As Borrus has noted: "A strict enforcement of U.S. antidumping law might otherwise have resulted in an effective embargo of E.E.C. steel. This could only have led to further deterioration of the European industry. . . . Through the pricing mechanism based on Japanese costs, American policy-makers could avoid such dislocation and the retaliation it was likely to engender, while still addressing the concerns of U.S. producers, labor and Congress."[46] In addition, the community's own anti-dumping policy, based on a reference price system, put anti-dumping proceedings on a "fast track." This reference pricing, along with the VER that the community had already

43. Harris, *U.S. Trade Problems*, 93.
44. Ibid., 227–29; and Patrick and Sato, "United States–Japan Trade in Steel," 223.
45. Harris, *U.S. Trade Problems*, 86.
46. Borrus, "Politics of Competitive Erosion," 95.

arranged with the Japanese, put these nations on a similar footing with the United States in regard to steel policy. The one major difference, which emerged later as a significant point of distinction, was the comprehensiveness of the E.C. adjustment and restructuring plan compared with the absence of such a U.S. plan.[47]

The decisions that produced the first TPM resulted from a number of considerations. First, U.S. demand for steel had generally been stronger than elsewhere during this period, and producers in other nations attempted to exploit this market potential. The appeal of the U.S. market, coupled with E.C. pricing practices, made it difficult for U.S. producers to retain their market share, and they pressured the administration to respond to industry needs. Wage and price studies had revealed that E.C. production costs were generally at least as high as U.S. costs despite lower-priced exports, which made anti-dumping investigations the logical avenue for enforcement of fair trade. Carter administration officials who were engaged in the difficult Tokyo Round negotiations, however, wanted to avoid E.C. retaliations and conflicts that execution of anti-dumping duties threatened to ignite.[48] The TPM offered the administration a way to maintain some control over anti-dumping investigations, provide trading partners with a degree of predictability, and offer the domestic industry some promise of fair trade enforcement. On this final goal, the TPM foundered, and two particular factors contributed to collapse. Because the yen depreciated significantly in 1979, Japanese production costs decreased at a time when U.S. domestic steel production costs were rising, which also caused the trigger price to decrease, allowing imports to compete comparatively freely

47. Ibid. The Davignon Plan involved strict anti-dumping procedures based on a reference price, orderly marketing arrangements with other nations that exported steel to the European Community, vigorous anti-dumping procedures based on a reference price, aggressive export efforts, and a restructuring plan, to facilitate the long-term competitiveness of the steel industry. The restructuring plan which required extensive E.C. involvement in industry policy and adjustment, was quite different from the generally noninterventionist nature of U.S. steel policy. These differences set the two trading entities at odds from the late 1970s onward. Steven Woolcock, "U.S.-European Trade Relations," *International Affairs* 58 (Fall 1982): 614–15.

48. Levine, *International Trade Policy Formulation*, 12.

with U.S. products. This situation, coupled with the ability of the E.C. countries to subsidize export prices without being charged with dumping (as long as products entered at or above the trigger price), convinced U.S. steel producers to abandon support for the TPM.

The Second Trigger Price Mechanism, 1980

U.S. domestic steel interests had become increasingly unhappy with the arrangement that had given E.C.-subsidized exports nearly free rein in the U.S. market. By 1980, pressure had built against the TPM, and U.S. Steel filed separate anti-dumping suits in May against Japan and the European Community.[49] As a result, the president, acting on his earlier threat, suspended the TPM, launching negotiations with representatives of the domestic industry to settle the matter before the suits were determined.

According to Patrick and Sato, Lewis W. Foy, chairman of Bethlehem Steel and the American Iron and Steel Institute, maintained that it was in the interest of the domestic steel industry to avoid a trade war but that the TPM was acceptable only if it were changed to "reflect faithfully the production costs of both Japan and the E.C."[50] The Carter administration sought compromise with Japan, which resented being charged with dumping, and also with the European Community, whose costs of production the TPM had never taken into account. The community agreed to provide data on production costs rather than have the costs determined unilaterally from U.S. sources.

In exchange for dropping the anti-dumping suits, officials offered the steel industry a revised TPM and a new program of government assistance involving tax credits for new investment, changes in the depreciation rate on capital investment, and more lenient treatment under both the Clean Air Act and the Clean

49. Harris, U.S. Trade Problems, 6–7. In the suits filed against E.C. countries, U.S. Steel charged that 75 percent of steel imported to the United States from these countries was dumped. Patrick and Sato, "United States–Japan Trade in Steel," 219.

50. Patrick and Sato, "United States–Japan Trade in Steel," 219–21.

132

Water Act.[51] In addition, writes Levine, the TPM was expanded to cover subsidization as well as dumping, even though "it was not specified just how TPM II would deal with subsidies." The steel industry found the offer attractive and withdrew the anti-dumping complaints. In the end, the trigger price was revised upward, which forced Japan to sell steel at prices well above production costs or face new anti-dumping charges, but which also raised TPM prices high enough to make it difficult for European producers to exploit the arrangement as they had exploited the first TPM. With a 12 percent upward revision of trigger prices, European steel would be in clear violation of the new arrangement. This change, coupled with the fact that the renewed TPM now covered subsidization, ultimately defeated the "TPM's primary purpose of maintaining peace with the E.C."[52]

Other events impacted U.S. commercial policy in this period; of particular interest were the changes in U.S. trade law implemented by the 1979 Trade Agreements Act. This package of measures was designed to implement the Tokyo Round negotiations and delineate the powers that the president would have in enforcing trade agreements, the most significant element being "reciprocity" in all trade agreements. On the face of it, this requirement appeared in keeping with the GATT's original intent as noted in its preamble. Closer examination, however, shows that the act actually further removed the United States from the principle of unconditional mfn treatment in relations with fellow GATT signatories.

Modifications in U.S. trade law reflected the fact that domestic political support for international trade agreements that opened U.S. markets further to imported goods could be achieved only if reciprocity were ensured. Addressing the OECD in 1980, Alan Wolff aptly explained that "the maintenance of the U.S. as an open market for other country's exports is highly dependent on the U.S. private sector's and the Congress' appreciation that there

---

51. Ibid., 222. The TPM was now 12 percent higher and also included a 15 percent market quota for those imports. Robert H. Ballance and Stuart W. Sinclair, "Re-industrializing America: Policy Makers and Interest Groups," *World Economy* 7 (June 1984): 204; and Woolcock, "U.S.-European Trade," 615.

52. Levine, *International Trade Policy Formulation*, 16.

is equity provided in terms of market access abroad and that injurious and/or unfair foreign competition particularly in our market will be remedied promptly."[53] The 1979 act reflected congressional determination to achieve reciprocity in dealings with other nations and to secure fair treatment for domestic producers.

As an integral part of this congressional mandate, the U.S. government signed the new code on subsidies and countervailing duties with two purposes in mind. First, the code limited export subsidies that the United States considered unfair trade instruments. Second, application of the code (which required that domestic industry must be injured by subsidized imports before countervailing duties could be applied, a departure from previous U.S. policy) was conditional on the trading partner implementing the code to U.S. expectations, thus giving it greater leverage over "recalcitrant" nations.[54]

Title I of the Trade Agreements Act of 1979, which implemented the international code on subsidies and countervailing duties negotiated in the multilateral trade negotiations (MTN), was officially recorded as Title VII of the Tariff Act of 1930.[55] The most important change in U.S. law regarding countervailing duties dealt with "eliminating the injurious effect" of subsidized imports. According to Harvey Kaye, the new law allowed "negotiated settlements of investigations and, under specified criteria, suspension of countervailing duty investigations upon agreement to eliminate completely net subsidies, to cease exports, to eliminate the injurious effect of subsidized imports, or to restrict the volume of imports of the merchandise under investigation."[56] If an

53. Alan W. Wolff, "The Trade Policy Context of Steel Sector Problems: Developing an International Approach," in OECD, *Steel in the 80s* (Paris: OECD, 1980): 248.

54. Hufbauer and Shelton Erb, *Subsidies*, 120–21.

55. Title I of the 1979 act became the new Title VII of the Tariff Act of 1930, Section 701.

56. Subsection 704 (c) (3) of the 1979 Trade Agreements Act allows "two governments to negotiate a quantitative restriction on importations of a particular product. . . . Once a quantitative restriction is successfully negotiated it constitutes an alternative remedy to the imposition of countervailing duties." Quoted in Harvey Kaye et al., eds., *International Trade Practice* (New York: McGraw Hill, 1981), Section 15, Part 6.

initial investigation on subsidized imports were launched, the latter remedy essentially offered a policy alternative to escape clause action as well as to the traditional, lengthy countervailing duty process. Along with reaffirmation of a reciprocal philosophy on the part of the United States, this action set the stage for a new round of trade disputes over steel.

Countervailing Duty Suits and the 1982 U.S.-E.C. VRA

Between October 1980 and July 1981, Levine notes, German, Dutch, and French currencies depreciated against the dollar, which made U.S. prices "extremely attractive to European producers, who could sell in their depressed home markets only at a loss." Reinstitution of the TPM in the last few months of the Carter administration, however, made selling on the U.S. market at competetive prices without being charged with dumping virtually impossible. The European Community, which claimed that the new trigger prices were now above their costs of production, wanted some provision "to allow E.C. sales in the United States without forcing them to undersell trigger prices."[57]

Under the first TPM, Canada had successfully argued that proximity and plant efficiency gave its steel producers a genuine cost advantage over the Japanese, on whose costs the trigger prices were set. In response, writes Levine, the U.S. "Treasury Department had established a 'preclearance procedure' under which foreign producers could submit to an informal investigation establishing that their fair value was below trigger prices, thereby removing the risk of provoking anti-dumping investigations by below-trigger sales."; European Community producers saw this process as a possible avenue to access the U.S. market without violating the TPM, and a number of them sought preclearances. U.S. and E.C. officials, however, were concerned that too many preclearance approvals would "provoke U.S. steelmakers into filing a new round of petitions."[58] In response, the Department of Commerce purposely delayed E.C. applications,

57. Levine, *International Trade Policy Formulation*, 18–22.
58. Ibid.

which caused a significant decline in community exports to the United States. Faced with this state of affairs, the E.C. Commission proposed to the United States that trigger prices be lowered by 10 percent. Pressure mounted from their firms to do something to change the arrangement. On the one hand, producers who did not want to violate U.S. procedures were losing market shares, whereas other firms were beginning to disregard the rules altogether and were selling well below trigger prices.

The U.S. Commerce Department, in an effort to modify the TPM procedure, would monitor imports, determine if dumping or subsidization and injury had occurred, and then negotiate with targeted firms to moderate pricing policies. In the meantime, the department and the E.C. Commission negotiated a trigger price reduction compromise at 5 percent, but, the compromise broke down in September 1981, writes Levine, at the same time that August import statistics "became available, showing the highest steel imports in U.S. history, much of it from the E.C." Despite efforts by the Commerce Department during the fall of 1981 to forestall anti-dumping and countervailing duty petitions by initiating seven cases and to seek a new negotiated understanding with the European Community, U.S. steel producers became frustrated with the process. In December, 132 anti-dumping and countervailing duty complaints were filed, and the second TPM was rendered useless. In addition a Section 301 complaint was filed in December 1981 with the USTR against "unfairly subsidized specialty steel imports from foreign producers."[59] As a result of this petition, the USTR requested these countries consult.

Meanwhile, the U.S. announced preliminary and affirmative countervailing duty determinations in June 1982 in response to the fusillade of petitions against subsidized carbon steel imports. These "determinations [concerned] certain steel products from Belgium, Brazil, France, Italy, Luxembourg, the Netherlands, South Africa, the United Kingdom and West Germany."[60] Because the major targets were members of the European Community, the

59. Ibid., 230–31. The petition named Austria, Belgium, Brazil, France, Italy, Sweden, and the United Kingdom.
60. Hans Mueller and Hans van der Ven, "Perils in the Brussels-Washington Steel Pact of 1982," *World Economy* 5 (November 1982): 262.

community immediately sought consultations with the U.S. government. At their request, the GATT Committee on Subsidies and Countervailing Duties met to examine "actions taken by the United States concerning certain steel products exported by the E.C."[61] Bilateral negotiations continued to take place outside the GATT dispute settlement framework, however.[62]

The Reagan administration, unlike its predecessor, was reluctant to intervene in the countervailing duty procedure, even within legally prescribed bounds.[63] Because of this reliance on U.S. administrative machinery, write Hans Mueller and Hans van der Ven, the "Reagan Administration had repeatedly voiced its resolve to stay out of the conflict and not to interfere with the steel industry's efforts to seek relief under the 'laws of the land.'"[64] The seriousness and extent of countervailing duty suits, however, brought vigorous E.C. protests, making the president's posture untenable and pressuring him into reaching a negotiated settlement with the community. After one unsuccessful attempt to have Washington suspend the suits, the E.C. Commission not only sought and obtained "'an exclusive mandate' to negotiate an overall agreement with the US Government"[65] but also threatened

61. GATT, *BISD* (Geneva, March 1983), 47.

62. Article 3 of the Agreement on Interpretation and Application of Articles 6, 16, and 23 of the GATT (Subsidies and Countervailing Duty Code) provides that the signatory whose products may be subjected to a countervailing duty has a right to consult "with a view to clarifying the factual situation and arriving at a mutually agreed solution." Article 17 provides for committee conciliation if a bilaterally acceptable solution is not forthcoming. Article 18 provides for establishing a panel to review the case and present findings to the committee if necessary; moreover, the committee is given the power to "authorize appropriate counter measures" if its recommendations are ignored. Agreement on Interpretation and Application of Articles 6, 16, and 23 of the General Agreement on Tariffs and Trade as quoted in Hufbauer and Shelton Erb, *Subsidies*, pp. 137–38, 147–48.

63. Stephen Woolcock, "U.S.-European Trade," 617. Several analysts have noted this shift in administrative orientation, which they mainly ascribe to the Reagan administration's commitment to enforce the laws against unfair trade and to take up the banner from Congress of reciprocity. The shift may also have occurred following completion of the multilateral trade negotiations of the Tokyo Round and abatement of diplomatically eased tensions after 1980.

64. Mueller and van der Ven, "Brussels-Washington Steel Pact," 262.

65. Benyon and Bourgeois, "Community–United States Steel Arrangement," 340.

retaliation against U.S. agricultural and fiber exports.[66] Previously, the European Community had begun to prepare its own countervailing duty case against the America's export aid program, Domestic International Sales Corporation, which provided subsidized credit for purchase of U.S. products. Initiated by the European Council, this latter effort was a purposeful tit-for-tat retaliation for use against the United States if a comprehensive settlement were not reached.[67] These added threats against U.S. exports clearly risked escalation unless diplomacy could intercede.

The European Community, guided by coherence of purpose in the dispute, held a strong bargaining position with the United States. As Benyon and Bourgeois note, E.C. officials perceived that the dispute and eventual agreement "demonstrated what good results could be achieved when the Member States showed the political will and solidarity to act as a community and enable that community to negotiate as one partner with the United States and thus as an equal partner."[68]

That the community might take solid retaliatory action against the United States provided an equally effective incentive for the Reagan administration to find a more acceptable solution.[69] The inherent dilemma was that pursuit of the countervailing duty process would target what the U.S. steel industry and the administration considered unfair trading practices, whereas a negotiated compromise would undermine U.S. enforcement efforts, which would seriously threaten relations with the European Community. As long as the European Community pressed so vociferously

66. Mueller and van der Ven, "Brussels-Washington Steel Pact," 262.

67. *European Report* no. 879 (10 July 1982): 8.

68. Benyon and Bourgeois, "Community–United States Steel Arrangement," 350–51.

69. Levine argues that the administration was not overly concerned about community-wide retaliation, expecting Germany and the Netherlands to block such action because their producers were competing fairly in the U.S. market without subsidization. This does not account, however, for the fact that the E.C. Commission now had the authority to deal with the situation for the entire community. The Commission pursued a unified position, negotiating in the interests of the community's collective steel policy, not simply those of individual members. See Carolyn Rhodes, "E.C. Supranationalism v. Bilateral Diplomacy" (Paper presented at the International Studies Association Annual Meeting, London, April 1989).

for a political settlement that ensured producers continued access to the U.S. market, the United States found it difficult to place enforcement of fair trade above mutual benefit. From April onward, the United States supported a negotiated settlement in place of unilaterally imposed countervailing duties if an acceptable agreement could be reached.

Throughout the summer and autumn of 1982 U.S. and E.C. officials conducted negotiations in Brussels and Washington. The first issue to resolve was whether the United States would accept an action other than countervailing duties (as allowed in U.S. law and in the new GATT Subsidies Code) that would limit the "injurious effect" of subsidized imports.[70] The second issue—the level of compensation warranted—pitted the E.C. view that many of its subsidies were not countervailable under the GATT against the U.S. Commerce Department's view that they were. In the end, negotiators suspended the countervailing duty procedure in favor of a bilateral settlement. The draft agreement resulting from these negotiations "provided that the entry into effect of the arrangement was conditional on the withdrawal of the petitions filed by the US industry in respect of imports originating in the E.C. and on the termination of all proceedings and investigations concerning CVD's [countervailing duties], AD [anti-dumping] duties and the petition based on Section 301."[71] In return, the arrangement provided voluntary E.C.-allocated export quotas on carbon steel, thus removing the "injurious effect" of subsidized imports without interfering with the community's steel restructuring policy, which relied on subsidization to temper reduced capacity.

This compromise, which was particularly attractive from the European point of view, would allow the E.C. Commission to determine which national industries received what levels of ex-

70. Gary Horlick, deputy commerce secretary in charge of the countervailing duty proceedings against the European Community, maintained that the administration fully intended to go through with the suits, a plan that was altered only in response to community demands for quantitative restrictions instead. Horlick, "American Trade Law and the Steel Pact between Washington and Brussels," *World Economy* 6 (September 1983): 359–60.

71. Benyon and Bourgeois, "Community–United States Steel Arrangement," 333.

ports to the United States rather than let U.S. countervailing duties price some E.C. steel producers out of the market. Vital to the commission's collective steel program was spreading the costs of a diminished U.S. market evenly across member states in relation to past market shares. A voluntary quota administered by the European Community would provide this flexibility, but U.S. countervailing duties would not; such duties would thrust costs onto the most heavily subsidized, whereas more efficient producers would hardly be affected. Although countervailing duties intentionally place extra cost burden on inefficient industries, this effect was not compatible with E.C. steel policy. To prevent states such as Britain and France from bearing the full cost impact, the European Community commission sought cooperation from states with more efficient industries, such as Germany and the Netherlands, which were clearly unhappy with a quota arrangement that forced them to pay for their neighbors' inefficiencies; nevertheless, these governments endorsed the plan.[72]

What diplomats saw as a good deal did not, however, satisfy U.S. steel producers, who initially rejected the offer. In addition, a new barrage of anti-dumping suits appeared likely to reach fruition when the Commerce Department on 10 August "piled on the agony by ruling that 15 steel companies from five E.E.C. nations had dumped steel in the American market."[73] This new development would add anti-dumping duties to imports to cover price differences between production costs in the various European countries and the U.S. sale price, *on top of* countervailing duties that dealt with subsidy rather than prices.[74] If both actions against "unfair" trade culminated in anti-dumping and countervailing duties, charges would be very costly. For example, France's Sacilor would have faced countervailing duties of 30 percent on struc-

---

72. Woolcock, "U.S.-European Trade," 616–17; and Horlick, "American Trade Law," 357.

73. *The Economist*, 14 August 1982, 60.

74. Harris, *U.S. Trade Problems*, 39. Countervailing duties are calculated as the proportion of the price advantage afforded a particular product because of the receipt of subsidies for its export. Whether the good is dumped makes no difference in the determination. Anti-dumping duties are applied only to compensate for the price advantage due to firms selling below cost.

tural steels and approximately 25 percent anti-dumping duties on steel sheet and strip, and British Steel faced 40 percent countervailing duties plus approximately 15 percent anti-dumping duties.[75]

The U.S. administration worked feverishly to appease steel industry demands in a manner acceptable to its trading partner; the key was inclusion of steel pipe and tube imports in the quota arrangement.[76] At the eleventh hour, the European Community agreed to this provision, and the steel industry pledged the U.S. government to withdraw its countervailing and anti-dumping suits. The letter exchange between Davignon and Baldridge, which constituted the agreement, did not establish whether E.C. subsidies were actually countervailable or whether E.C. industries had dumped their products. In fact, Davignon's letter of 21 October 1982 explicitly stated that: "In entering into this Arrangement, the E.C. does not admit to having bestowed subsidies on the manufacture, production or exportation of the products that are the subject of the countervailing duty petitions to be withdrawn or that any such subsidies have caused any material injury in the U.S. Neither does it admit that its enterprises have engaged in dumping practices which are the subject of the anti-dumping petitions to be withdrawn or that any such practices have caused any material injury in the USA."[77] This E.C. disclaimer allowed the negotiated settlement to sidestep any admission of wrongdoing. Terms of agreement made no formal connection between its willingness to voluntarily restrain exports and the legality of subsidies under U.S. law or under the new GATT code.

The agreement restrained exports to the United States to average 5.44 percent of the U.S. market for carbon and certain alloy steel products, including steel pipe and tubing. Each product cate-

75. *Economist*, 14 August 1982, 60.
76. *The Economist*, 9 October 1982, 78. The delay on steel tubing resulted mainly from the reluctance of the Germans, who were the biggest suppliers of steel pipe and tubing to the United States and whose exports of these products were not even part of the original countervailing duty suit. *Economist*, 22 October 1982, 52.
77. *Official Journal of the European Community*, L307/12. The wording of the letter from Baldridge to Davignon on 21 October 1982 includes the same assurance verbatim. Ibid., L307/26.

gory was assigned a separate limit, and the ECSC would issue export licenses to allocate and regulate such exports from various E.C. steel producers.[78] The United States was assured that this restructuring included a target date for eliminating subsidies to help industries adjust to reduced capacities. Although not a new offer but rather an integral component of the community's Davignon plan, this factor was persuasive.[79] The VER agreement with the United States would expire at the end of December 1985, at the same time that these subsidies were to be discontinued, directly linking the two.[80]

Although the European Community hoped to achieve predictability and cooperation for three full years with the E.C.-U.S. VRA, unfolding events in 1982 demonstrated that successful management of the trade crisis was temporary. Having barely reached an acceptable compromise on E.C. carbon steel imports, the U.S. steel industry sought to impose penalty duties on specialty steel from France, Germany, and the United Kingdom. In early 1983, countervailing duties were imposed on imports from these three E.C. member countries. Because the 1982 agreement did not include specialty steels, U.S. manufacturers did not refrain from filing countervailing duty suits.[81]

As Mueller and van der Ven note, President Reagan announced in July 1983 that the United States "would grant its domestic specialty steel industry protection from imports through a combination of tariffs on imported stainless steel sheet, strip, and plate and quotas on stainless steel bar, rod, and alloy tool steel."[82] U.S. Trade Representative William Brock defended this decision on the grounds that the domestic steel industry's "difficulties stem from persistent excess productive capacity, some of it uneconomic and supported by subsidies, as well as trade restrictive and distortive practices used by many of our trading partners to protect their

78. Ibid., L307/13–15.
79. Mary Frances Dominick, "Countervailing State Aids to Steel: A Case for International Consensus," *Common Market Law Review* 21 (June 1984): 386.
80. *Official Journal*, L307/13.
81. *International Herald Tribune*, 15 May 1985, 11.
82. Mueller and van der Ven, "Brussels-Washington Steel Pact," 274.

industries and stimulate exports."[83] The Europeans immediately protested that this violated the GATT's conditions for invocating Article 19 of the GATT as well as punishing twice those countries whose exports were assessed countervailing duties earlier that year.[84] Under the auspices of Article 19, the European Commission announced retaliation against the quota-introducing country, as well as protest against U.S. actions before the GATT Council.

By January 1984, the European Community had compiled a list of quotas and restrictions against U.S. chemicals, plastics, burglar alarms, skis, and rifles—worth about $120 million per year—to be used in retaliation for American tariffs and quotas on specialty steels. This announcement followed negotiations in which the community attempted to arrive at compensation agreeable to the Americans, but after the United States refused E.C. proposals, the commission took the list to GATT for a "third-party" opinion.[85] When the United States continued to balk, the European Community refused to grant any further extensions on negotiations and in April 1984 unilaterally imposed the compensatory measures.[86]

European Community officials also worried about two January petitions by U.S. steel producers, one by Bethlehem Steel, America's second largest steelmaker, and the other from Gilmore Steel. The Bethlehem petition asked the ITC for "across-the-board limits on imports of foreign steel" set at 15 percent of the U.S. market, "compared with their present share of about twenty-two percent."[87] If successful, this action would revoke the European Community's quota agreement with the United States, a most worrisome prospect. The Gilmore suit, which was more limited, charged that certain steel products from Belgium and West Germany were being dumped on the American market, thus resulting in injury to the company.[88] Given the then high value of the dol-

---

83. *Europe*, September–October 1983, 48. One of the suits filed against British Steel was finally upheld in the spring of 1985 by a ruling of the U.S. Court of International Trade. *International Herald Tribune*, 16–17 March 1985, 11.
84. *Europe*, September–October 1983, 48.
85. *Economist*, 9 July 1983, 70.
86. Ibid., 21 January 1984, 63.
87. Ibid.; and *Europe*, January–February 1984, 46.
88. *Europe*, March–April 1984, 50.

lar, this charge was not likely to stick but added to the community's uncertainty about its U.S. trade agreement and, consequently, the exports of its steel producers. Pressure from the steel industry for protective action was also building in Congress. Bethlehem Steel had lobbied Congress for a bill to mandate a 15 percent protective quota if the Reagan administration failed to act favorably. At the same time, a domestic content requirement for all automobiles sold in the United States, which would have directly benefited U.S. steel producers by mandating that components be manufactured in the United States, was gaining momentum.

In 1984 the ITC initially ruled that steel imports were injuring the domestic industry, and pressure for protection mounted. To avert the quota, however, the Reagan administration decided to seek actively a comprehensive set of bilateral export restraint agreements.[89] Because the 1982 U.S.-E.C. agreement had not included semifinished steels and because these imports from Europe had risen, the United States initiated negotiations with the European Community in early 1985 for a restraint agreement including these products.[90] The United States had accused the community of violating the 1982 agreement by diverting exports from the categories specified in the quota arrangement into semifinished steels. The European Community denied the charge, arguing that the high value of the dollar had caused increased European purchases.[91] To deter the United States from limiting imports of its semifinished steel, the European Community in April 1985 announced "a list of American farm exports which could be hit by restrictive measures if Washington carries out its threat to reduce their already limited steel shipments any further."[92]

Because the 1982 agreement would expire at the end of 1985, both sides wanted to prevent this particular dispute from ruining chances for the successful completion of a VRA renewal; yet, American steel producers supported inclusion of semifinished steel in the next arrangement as adamantly as European steel pro-

89. *Economist*, 21 January 1984, 63.
90. Ibid.
91. *Economist*, 2 March 1985, 83; and *International Herald Tribune*, 19 March 1985, 13.
92. *International Herald Tribune*, 28 February 1985, 7.

ducers favored exclusion. As tensions mounted, the United States initiated a special purchase of steel pipe from European producers in exchange for an E.C. commitment to negotiate the semifinished steel issue. By exporting an extra one hundred thousand tons of steel pipe to the United States for a Texas-California pipeline, this sale allowed the European Community to "exceed the quota limiting its 1985 exports to 7.6 percent of the U.S. market."[93] This conciliatory action put export restraint discussion back on track. On 31 October 1985, a four-year VRA renewal was announced that limited the European Community to 5.5 percent of the United States finished steel market, a reduction from the 6.6 percent total share held in 1985. This plan also extended the pipe and tube arrangement until 1989, however, and set total export levels at slightly more than those of the 1982 accord (5.46 percent). At first, semifinished steel was not included, but the two sides announced in December that it also would be limited.[94]

Levine, who participated in the 1982 E.C.-U.S. steel negotiation, concluded that although "legalistic import protection procedures . . . enabled the industry to achieve a quota arrangement with the E.C., those same procedures prevented the industry from achieving its real goal (control on imports from all countries), and limited its ability to control imports from E.C. producers."[95] This meant that dissatisfaction within the U.S. industry with limitations prompted renewed protectionist pressure for global quotas, not simply enforcement of fair trade, which had proved less than satisfactory. These actions turned prophetic, as the next three years demonstrated; not only was the European Community expected to restrain exports, but so were other major suppliers, including Japan.

United States–Japan VRA, 1985

Although the October steel arrangement allowed a temporary lull in trade conflict between the community and the United

---

93. Ibid., 8–9 June 1985, 13.

94. *International Trade Reporter*, 6 November 1985, 1388, and 18 December 1985, 1572–73.

95. Levine, *International Trade Policy Formulation*, 111.

States, no such salve was available for U.S.-Japanese relations. Before the E.C. agreement had even been completed, the U.S. steel industry turned its attention to other significant steel exporters. Not wanting a flood of imports to replace those recently curtailed and suffering as well from a higher dollar and reduced demand due to the Reagan administration's Soviet pipeline construction embargo, domestic steel producers immediately targeted Japan.

Charging an undervalued Japanese yen and Japanese diversion of European-bound steel to the U.S. market, U.S. Steel chairman Roderick threatened a Section 301 suit against Japan and asked for an import surcharge to offset the yen's undervaluation. Although a GATT conference on revitalization of free trade was scheduled within less than a month, the U.S. steel industry appeared bent on increased protection, despite Japanese imposition of a voluntary export restraint of approximately six million tons a year since the late 1970s. As one report noted, "although Japan's 7.2% share of the American market so far this year [1982] is up from the 5.5–6% consistently achieved in 1978–1981, it is exactly the same as the level reached in 1977, the year before the 'diversion' from Europe began."[96] Although the 301 suit was terminated, congressional consideration of the 15 percent comprehensive quota on steel imports would seriously affect Japanese imports. When he imposed the escape clause quota on specialty steel, President Reagan noted that these actions would protect against "subsidized foreign steel competition,"[97] a particularly irksome prospect to the Japanese, whose exports were not subsidized but whose steel was included in the quota. Japan claimed once again to be caught in the cross fire of an American-E.C. steel dispute. Still, it did not threaten retaliation but continued to pursue cooperation with the United States to avoid conflict that might close markets even further.

After experiencing nearly fifteen years of U.S. protectionism, Japanese steel firms strategized direct investment in U.S. steel firms in addition to their accommodative export restraint policy. In February 1984, Nisshin Steel, one of the top six producers,

---

96. *Economist*, 16 October 1982, 87–88, and 18 December 1982, 84.
97. *Economist*, 9 July 1983, 70.

bought 10 percent of Wheeling-Pittsburgh Steel, ranked "eighth among American steelmakers."[98] In April, Nippon Kokan, the second largest steel firm in Japan, bought half of National Steel.[99] These Japanese investment actions in U.S. firms reflected efforts to secure a portion of U.S. sales of steel without the complications of import restrictions. The strategy was sound, given mounting protectionist pressure in the United States. The Reagan administration, although it felt doubly pressured from the ITC recommendation and from the pending import quota bill in Congress, recognized the weight of both issues during the 1984 presidential campaign in which Reagan's opponent, Walter Mondale, promised to hold imports to 17 percent of the U.S. market. As we have seen, the president deflected this pressure and announced his intention to seek voluntary restraints rather than allow Congress to impose quotas unilaterally.

The administration sought voluntary restraints from those suppliers whose exports to the United States had surged during the previous year and especially from those that had used subsidies and dumping to "prey" on the American market. If suppliers failed to voluntarily restrain exports, mandatory quotas would be imposed.[100] The administration immediately launched negotiations with the Japanese, South Koreans, and Brazilians on limiting their exports to the United States. Because the U.S.-E.C. steel arrangement was still in effect, E.C. states were not targeted (although the 1985 VRA renewal was part of the overall calculation), nor was Canada. Japan's 84 percent surge in imports in 1984, along with its long-range import threat to U.S. industry, made that country the target of U.S. protectionism.

Once again Japanese steelmakers were frustrated by the new policy. First, Haruki Kamiya argued, their industry had for many years exercised restraint in the U.S. market, maintaining their "historic share" and not more.[101] Second, Japan was not using

---

98. Ibid., 11 February 1984, 69.
99. Ibid., 18 April 1984, 71–72.
100. *International Herald Tribune*, 20 September 1984, 1.
101. See statements by Haruki Kamiya, executive vice president of Nippon Kokan K. K., Japan's second largest steel company, as quoted in ibid., 22 November 1984, 1.

unfair trade tactics to maintain that market share but was genuinely competitive. Despite this dismay over inclusion in the plan for restrictions, Japan agreed to limit steel exports to 5.8 percent of the U.S. market, compared with an average of 6.3 percent over the previous ten years. In exchange, the United States agreed to secure withdrawal of any anti-dumping cases pending against Japan.

Although VRA details were not finalized until March 1985, Japan was the first to reach agreement with the United States on voluntarily reducing sales. Japan's reaction replayed previous interactions, again accommodating the United States in its efforts to protect a chronically uncompetitive steel industry. Concerned about losing an even larger share under mandatory quotas as well as about maintaining good relations with the United States during a period when the U.S. bilateral trade deficit had reached a record $37 billion, Japan did not threaten retaliation but publicized willingness to reach agreement to engender goodwill.[102] Japan's two-pronged strategy of direct foreign investment and accommodative export restraint, at least for the time being, avoided even greater restrictions on access to the U.S. market.

The Japan-U.S. VRA, coupled with similar U.S.-instigated arrangements and following so closely the E.C.-U.S. agreement, illustrated the underlying nature of U.S. strategy. Ostensibly aimed at subsidized exports to the United States (whether the result of direct government subsidization or currency undervaluation), U.S. counteractions were launched to enforce fair trade but also to protect the domestic steel industry from competition.

Protectionism, Reciprocity, and Bilateral Cooperation in Steel Trade

A number of observations can be made from this sectoral study about U.S. trade policy, protectionism, reciprocity, and the GATT regime. Not surprisingly, this case study demonstrates that U.S. trade policy in the steel sector has been guided by protectionist

102. Ibid., 7 December 1984, 17.

motivations as well as by fair trade considerations and, paradoxically, that each has given way to the other from time to time.

Little doubt exists that U.S. trade policy for steel became protectionist after 1968. Initially, escape clause actions and congressional threats of mandatory quotas created protectionist leverage that enabled the U.S. executive to negotiate voluntary export restraint agreements with major importers. These VRAs clearly resulted from the protectionist coercion of the United States. Then, with passage of the 1974 Trade Act, which made fair trade enforcement options more appealing to U.S. steel producers, Section 301 and anti-dumping duty cases began to replace Section 201 and congressional sources of protection. As Chapters 3 and 4 explain, institutions of fair trade had coexisted with norms of liberalism in the United States since the new trade regime was created. As Judith Goldstein observes, it was not until "competition intensified" in the 1970s that "producers found that state-society relations in most nations qualified them for state aid under unfair trade statutes,"[103] and the 1974 modifications made enforcement of fair trade an attractive avenue for assistance.

Normatively, anti-dumping duty provisions, as we have seen, were aimed against importers' predatory behavior and, if fairly enforced, could check foreign producers' unfair competition. In this regard, anti-dumping duties as forms of reciprocity against unfair trade are useful instruments of the GATT regime and domestic fair trade enforcement. As this set of cases reveals, however, anti-dumping petitions can be exploited as a means of protectionist disruption, creating a good deal of uncertainty for the fair importer as well. The first TPM was devised in part to address this issue by clarifying what constituted fair prices and by recognizing the genuine lower costs of production enjoyed by most Japanese firms. Yet doing so made it possible for European firms, whose production costs were much higher, to sell below cost in the U.S. market without being charged with dumping. This outcome exploited the administrative arrangement that had been

103. Judith Goldstein, "Ideas, Institutions, and American Trade Policy," in G. John Ikenberry et al., eds., *The State and American Foreign Policy* (Ithaca: Cornell University Press, 1988), 204.

designed to remove much of the uncertainty created by multiple independent anti-dumping petitions. Ironically, this also meant that Japanese and U.S. producers would have to compete with state-aided steel from the European Community, despite the original intent of the anti-dumping law.

Instead of enforcing fair trade and rewarding genuinely efficient production, the first TPM, in effect from May 1978 to March 1980, produced a somewhat opposite result by allowing E.C. producers to continue to sell below cost of production. The Carter administration's decision to intervene in the countervailing duty process was motivated in large measure by pressures from the European Community and by considerations of the Tokyo Round of multilateral trade negotiations, which, it was feared, would be disrupted by a proliferation of multiple dumping disputes. Paradoxically, regime considerations and international relationships motivated the U.S. government to modify the anti-dumping process in order to maintain the constructive momentum of the negotiations while satisfying domestic demands for protection and enforcement of fair trade. In doing so, however, this action reinforced expectations of managed trade rather than rewards for efficiency and fair trade.

The first TPM was replaced because it failed to secure for the domestic industry the contradictory goals of fair trade enforcement and blatant protectionism. On the one hand, the European Community had been licensed to dump in the U.S. market by the arrangement, much to the disgruntlement of the U.S. steel industry; on the other hand, currency changes allowed Japanese steel products to enter the U.S. market at lower prices than ever before, which frustrated steel producers, as the TPM failed to protect them. U.S. steel producers, who were just as interested in protection as in fair trade enforcement, scrapped their deal with the government and negotiated a second TPM that lasted even more briefly, from March to October 1981. This agreement, which resulted from continued need to address the domestic steel industry's demand for protection and fair trade enforcement, was short-lived because of failure on both counts. In particular, the plan did not adequately address the issue of how to deal with subsidized E.C. firms, whose competitiveness resulted directly

150

from that subsidization. Turning again to U.S. fair trade law, U.S. steel producers used countervailing duty procedures to target this unfair competition.

For a short time, the new Reagan administration appeared to prefer execution of U.S. countervailing duty law over mediating disputes with the European Community, but at this point in the ongoing trade conflict, the community escalated pressure on the U.S. government, threatening retaliation if a negotiated settlement did not replace U.S. countervailing duty procedures. This reciprocal leverage over U.S. trading interests in the E.C. market made avoiding a diplomatic solution very difficult. In the end, the mutual political benefits from a VRA with the European Community outweighed considerations of fair trade, and bilaterally negotiated trade management was preferred over the enforcement of countervailing and anti-dumping duties. This choice was further substantiated by U.S. negotiation of comprehensive voluntary export restraints in steel, even with those nations, including Japan, that were not charged with unfair trading practices.

Two general observations can be made about the role reciprocity played in this sector. First, in most cases, when the United States used reciprocity as a tool of fair trade enforcement in the form of anti-dumping or countervailing duties, intervention of the executive, which was concerned about conflict with GATT partners, undermined the enforcement effect. Ironically, considerations of how enforcement would affect foreign trade relations convinced administration officials to sidestep direct execution of anti-dumping and countervailing duty processes, even though they were legitimate GATT actions. That the domestic steel industry preferred protection over enforcement of fair trade if the two goals did not prove harmonious rendered reciprocal fair trade policies ineffectual. Interestingly, reciprocity was clearly part of the domestic industry's strategy for obtaining protection, yet it was not desired when other forms of protection could be achieved diplomatically. Use of reciprocal strategies as a means of fair trade enforcement would not secure U.S. producers from genuinely competitive actors such as Japan and might threaten a rift with the European Community, whose trading relationship was highly valued.

Reciprocity, U.S. Trade Policy, and the GATT Regime

The two largest trading entities in the world colluded against the GATT's norms of liberal and fair trade to accommodate each other's interests. Once these two giants in the steel sector had agreed on the 1982 VRA, given that the European Community had already secured similar arrangements with its steel importers, America's trade partners found it very difficult to resist U.S. demands for compliance with a comprehensive "voluntary" quota system.

Between 1968 and 1985, U.S. actions in this sector, reciprocal as well as unilateral, were generally motivated by protectionist goals. As was true before 1934, reciprocal policies were manipulated to achieve protectionist goals rather than to achieve genuine fair trade. Had U.S. reciprocal responses been carried through according to GATT regime norms of liberal and fair trade, the result would have been much different. Efficient importers would have been rewarded by a freer market in which subsidized importers would have been penalized. The European Community, however, also pursued a retaliatory strategy rather than accept U.S. enforcement of GATT rules, which contributed to the U.S. decision to accommodate community interests rather than to pursue a fair trade enforcement strategy. When reciprocal strategies based on fair trade were modified by foreign retaliation and domestic protectionism, their result was no different than that of coercive protectionism. Yet reciprocity did prove uniquely useful as a bargaining tool in this sector when the European Community pursued it in response to U.S. protection or fair trade actions.

This leads to a second observation about the role of reciprocity: generally, its use as a bargaining strategy advanced the interests of the actor who used it. For example, the United States was unable to end dumping and subsidization of products exported to its market, but its rigorous use of the anti-dumping and countervailing processes prevented the steel industry from competing with an unimpeded influx of below-cost-of-production exports. At the same time, the European Community, which refused to tolerate U.S. anti-dumping and countervailing duty suits without resistance, effectively used retaliatory threats to press the U.S. executive into compromises that made the U.S. market far less restrictive and much more predictable for its producers. When the community used reciprocal responses to U.S. policies that had the potential to retaliate meaningfully against U.S. interests, it leveraged a cooperative arrangement that accommodated interests on both sides of the Atlantic. Although this resulted in collusion, European Community interests were served in a way that would have been less likely had the United States been immune from retaliation.

In comparison with Japan, for example, the European Community not only used diplomatic efforts to persuade U.S. decision makers but also threatened tangible retaliation against the United States if the latter dismissed its concerns. On the other hand, Japan registered dismay, concerns, and willingness to cooperatively restrain exports to prevent more extreme disruption, yet it did not threaten retaliation, which might have taken away some of the unilateral protectionist prerogative from Washington. To fully explain this difference would require comparative analysis of domestic and historical factors that produced the respective approaches, but differences in market interdependence and relative vulnerability at the international level appeared to be important contributing factors. The European Community was more clearly an equal partner of the United States during the period of study, both in economic size and in market interdependence. The United States considered exports to the community important in a way that exports to Japan were not. Moreover, Japan in the 1970s and early 1980s was not in a position to threaten the United States with retaliation and had no viable alternative to accommodative strategy. On the other hand, the European Community, which had the potential to leverage a more acceptable compromise, acted on it.

Potential leverage is a necessary but not sufficient requisite for a more favorable settlement. Potential must be actualized as a credible threat. In terms of bargaining strength and willingness to use a reciprocal strategy, Japan and the European Community proved very different, and these differences were reflected in the community's ability to shape U.S. steel trade policy, which Japan could not do. Simply, the United States had to reckon with the European Community in a way that it did not with Japan, which demonstrates that reciprocity can usefully contain trading partners' actions under certain interdependent circumstances. Although on a much smaller and more specific scale, the potential for retaliation in this case can be compared to the retaliations of the 1930s that pressed the United States into cooperation. On the one hand, U.S. fair trade actions forced the European Community to modify export policies, even if such actions were not in strict compliance with original GATT liberal norms; on the other hand, E.C. retaliatory threats forced the United States to seek a more amenable bilateral compromise. Mutual reciprocal activity produced mutually acceptable arrangements, even if they ran counter to GATT's original free trade intent.

Clearly, U.S. and E.C. policy actions in the steel sector affected the GATT regime and its liberal trade principles. Unlike coercive protectionism, reciprocal strategy that carried through the enforcement capabilities of U.S. trade law could have reinforced GATT regime rules; U.S. domestic steel producers, however, as well as E.C. interests, preferred managed trade to liberal fair trade, which sacrificed efficiency and fairness to the sovereign protectionist concerns on both sides of the Atlantic. Particularly noteworthy was the U.S. desire not to derail the multilateral trade negotiations and a later desire not to begin a trade war with the European Community, both of which motivated U.S. officials to interfere with enforcement of U.S. fair trade law and to favor bilaterally managed trade over that prescribed by the GATT. Moreover, changes in GATT rules on subsidy dispute settlement and in U.S. trade law facilitated this shift.[104] Dispute settlement in this sector demonstrates that a political interpretation of reciprocity dominated, one in which mutual benefit of managed trade (compensation for illiberal actions) took precedence over reciprocal enforcement of liberal fair trade rules.

Protectionist coercion and retaliation in steel produced a new sectoral regime based on bilaterally managed trade and reciprocal concessions that departed partially from original GATT norms. This departure sacrificed principles of comparative advantage and

104. Carolyn Rhodes, "Managed Steel Trade, the GATT Subsidies and Countervailing Duty Code, and the 1979 United States Trade Act," *World Competition Law and Economic Review* 12 (December 1988): 37–47.

Table 5. Steel imports as percentage of U.S. supply

Year	Total	E.C.	Japan	Canada	Other
1990	17.5	5.6	3.2	3.0	5.7
1989	17.9	5.8	3.8	3.1	5.2
1988	20.3	6.1	4.2	3.1	6.9
1987	21.3	5.0	4.5	3.8	7.0
1986	23.0	7.3	4.9	3.6	7.2
1985	25.2	7.2	6.2	3.0	8.8
1984	26.4	6.4	6.7	3.2	10.1
1983	20.5	4.9	5.1	2.9	7.6
1982	21.8	7.3	6.8	2.4	5.3
1981	18.9	6.1	5.9	2.7	4.2
1980	16.3	4.1	5.0	2.5	4.7
1979	15.2	4.7	5.5	2.0	3.0
1978	18.1	6.4	5.6	2.0	4.1
1977	17.8	6.3	7.2	1.7	2.6
1976	14.1	3.2	7.9	1.3	1.7
1975	13.5	4.6	6.6	1.1	1.2
1974	13.4	5.4	5.1	1.1	1.8
1973	12.4	5.3	4.6	0.9	1.6
1972	16.6	6.0	6.1	1.1	3.4
1971	17.9	7.0	6.7	1.2	3.0

Sources: Years 1971–80 taken from Selected Statistical Highlights, *Annual Statistical Report* (Washington, D.C.: American Iron and Steel Institute, 1980), 8. Years 1981–90 taken from Selected Statistical Highlights, *Annual Statistical Report* (Washington, D.C.: American Iron and Steel Institute, 1990), 6.

nondiscrimination to maintain traditional market shares and cooperative management. No escalating spiral of retaliations occurred, however, and trade flows were maintained (see Table 5). Even though managed trade resulted, the use of limited retaliations and threats of retaliation actually checked the exploitative activity of trading partners and produced cooperative outcomes.

6

U.S. Trade Relations
in Automobiles

Two distinct bilateral relationships have dominated U.S. trade in automobiles. The first, which developed in the early 1980s, emerged from increasing competition between U.S. carmakers and Japanese imports, a relationship characterized by U.S. demands for export restraint and Japan's acquiescence to maintain market access. The specific Japanese-U.S. relationship in this sector resulted from negotiations in which the United States utilized coercive protectionist threats to induce Japan to voluntarily restrain exports. More generally, U.S. concerns over the growing trade deficit with Japan made friction over this particular bilateral problem part of the much wider issue of reciprocal trade relations. The auto sector has increasingly symbolized Japan's penetration of the U.S. market in the absence of balanced treatment and mutual benefit in Japan for U.S. products. U.S. retaliatory threats from this bilateral dispute became part of the larger U.S. strategy in the 1980s of tying access to the American market with reciprocal Japanese market liberalization.

The second U.S. trading relationship involving automobiles was forged during the 1960s, when Canada threatened to close its market to U.S. exports unless American auto manufacturers agreed to invest in production facilities in Canada. After threats and counterthreats by both Canada and the United States during the negotiations, the outcome was managed integration of automotive industries in the neighboring countries.

156

The following analysis of these two distinctive cases demonstrates that the actor who threatened coercive protectionism or retaliation against a trading partner successfully leveraged specific cooperative responses. As in the steel sector, when the other trading partner responded with a reciprocal strategy, the interaction produced a cooperative outcome that required compromise on both sides. In each case, the economic power relationship between the United States and its trading partner was highly asymmetrical, which led to the expectation that the United States would dominate in outcomes of dispute settlements, but this was not true in both cases. In the bilateral relationship between it and the United States, Japan pursued an accommodative strategy whenever the United States initiated coercive protectionist demands. In the bilateral relationship between it and the United States, Canada used an aggressive coercive policy to exact certain U.S. trade and investment concessions, thus forcing the United States to accommodate Canadian interests. This comparison indicates that even in an asymmetrical relationship, the smaller trading partner can effectively use leverage against the larger when the two economies are interdependent and market access is at stake.

Japanese-U.S. Relations

The 1970s challenged the U.S. automobile industry to adjust; for the first time, foreign competition seriously threatened a market that had been exclusively reserved for domestic producers. By the end of the decade, Detroit's demands for protection had reached a crescendo. Culminating in a complaint filed with the ITC for emergency quota protection against Japanese imports, pressures on the U.S. auto industry became too strong to ignore. Consequently, in 1981 the U.S. government began negotiations with the Japanese government for voluntary limitations on exports of vehicles to American[1] a voluntary restraint that was then

1. U.S. Trade Representative William Brock adamantly denied that formal negotiations took place, though Secretary of State Alexander Haig reported that the U.S. government had indeed given the Japanese government an ultimatum

157

renewed several times without U.S. government request. How this state of affairs developed and why the Japanese were willing to limit their exports provide an interesting story that sheds light on the origins and nature of U.S. coercive protectionism and demonstrates how this tactic became a component of fair trade reciprocity in this sector.

The 1981 Voluntary Export Restraint

A series of shocks jolted U.S. car manufacturers out of complacency during the 1970s. Because of inflation, high wage contracts, and lower efficiency levels, prices of U.S. automobiles skyrocketed at the staggering rate of 145 percent between 1973 and 1981.[2] At the same time, the oil price increases following the Yom Kippur War in October 1973 made Detroit's heavy, fuel-inefficient cars unattractive to increasing numbers of buyers. Faced with the choice between expensive fuel-guzzling U.S. cars and smaller, cheaper fuel-efficient Japanese cars, the U.S. public was shifting its loyalty to foreign imports. In 1970, foreign-made automobiles accounted for 15.3 percent of the U.S. market, which by 1982 had nearly doubled to 27.8 percent; in 1983, Japanese imports accounted for 21.5 percent of all automobiles sold in the United States.[3]

That Japan manufactured cars to match the new American consumer demand put U.S. carmakers at a competitive disadvantage, providing an opportunity for Japanese firms to penetrate the U.S. market with high-quality cheaper products. Although U.S. car manufacturers launched impressive new investment and retooling programs to cut costs and produce more competitive products, they were unable to recapture the market they had lost by 1980.

---

and that "talks" did take place publicly in April 1981. Liberty Mahshigian, "Orderly Marketing Agreements: Analysis of United States Automobile Industry Efforts to Obtain Import Relief," *Hastings International and Comparative Law Review* 6 (Fall 1982): 175.

    2. Robert H. Ballance and Stuart W. Sinclair, "Re-industrializing America: Policy Makers and Interest Groups," *World Economy* 7 (June 1984): 202.

    3. Sean D. Murphy, "International Joint Ventures in the United States: The GM-Toyota Deal," *Columbia Journal of Transnational Law* 22 (1984): 508.

Faced with layoffs, the United Auto Workers Union (UAW) filed a request on 12 June 1980 with the ITC for import relief under Section 201 of the 1974 Trade Act. Within two months, Ford Motor Company became a party to the request; but the ITC, according to Mitsuo Matsushita and Lawrence Repeta, after holding public hearings in October, announced that "although the U.S. automobile industry had suffered severe injury, foreign automobile imports were not a substantial cause of this injury."[4] The commission decided against relief on a three-to-two vote, with both Republican appointees voting for Section 201 relief and the three Democrat appointees voting against. Dr. Paula Stern, who voted with the majority, was careful to point out that "there is no question that domestic producers face serious problems; . . . however, on balance I have found that the decline in demand is due to general economic conditions—recession, [the] credit crunch, rising costs of our car ownership—and a major unprecedented shift in demand from large to small cars [which] brought the domestic industry to its present weakened state."[5] Blocked in their request for Section 201 relief, write Robert Ballance and Stuart Sinclair, the UAW and Ford appealed to Congress to "empower the Administration to negotiate restrictions on the imports of Japanese cars."[6] This effort aimed to circumvent the fact that the president did not have the authority under the 1974 Trade Act to unilaterally impose quotas in the face of an ITC no-injury decision. In this regard, the act was consistent with the GATT Article 19 escape clause provision for emergency import relief: granting import relief in cases where injury was not linked to imports would violate GATT rules as well as U.S. law.[7]

During this same period, the Carter administration had nego-

---

4. Mitsuo Matsushita and Lawrence Repeta, "Restricting the Supply of Japanese Automobiles: Sovereign Compulsion or Sovereign Collusion?" *Case Western Reserve Journal of International Law* 14 (1982): 49.

5. *Far Eastern Economic Review*, 21 November 1980, 48.

6. Ballance and Sinclair, "Re-industrializing America," 206.

7. As Matsushita and Repeta note, "The question whether the President has power to negotiate an orderly marketing agreement independent of that Act [Section 201 of the 1974 Trade Act] (and despite a finding by the ITC of no injury due to imports) is unresolved." Matsushita and Repeta, "Supply of Japanese Automobiles," 49–50.

tiated with the Japanese government to remove barriers to imported automotive components that the United States was producing at competitive rates. As the assistant secretary of state for economic and business affairs reported to the Subcommittee on International Trade of the Senate Finance Committee in December 1981:

> In April 1980, the United States asked the Government of Japan to eliminate import duties altogether on all automobile parts, including original equipment and replacement parts. After extensive negotiations, the Japanese obtained Diet approval for the elimination of tariffs on 38 automotive parts categories and for a substantial reduction of the tariff on tires and tirecases. These reductions—which went into effect on April 1, 1981—were on items the U.S. Government, in consultation with the U.S. industry, had identified as of greatest interest to our firms.[8]

Coupled with the ITC ruling later that year, this effort to derive some reciprocal benefit from the increase in automobile trade illustrates how seriously the Carter administration had taken the economic challenges facing domestic producers but also how much it preferred remedies that would expand rather than restrict trade.

Congress, however, had other ideas. After the ITC ruling, legislation appeared that would limit imports of Japanese automobiles to 1.6 million per year for a period of three years. The Danforth-Bentsen Bill, which was blatantly protectionist, showed no regard for the GATT international trade rules, given the ITC no-injury ruling. That the ITC decision had been divided, however, lent legitimacy to congressional demands for import relief. Even those who voted in the majority against escape clause action recognized imports as an "important cause" of the problem, and Vice-Chairman Michael Calhoun stated that "'particular foreign manufacturers' should not take advantage of a depressed United States

---

8. Robert Hormats, "Auto Parts Industry," *Department of State Bulletin*, February 1982, 40.

market."[9] Armed with such views from the ITC, congressional proponents of automobile import protection were in a good position to have their legislation seriously considered. Other efforts were also being proposed, including a Senate resolution that would have empowered "the President to enter negotiations with foreign governments to persuade them to voluntarily limit their export of automobiles and trucks to the United States."[10]

As pressure built in Congress for protectionist action against Japanese imports in early 1981, President Reagan, who had just taken office, was reminded of his campaign promise to take action against Japanese imports, and a task force was organized to consider the best policy options open to the president.[11] The most attractive option was to convince the Japanese government to force export limits on vehicle manufacturers, as evidenced by a letter from Attorney General William French Smith to U.S. Trade Representative William Brock on 18 February 1981. Concerned with the antitrust restrictions that U.S. law might impose on Japan's government-negotiated export restraints, the Reagan administration requested an opinion from the attorney general. In his reply, French Smith stated that:

> Generally speaking, an agreement among foreign private companies to reduce the numbers of automobiles they export to this country would most likely violate United States antitrust law. However, we believe that if such an agreement were formally mandated by a foreign government, the formal mandate would provide a defense to any subsequent antitrust challenge. . . . [However,] foreign or United States governmental "approval," "urging," or "guidance" of such behavior cannot safely be relied on as a defense; if the foreign government does not provide adequate protection by mandating the restraints in a legally binding manner, private antitrust suits could jeopardize the effective implementation of any agreements that are negotiated.[12]

9. Robert J. Leo, "An Update of the Japanese Automobile Export Restraint," *Brooklyn Journal of International Law* 8 (1982): 163.
10. Matsushita and Repeta, "Supply of Japanese Automobiles," 50.
11. *Economist*, 14 March 1982, 65.
12. Rodney C. Grey, *United States Trade Policy Legislation: A Canadian View*

Clearly, this letter indicates the Reagan administration's interest in securing an agreement with the Japanese, although previous U.S. experience with voluntary restraint agreements suggested the need for caution.[13] Besides avoiding antitrust complications, the administration was interested in convincing the Japanese government to enforce quotas specifically on its automobile exports to the United States. French Smith's opinion gave them leverage for a Japanese-enforced arrangement if one could be agreed on.

Informal talks were already underway in February, and discussions continued off and on through April. After no agreement followed Japanese foreign minister Masayoshi Ito's late-March visit to Washington, the United States sent a trade delegation to discuss U.S. proposals for Japanese export restraints and the American industry's plan for revitalization.[14] Arriving on 6 April, the U.S. delegation had been officially instructed by Secretary of State Haig not to enter into actual negotiations with the Japanese but to continue to "exchange views."[15] The Japanese were divided on whether to acquiesce to U.S. pressures and adopt the kind of compulsory export quotas that were expected by the United States. On the one hand, the Ministry of International Trade and Industry (MITI) wanted the automobile industry to "exercise prudence" in exportation to the United States to avoid mandatory import quotas and other protectionist measures that might punish the Japanese for noncooperation. On the other hand, the Japanese automobile industry considered the U.S. industry's predicament of its own making, to be solved domestically rather than at the cost of Japanese manufacturing interests.[16]

(Montreal: Institute for Research on Public Policy, 1982), 31. Letter from William French Smith to William Brock dated 18 February 1981.

13. Questions arose following a suit filed by the Consumers Union of the United States against the U.S. government in the wake of a VRA on steel products between the U.S. government and producers within the ECSC in 1968. See Chapter 5.

14. *Far Eastern Economic Review*, 10 April 1981, 90.

15. Alexander Haig, as quoted by Mahshigian, "Orderly Marketing Agreements," 175, n. 109. Haig exemplified the administration's official view of the entire process by asserting that "we are merely exchanging views on this sensitive and complex matter, and we will continue to do so."

16. Leo, "Japanese Automobile Export Restraint," 168–69.

In the end, MITI's fear that Congress would impose quotas if Japanese action was not forthcoming overshadowed resentments over being unfairly targeted to pay the costs of Detroit's poor production and marketing performance. During a visit to Tokyo by U.S. Trade Representative Brock, a voluntary restraint agreement was announced.[17] Japanese officials believed no action would have meant the alternative of handing over their export policy to the United States. Senior trade official Naohiro Amayal maintained that "there was no option but to take such steps . . . to avoid worse consequences." The United States had coerced Japan into voluntarily restraining exports or facing more restrictive protectionism. Although they risked a proliferation of export restraint demands from other importing countries, Japanese officials believed that to lose control of their most important market and risk future access for other products besides automobiles would possibly damage the world trading system. They reasoned that they would risk more rigid protectionism worldwide if they did not ease the pressure from their exports. In the words of Prime Minister Zenko Suzuki, the decision to restrain automobile exports would actually "protect the free trade system."[18]

On 1 May 1981, the agreement was announced between the U.S. and Japanese governments for limitation of automobile exports to the U.S. market. Offering to restrict exports for a three-year period, the Tokyo government based its proposal on the following considerations. First, the Japanese government did not accept responsibility for the plight of U.S. manufacturers; rather, Japan's willingness to restrain was temporary and predicated on U.S. agreement to revitalize its own industry. Second, Japan reviewed other cooperative efforts that had been and were still being undertaken for America's benefit, stressing an accommodative rather than confrontational strategy. Third, the restraint agreement was subject to the condition that U.S. protectionist measures

17. Ibid., 170. Brock claimed at the time that his presence in Tokyo was only coincidental.
18. *Far Eastern Economic Review*, 8 May 1981, 51. See Kent Jones, "The Political Economy of VER Agreements," *Kyklos* 37 (1984): 89, for a general discussion of the reasons why an exporting nation might favor a VRA over other types of restrictions.

against Japanese exports would be deflected by this cooperative act.[19]

The agreement provided Japanese exporters a relatively firm and somewhat liberal expectation of the U.S. market for the next few years, without fears of major protectionist disruptions. The Japanese government was given the opportunity to reiterate its cooperative position in the entire affair; in return, U.S. industry received relief from imports. The U.S. government also found a politically acceptable middle ground between protectionists and free traders. The Reagan administration diplomatically achieved results for the beleaguered American industry while it avoided unilaterally imposing import restrictions that would violate GATT Article 19 requirements. Japanese firms were in turn able to garner quota rent from the supply constraints, which paid high dividends. Even though Japanese automobile manufacturers were punished for their competitive success, says Kent Jones, the VER paradoxically caused a "deterioration in the importing country's terms of trade," which in turn led "to the creation of an economic rent transferred to the restraining exporters." As Jones explained in his 1984 analysis of voluntary export restraint agreements:

> The advantages of a VER to exporting firms derive from the quantitative limit it places on export supply, which calls for competition-reduction measures in the export market, and for the creation of monopoly rents. In order to implement export restraint, the government must form (or allow the formation of) an export cartel. Such an arrangement tends to favor the established firms in the industry by introducing a forum through which the export market is to be organized. The cartel provides the possibility for existing firms to capture guaranteed export market shares and to keep potential newcomers from entering the export market. Although profits for some firms may thereby be constrained, this is compensated by a reduction in the *variance* of profit levels as long as the VER limit is operational, and thus the *risk* associated with fluctuating market conditions.[20]

19. See the text of the Japanese statement as cited by Leo, "Japanese Automobile Export Restraint," 159–60.

20. Jones, "VER Agreements," 86 and 89–90.

Though smaller car exporters chafed under the restraint, firms with an established export share did very well.

Another result of the voluntary restraint was a shift by Japanese manufacturers in their product mix from smaller cars to larger, higher-valued cars, with two important effects. The Japanese not only were positioned to capture the quota rent from the reduced supply, but they were also able to secure greater profits from each product by increasing the proportion of higher-valued intermediate automobiles sold in the U.S. market.[21] After successfully negotiating joint ventures with the Japanese, where direct American investment in Japanese firms was exchanged for agreements to import Japanese subcompacts under their U.S. name, American manufacturers found themselves faced with competition in the midsize luxury car market.

Japanese VRA Renewals

Despite the VRA, the domestic industry blamed the sluggish U.S. economy for its import problems. The House of Representatives twice approved a "domestic-content" bill, once in December 1982 and again in November 1983, which Sean Murphy writes would have required that "by 1986 the domestic content of automobiles must reach 90 percent for firms selling over 900,000 vehicles."[22] This legislation was "aimed chiefly at Japanese manufacturers."[23] Although complaints did not always target automobile imports, they often threatened automobile protection to get at other irritants. The state of the economy, which included high interest rates, a high dollar, and a bilateral trade deficit with Japan, turned political attention to Japan's import policies as well as its exports.[24]

Demands that the Japanese government open its market in exchange for U.S. efforts to *refrain* from taking reciprocal restrictive actions against their imports ran rampant. Congress, led by Rep-

21. Philip Turner and Jean-Pierre Tuveri, "Some Effects of Export Restraints on Japanese Trading Behavior," *OECD Economic Studies* (Spring 1984): 99.
22. Murphy, "International Joint Ventures," 509–10.
23. Ballance and Sinclair, "Re-industrializing America," 206.
24. *Far Eastern Economic Review*, 5 February 1982, 72.

165

resentative Danforth, pressed for reciprocity in Japanese treatment of U.S. exports while negotiations between the U.S. trade representative and the Japanese government attempted to secure concessions on raw materials and high-technology products.[25] As Deputy U.S. Trade Representative David McDonald warned, Japan was expected to "open its market or sacrifice some of its access to the U.S. market,"[26] and often the threat against Japanese exports aimed directly at the automobile sector.[27] Although no legislation specifically to protect the U.S. automobile industry became law during this period, pressure on the Japanese never lifted. Proving themselves cooperators in this area did not make them invulnerable to reciprocity demands in other commercial relations between the two countries.

More and more, the U.S. Congress and even members of the administration became dissatisfied with the overall trading relationship between the United States and Japan. Policymakers found the burgeoning bilateral trade deficit increasingly uncomfortable. Instead of accepting results of past negotiations under GATT auspices as the basis of reciprocal relations between the two GATT members, legislators in particular were more and more unhappy with persistent trade barriers in market sectors of potential significance to the United States. Consequently, what William Cline and others have described as "aggressive reciprocity" emerged as a popular congressional policy option.[28] This concept, very similar to U.S. policy before World War I, was predicated on strictly bilateral measures of reciprocal trade. As R. J. Wonnacott put it:

Aggressive reciprocity is based on a very special and controversial concept of equal treatment. In trade negotiations in the past [under the GATT], the attempt, by and large, has been to equalize *changes*

25. Ibid., 73; Keith A. J. Hay and Andrei Sulzenko, "U.S. Trade Policy and 'Reciprocity,'" *Journal of World Trade Law* 16 (November–December, 1982): 472–73; and *Far Eastern Economic Review*, 18 December 1981, 43.

26. *Far Eastern Economic Review*, 18 December 1981, 43.

27. Ballance and Sinclair, "Re-industrializing America," 96.

28. William R. Cline, "Reciprocity: A New Approach to World Trade Policy?" in William R. Cline, ed., *Trade Policy in the 1980s* (Washington, D.C.: Institute for International Economics, 1983), 121–58.

in protection, but this new concept of reciprocity attempts to equal-ize *existing levels* of protection. In other words, the United States would be raising trade barriers against trading partners whose levels of protection might not have changed at all; their only offense might be that their *existing* barriers are judged *by Americans* to be higher than those of the United States.[29]

The United States had previously adhered to the principle that trade barrier concessions were to be negotiated on a mutual and reciprocally advantageous basis *at a given time*. A new policy of "aggressive reciprocity" would allow U.S. policymakers to exact reciprocal payment in trade barrier concessions for asymmetries in protection levels that had developed *over time*. Moreover, the United States could single out certain sectors that were protected against U.S. products, even though previous tariff negotiations had proven reciprocally satisfactory in other areas. In its desire to see new Japanese markets opened to U.S. goods, Congress threat-ened leverage against Japanese automobile imports if this action would convince the Japanese to allow freer access in other areas. Whereas the Japanese had hoped to achieve a predictable market by supervising a voluntary export restraint, both the U.S. admin-istration and Congress were making future imports uncertain. The only positive note for the Japanese came in 1983, when car sales appeared to be leading the U.S. economy into recovery, thus removing some pressures against Japanese imports as demand for U.S. cars increased.

Considerable growth in the U.S. market had occurred in 1983, and all automobile sales had risen about 14 percent between 1982 and 1983. MITI, which wanted exports to expand accordingly, suggested that exports be raised to 2.2 million cars for 1984 to maintain the Japanese market share at the 22 percent level of 1983. Because of General Motors' (GM) large stake in smaller Japanese companies' exports, MITI gained GM's support to in-crease the quantity of exports if quotas were also reallocated in favor of the company's Isuzu and Suzuki partners. At the same time, demand for new cars was giving Detroit's manufacturers a

---

29. R. J. Wonnacott, *Aggressive U.S. Reciprocity* (Montreal: Institute for Re-search on Public Policy, 1984), 10.

new lease on life; each of the Big Three advanced in profits after 1982.[30] Sales of U.S.-made cars were soaring, while Japan's VRA reined in Japanese sales. By the time the VRA came up for review at the end of 1983, Japanese domestic pressure was increasing on MITI to shift the quota upward.

Countervailing pressures continued in the United States, however, for existing restraints. According to Murphy, Ford and Chrysler argued that "restrictions would be needed for years if the U.S. auto industry is to survive,"[31] and Congress pressed for extension. With two of the Big Three automakers supporting the VRA and reciprocity legislation still pending in Congress, an extension of some kind appeared likely. Following fall 1983 negotiations between MITI and U.S. Trade Representative Brock in Japan, officials announced a compromise VRA extension that set the Japanese quota at 1.85 million cars for 1984. Furthermore, U.S. automobile companies were also enlarging investment in Japanese production. The three major car-manufacturing companies had already secured an interest in Japanese production of subcompacts. As Ballance and Sinclair have noted, this interest mainly took the form of "outsourcing," where Japanese-produced cars were sold through U.S. car dealerships. A new development that offered something for American labor as well as for car companies was emerging as an important investment alternative to outsourcing, however.

Joint ventures between U.S. manufacturing companies and Japanese companies, with much of the manufacturing done in the United States, were turning around the traditional U.S. approach. Instead of U.S. companies being sole owners and using foreign direct investment to capture markets abroad through foreign subsidiaries, these ventures began to facilitate the foreign direct investment of Japanese companies in the U.S. market. General Motors, which already held the largest interest in Japanese manufacturing with investments in Isuzu and Suzuki and also the largest share of

---

30. *Economist*, 22 October 1983, 79; 30 July 1983, 63–64; and 5 May 1984, 66–67.

31. *New York Times*, 2 November 1983, D1, as quoted by Murphy, "International Joint Ventures," 508–9, n. 17.

the U.S. market, agreed in February 1983 to collaborate with Toyota, the largest of the Japanese companies, and produce Toyota-designed subcompacts in an American plant in Fremont, California. As Ballance and Sinclair observe, GM "could offer a full product line without incurring development costs. Thus, the American firm would limit its potential losses if consumer preferences continue to swing away from small cars."[32]

For Toyota, the advantages were numerous. The company would benefit from sales without facing the obstacle of domestic content requirements. They could circumvent the uncertainty of U.S. policies toward automobile imports through such ventures. Just as the U.S. firms had penetrated foreign markets by local production, so could the Japanese. For some time, Japanese business and policy leaders had considered foreign direct investment their best option. As early as 1978, Toyota's assistant director of finance Ikegami predicted that "in the future, we risk having to manufacture our cars outside of Japan."[33] Toshihiro Tomabechi noted that although aware of their market's vulnerability to the vagaries of foreign protectionism, "Japanese industries are looking to increase overseas investments as a way of broadening their base for future growth while reducing dependence on export *per se*. Where circumstances permit, partnerships and joint ventures with the right American partners remain far and away the most attractive option."[34]

After three years of import restraint, the VRA had clearly produced interesting effects. First, the export unit values of Japanese cars rose dramatically; for the U.S. consumer, this meant a 35 percent price increase between 1980 and 1983,[35] due to both the direct supply restriction and the Japanese manufacturers' shift to

32. Ballance and Sinclair, "Re-industrializing America," 206–7.
33. Raymond R. Sekaly, *Transnationalization of the Automotive Industry* (Ottawa: University of Ottawa Press, 1981), 216.
34. Toshihiro Tomabechi, "The U.S.-Japan Connection in the Changing World Marketplace: A Trader's Perspective," *Journal of International Affairs* 37 (Summer 1983): 45. At the time of his speech, Mr. Tomabechi was president of Mitsubishi International Corporation, New York.
35. Turner and Tuveri, "Export Restraints on Japanese Trading," 100.

larger, more luxurious models.[36] Japanese firms also sought ways around U.S. threats of protectionism by investing directly in U.S. production. Both responses demonstrate these industries' far-sighted, flexible reactions to challenges posed by the menace of American trade restrictions. They also evidence the importance of the American market to Japanese automobile firms and Japanese willingness to pursue alternative marketing and production strategies to maintain their companies' market hold.

The success with which the Japanese adapted to the constrained U.S. market, coupled with the significant pressures that Congress continued to exert against Japanese imports, influenced the Japanese government to renew the formal export restraint agreement for 1984. Although demand for foreign automobiles appeared even greater that year and Japanese exporters wanted restraints lifted, costs of keeping them in place (especially at higher levels than before) were far lower than had been originally anticipated. Clearly, the VRA and Japanese direct investment in American production allowed Japan to pursue an accommodative policy toward the United States at a very low cost without significantly altering its long-range marketing strategy. Although the United States had followed a confrontational policy toward Japan in demanding specific reciprocal treatment for American exports in exchange for continued access to the American car market, Japan's interests lay in nonretaliation and cooperation. Moreover, as we saw in the steel trade relationship, both Japan's commitment to cooperation and its market dependency constrained that country from pursuing a less acquiescent strategy.

Unlike 1983, the following year did not witness renewed demands for another extension of the Japanese VER from the Reagan administration. By May 1984, U.S. Trade Representative Brock stated publicly that recovery for U.S. automobile manufacturers was so healthy and enduring that he saw no need to extend

36. It was estimated in 1984 that "in the Japanese market, Japanese firms aim to make a profit of only . . . $85–125 each on such mass-produced cars as the Toyota Corolla or the Nissan Sunny. In the American market, thanks to quotas and sales of higher-value cars, they make more than $2,000 a car." *Economist*, 14 July 1984, 68.

after the current agreement expired in March 1985.[37] In February 1985, the Reagan administration officially announced that the United States would not renew the VER; "reciprocity," however, was implied in the overall commercial relationship as a result of American willingness to forgo such protection.[38] As with the scenario during the 1983 renewal discussions, General Motors supported an end to import curbs, whereas Ford and Chrysler, whose stake in "captured imports" was far smaller, remained opposed.[39]

MITI's decision was very interesting. On 28 March 1985, officials announced that the voluntary restraint would be renewed for another year but at a rate considerably higher than that of the previous twelve months. Under the Reagan administration's green light to unleash exports, Japanese officials obviously felt free to liberalize the export quota from 1.85 million units during 1984–85 to 2.3 million units for 1985–86.[40] This 24 percent increase would allow Japanese carmakers to benefit from the booming U.S. market without inundating it. They had learned the benefits of cartelizing automobile supply, and they were not anxious to depress prices or stimulate protectionist reactions by overexporting.

The Japanese government stressed that some restraint would continue to rein its record trade surplus with the United States, which amounted to $34.7 billion in 1984. This gesture, said Minister of International Trade and Industry Keijiro Murata, "was intended to foster good relations with the United States by providing for 'moderation' in growth of auto exports."[41] Although critics in the United States argued that the quota was set high enough to produce no effect, Japanese officials maintained that exports could easily reach levels of 2.6 to 2.8 million cars with no curbs in place.

The Reagan administration, however, did not want unilateral renewal to substitute for liberalization of the domestic Japanese market in present negotiations. In January 1985, Prime Minister

---

37. Ibid., 5 May 1984, 66.
38. *International Trade Reporter*, 6 March 1985, 325–26.
39. *Economist*, 12 March 1985, Survey 5.
40. *International Trade Reporter*, 3 April 1985, 476.
41. *International Herald Tribune* (Paris), 30 January 1985, 13.

Yasuhiro Nakasone had pledged the Japanese government to "a bold step" toward opening Japan's markets to U.S. electronics, telecommunications, and medical and forest products.[42] As part of the U.S. drive for reciprocal treatment for U.S. products, the two government leaders met to discuss acceptable changes in Japanese import politics; Nakasone promised Reagan to back personally measures to reduce barriers to U.S. imports, after which the two governments entered into formal negotiations.

The Reagan administration had expected the Japanese government to make concessions in these important market sectors in return for reopening the U.S. market to Japanese automobile imports. When the Japanese announced in late March their intention to retain export controls, the administration worried that such a gesture would sidestep improving market access for U.S. imports. This interpretation was plausible. Between the first of the year, when President Reagan and Prime Minister Nakasone discussed the burgeoning Japanese trade surplus, and the Japanese announcement on 1 April that voluntary restraint would be renewed at higher levels, negotiations between the two countries had produced nothing tangible. Despite congressional threats of special import surcharges on Japanese imports and William Brock's personal diplomacy, by late February the two negotiating teams had no agenda for future talks.[43]

When President Reagan requested no renewal of the automobile VRA on 1 March, a sweetened tactic appeared coupled with the hard-line push for trade barrier concessions, but the Reagan administration had not really shifted strategy. As far back as May 1984, the administration had announced that it would not seek a new VRA because of the vigorous rebound in demand for American cars. Nonetheless, this tactic influenced public opinion and created greater pressure on the Japanese by removing any Japanese excuse for failing to take definitive action on import barriers. In fact, the president's speech specifically noted that he hoped for "reciprocal treatment for American products as a result

42. Ibid., 28 March 1985, 11.

43. *International Herald Tribune*, 13 February 1985, 10; and 26 February 1985, 17; and *Far Eastern Economic Review*, 11 April 1985, 63.

of his willingness to let the VRA expire." Although White House spokesperson Marlin Fitzwater stated that "Mr. Reagan's decision was not based on assurances from the Japanese that they would accept more U.S. products, [but] on his conclusion that it was in the best national interest of the U.S.," clearly this treatment was expected. Following President Reagan's announcement but before the Japanese would announce their intentions on automobile exports, VER termination was widely accepted. William Brock predicted that without any restraint, sales of Japanese imports were likely to rise to 2.6 million per year. Although Ford and Chrysler vociferously opposed the administration's policy, Chrysler had already moved quickly to import an additional 200,000 Mitsubishi-made cars in anticipation of increased imports. General Motors, which supported the president, announced a plan to "increase the volume [of imports from Isuzu and Suzuki] to several thousand cars a year."[44]

Expecting that the Japanese government would not renew the VER without pressure from the U.S. government, U.S. politicians and business leaders, many of whom did not support the president's conciliatory gesture, added their demands for "reciprocity" to those of the president. The entire month before the anticipated Japanese termination announcement was filled with as intense protectionist pressure as the Reagan administration had witnessed. Amid charges that the administration was giving Japanese workers jobs by stealing them from Americans and that the Japanese were "in the back yard taking over the country [while the United States was] trying to deal with things in the front yard," a Japanese envoy observed that "the sentiment in the United States is like that before the outbreak of a war."[45]

Americans became more and more adamant that Japan open markets to U.S. goods. Even those who saw the major cause of the growing U.S. trade deficit as "a dollar overvalued by an average of 40 percent against a basket of currencies" argued that "the

44. *International Herald Tribune*, 2–3 March 1985, 9.
45. Ibid., 5 March 1985, 3. Lee Iacocca, chairman of Chrysler Corporation, was so quoted at a special meeting of Democrats. The reaction to his remark comes from a statement by Saburo Okita, head of a Japanese government advisory committee on U.S.-Japanese trade relations in ibid., 19 March 1985, 6.

Reagan administration had made a mistake in not getting a *quid pro quo* from Japan when it announced that it would no longer press for continuance of voluntary auto quotas after March 31."[46] Meanwhile, Tokyo negotiations had slogged along without much progress until 18 March, when the Japanese government announced plans to abolish tariffs on electronics products in preparation for a renewed round of negotiations. In a move of considerable symbolic importance for U.S. negotiators, who had debated the point for over a year, the Japanese government proclaimed the imminent submission of legislation that qualified computer software for fifty-year protection under Japanese law. Such legislation ensured that software would be considered intellectual property much like books and would thereby be protected when U.S. companies or individuals ventured into the Japanese software market.

The United States did not perceive such incremental progress in Tokyo as very significant. Despite Japanese efforts to appease U.S. demands, Nobuo Matsunaga, who would become Japan's new ambassador to the United States at the end of March, reported that "we are facing a critical situation now [concerning U.S.-Japan trade relations]." In response, the Japanese government ordered studies and policy plans to offer "new concessions to open Japan's markets to foreign imports," followed by another round of "market-opening measures in April."[47] Possibly to demonstrate immediate good faith in easing trade tensions between the two countries without incurring significant costs to Japanese automobile manufacturers, the Japanese government then announced continued voluntary restraint at a substantially higher level than before. Good intentions in market liberalization did not satisfy Congress, however, and the Senate Finance Committee unanimously approved a resolution "calling on President Reagan to demand that Japan buy enough additional U.S. imports to offset the impact of increased car shipments."[48] The measure, which

---

46. Ibid., 13 March 1985, 9. Conclusion of a report prepared by Data Resources and under the auspices of its chief economist, Roger Brinner.

47. Ibid., 18 March 1985, 7, and 19 March 1985, 6 and 11.

48. *Financial Times*, 28 March 1985, 6.

directly attacked Japan as an "unfair" trader, placed much of the blame for the American trade deficit on closed Japanese markets. Two days later, the Senate on a vote of ninety-two to zero signaled support for the committee's resolution that also demanded the president "retaliate with tariffs or quotas against Japan unless it took steps to open its markets."[49] If passed, other retaliatory legislation would impose a 20 percent surcharge on all Japanese imports for three years.[50]

While sentiments against Japanese trade policies ran high in Washington, *Financial Times* announced that the U.S. trade deficit had widened to $11.4 billion for February: "Exports suffered their steepest decline in seven years. . . . As usual, the United States sustained its largest trade deficit with Japan. This was $4.2 billion."[51] Such statistics added fuel to a fire already raging in Congress; moreover, the Japanese decision to maintain a high automobile export restraint left many in Washington suspicious that such conciliatory gestures were meaningless ploys to avoid serious market liberalization. In fact, some reports characterized the Japanese decision as an "embarrassment" to the administration and a direct snub to President Reagan's invitation to let the quotas expire on 1 April. In addition, the White House was not pleased that the Tokyo government might consider restraint renewal to escape from earlier promises of liberalization. Spokesperson Larry Speakes emphasized that "the United States does not accept the new auto limitation as a substitute for—or in any way linked to—a more open market in Japan for U.S. exports."[52]

With pressure in Washington mounting, Prime Minister Nakasone, in a dramatic television appearance, announced a three-year program to liberalize Japanese markets and urgently appealed to the Japanese to buy more U.S. goods. Reactions in the United States were mixed. The administration, which did not want a trade war with Japan, reacted favorably but with caution. Donald T. Regan, White House chief of staff, commented that

49. *International Herald Tribune*, 1 April 1985, 1.
50. *Financial Times*, 28 March 1985, 6.
51. Ibid.
52. *International Trade Reporter*, 3 April 1985, 476.

"Prime Minister Nakasone's statement is an unprecedented appeal to the Japanese people to embark on the path to free trade" and praised Nakasone for his efforts to transform "deeply entrenched habits and attitudes." Regan also stated, however, that the package "contains few new or immediate" measures that would affect U.S. exports. Congress was not so understanding; support for retaliatory action against Japan was as strong as ever. As Senator Robert Packwood, head of the Senate Finance Committee, explained, although Nakasone's "heart is in the right place, our patience has worn beyond the breaking point."[53] He did not think that the prime minister's actions would deflect Congress from enacting retaliatory legislation. Sponsors of the measures to punish Japan for import restrictions remained firmly behind their legislation.

Such intransigence could not, however, be attributed wholly to protectionist sentiments from congressional leaders who demanded reciprocal treatment for U.S. exports. As Stephen Cohen comments, past Japanese liberalization packages had often been "recycled versions of previously announced actions," and promises of further market liberalization were not very credible given the record.[54] Even had no aggressively retaliatory fervor gripped Washington at the time, Americans were understandably less willing to be cajoled into conciliation over unfulfilled intents and promises.

In Japan, reaction to persistent U.S. threats and demands mixed worry with resentment. On the one hand, officials took congressional threats very seriously, seeing the loss of important U.S. markets as intolerable; on the other hand, some talk surfaced about a strategy of counterretaliation. Suggestions about how Japan might "punish" the United States for insisting that Japan bear more costs of the bilateral trading relationship included shifting cotton and corn purchases from U.S. farmers to Chinese sources. Such a move would seriously affect an already-beleaguered U.S.

53. *International Herald Tribune*, 11 April 1985, 1.

54. Stephen Cohen, *Uneasy Partnership: Competition and Conflict in U.S.-Japanese Trade Relations* (Cambridge, Mass.: Ballinger Publishing, 1985), 40–41.

industry and, at the same time, provide China with foreign exchange to buy more from Japan.[55] The Japanese government, however, continued pursuit of a policy to "placate rather than provoke Washington," a strategy that appeared to be successful in the short run. The clamor for retaliation against Japan ebbed in the aftermath of Prime Minister Nakasone's public appeal, and the Reagan administration welcomed his "promises," even though U.S. industrial leaders were cautiously optimistic. Congress remained skeptical, but the momentum for retaliatory legislation had flagged. The bilateral crisis had been defused.[56]

One month later, a MITI white paper recommended that Japan reduce "dependence on exports, increase imports, and stimulate domestic demand as a means of reducing international trade tensions."[57] This paper revealed an important new phase in the attitude of the Japanese government: acceptance of Japan's part in maintaining the world trading system. Although they had long accepted that Japan could not depend forever on such a singularly export-oriented policy, the Japanese found opening their doors to foreign goods domestically unpalatable. The intensity of this trade conflict with the United States possibly provided the Nakasone government enough leverage to convince the Japanese people to metamorphose to some extent their role in world trade. As Chalmers Johnson surmised: "Some good may come out of all this bilateral bickering. In the long run Japan must make reforms and begin to assume the responsibilities of a rich nation."[58]

Conclusions about Coercive Protectionism and Reciprocity in U.S-Japanese Auto Trade

The VERs on automobiles, entwined with the larger American-Japanese debate over trade reciprocity, demonstrate the complexities in identifying particular strategies and evaluating their rele-

55. *Far Eastern Economic Review*, 11 April 1985, 66.
56. Ibid., 9 May 1985, 66–67.
57. *International Herald Tribune*, 18 June 1985, 11.
58. Chalmers Johnson, "Both Japan and the U.S. Are to Blame for Trade Tensions," in ibid., 19 April 1985, 4.

vance as causal factors in achieving policy objectives. The United States, after obtaining an agreement from Japan to voluntarily restrain automobile exports to the U.S. market, continued to press the Japanese government to liberalize its import market. As demands for Japanese market liberalization were as much a part of the context of the VER as were U.S. demands for import protection from rising automobile imports, the Tokyo government, coping with one or the other, had to take both into account.

The initial effective U.S. use of coercive protectionism to secure voluntary restraints from Japan in turn raised the possibility of coercion to induce broader Japanese liberalization. Consequently, U.S. coercive protectionist threats over automobile trade became part of a larger reciprocal strategy to pressure Japan into liberalizing import policies, even though they originated as purely protectionist measures to appease domestic industry interests. The Japanese government faced two difficult problems. Those abroad saw Japan as a noncooperator, a free rider on the GATT liberal regime, whereas those at home saw overaccommodation. Relatively speaking, the Japanese import market was becoming considerably more liberal than it had been at the beginning of the 1970s, but the cumulative protective effect of persisting import barriers remained significant. Despite separate bilateral negotiations on post–Tokyo Round agreements between the two nations that would reduce obstacles to U.S. exports, Japan's efforts were viewed as too little, too late.

Although foreigners saw a poor cooperator, the Japanese perspective was just the opposite. Increasingly, writes Tomabechi, the Japanese viewed American claims as attempts to whitewash their own economic problems, "deliberately misconstruing . . . the trade issue [in] an attempt to make Japan a scapegoat for problems of America's own making." Officials pointed out that Japan had recently initiated a "broad range of measures to open further her market on five different occasions." Citing as examples the "series of reforms on the standards and certification systems which go beyond the requirements under the GATT Standards Code" and the fact that Japan had never imposed any countervailing or anti-dumping duties, the Japanese defended their actions as genuine efforts to liberalize.[59] Observers in the GATT and elsewhere agreed.[60]

Regardless of which perspective was correct, the U.S. perception remained that Japan had not done enough to open its market to foreign trade. Unable to alter this view, the Japanese government in the 1980s occupied the unenviable position of preempting Congress from mandatory import quotas on automobiles while avoiding U.S. retaliation for not liberalizing its own import policy. As we have seen, the U.S. market is not only strategically important to Japanese carmakers but also to other sectors, including steel, televisions, and electronics. To risk a trade war and suffer the costs of U.S. retaliation would have been extremely burdensome for such an export-oriented society. To maintain substantial portions of their U.S. market and an element of predictability for their automobile market, the Japanese agreed to voluntary export restraint. Leaders also hoped that cooperation would prevent implementation of the retaliatory legislation pending in Congress.[61]

The VER renewals since 1984 appear to have been motivated by the same considerations. Although pressure from Congress for Japanese market liberalization never disappeared with restraint announcements, much of the impetus for retaliatory legislation dwindled, and no binding measures ever reached the president's desk. Moreover, the Japanese government recognized that a flood of Japanese car imports, whenever the gates were opened, might provoke another round of demands for protection from the U.S. auto industry. Coupled with the quota rent garnered from supply limits, this consideration made continuation of the VER attrac-

59. Tomabechi, "U.S.-Japan Connection," 46.

60. Richard Blackhurst, chief economist, GATT Secretariat, interviewed by author on his return from Japan, April 1985, to Geneva, Switzerland; and Kenneth W. Abbott and Conrad D. Totman, " 'Black Ships' and Balance Sheets: The Japanese Market and U.S.-Japan Relations," *Northwestern Journal of International Law and Business* 3 (1981): 103–54.

61. Peter Ingersoll, "Toward a Bilateral Partnership: Improving Economic Relations," *Journal of International Affairs* 37 (Summer 1983): 22. Ingersoll was U.S. ambassador to Japan during 1972 and 1973 and cochairman of the Japan-U.S. Economic Relations Group for 1979–81.

tive. For Japan, accommodation at the least possible cost was preferable to risking the potentially high costs of confrontation. Given the asymmetry of the two actors' market dependence and the structure of the VER option, Japan could gamble at a very low cost that VER cooperation would patch the bilateral disagreement over market liberalization and deflect American retaliation. When the Japanese opted to renew the VER again in 1985, with no request from the U.S. government, they used a much less valuable bargaining chip to bid against U.S. demands for market liberalization, and the Reagan administration raised the stakes. The U.S. government would not accept the exchange Japan had in mind when clearly Japan had something to offer in return for America's willingness to remove all restraints on automobile exports. Although useful to both sides, the VER was an acceptable demonstration of cooperation but lost much of its usefulness as a bargaining concession once the Reagan administration withdrew support. Public opinion, and therefore Congress, might be somewhat influenced, but not enough to prevent attention toward Japan's imports.

Trade in the automobile sector per se faded as debate with Japan focused on import policies. Domestic demand between the summers of 1983 and 1985 continued to fuel recovery of the U.S. automobile industry, and pressure for import protection subsided. The Reagan administration, which preferred not to take protectionist action, was relieved not to seek Japanese cooperation on another restraint agreement, saw the bargaining advantage that this provided, and used Japan's own accommodative tactic to coerce cooperation elsewhere. By "giving" Japan the concession of no VER extension, the U.S. government exacted payment of trade liberalization in reciprocation, just as Japan had *tried* to offer the VER extension in exchange for U.S. demands. Throughout the dispute over automobile exports and Japan's import policies, the United States effectively pursued a coercive strategy at the least possible cost. In the first instance, the government accommodated domestic manufacturers with unilateral coercive protectionism, then sought a reciprocal strategy that coupled U.S. market access with balanced treatment from Japan for U.S. exports.

For the Reagan administration, securing this voluntary restraint agreement with Japan was inexpensive and politically beneficial. Groups that opposed protection against Japanese imports were diffuse and ineffectual, whereas the UAW, Chrysler, and Ford had successfully garnered massive public and congressional support for relief, particularly against Japan.[62] The Reagan administration could place the responsibility for restraints on Japan without officially setting import limits itself. With regard to Japan's import policies, the administration could buttress its own demands for liberalization with congressional retaliatory fervor in reserve to threaten Japan if no agreements were forthcoming, all without much risk. The administration preferred to maintain a free trade stance, but retaliation was very popular at home. Abroad, such threats could also be useful, even if unpopular, because they demonstrated the U.S. willingness to punish "unfair trade." Although costs to U.S. consumers would be high, the benefits to the potentially unemployed in the auto sector would be politically preferable in the short run.

Therefore, the U.S. administration could press Japan at every turn to further liberalize the import policies and still obtain voluntary export restraint without surrendering one demand for the other. Though Japan may have effectively defused some of the pressure with the first two VER announcements, the Japanese could never escape the threat, which the U.S. government knew. While Japan pursued accommodation that gave away as little as possible in incremental steps, the United States pursued a coercive policy backed with threats they never had to use. The U.S. government wanted the Japanese to act positively without direct resort to measures that might violate GATT rules, and the Japanese wanted to prevent Americans from imposing costly import restrictions on Japanese interests: both achieved their goals. The United States limited coercion to *threats* of retaliation, although Japan and even the Reagan administration never knew when congressio-

62. Japan has consistently been singled out in public opinion polls and in legislation in Congress for its "unfair" trade practices. Long after this particular phase of the dispute died down, a *Wall Street Journal* poll (11 October 1985, 1) indicated that 70 percent of those surveyed supported import limits on goods from Japan, whereas surveyed sentiment against other trading partners was much lower.

nal resentment might force the administration's hand. In return, the United States obtained a series of agreements with Japan for import liberalization and the VERs, when judged politically useful. Japan, on the other hand, benefited from the quota rent from export restraints and restricted concessions to those items that were politically least difficult.

In another sphere of the trading relationship, the dynamics and outcome can be similarly explained. As U.S. protectionist pressure built against Japanese automobile imports, Japanese carmakers stepped up their goal to invest directly in the U.S. market and to enter into joint ventures with U.S. car companies in two distinct ways. First, U.S. companies were allowed to invest in Japanese production facilities in Japan, which gave them a stake in the lucrative flow of exports to the American domestic market. Second, Japanese companies invested in U.S. production facilities to circumvent the insecurity of potential import barriers. Japanese industries benefited from both schemes. Through an interest in importation of Japanese-made subcompact cars into the United States, American carmakers' profits depended in part on continued imports. Although Ford and Chrysler maintained support for import protection, they did so because their share in Japanese production was considerably lower than was that of General Motors, the giant in both U.S. production and investment in Japanese production. From the outset of this trade dispute, GM favored free trade, thus splitting the auto lobby.[63]

In the case of direct Japanese investment in U.S. automobile production, Japanese companies obtained the benefits of a domestic industry by avoiding import restrictions on fully manufactured automobiles. They also provided U.S. labor with expanded employment opportunities, which lifted some pressure from labor for domestic content legislation. Although incremental, such inroads into the U.S. economy provided Japanese manufacturers with more potential to influence the views of policymakers.

Japanese firms were already negotiating establishment of plants in the United States, and U.S. firms had also acquired stakes in

63. Ballance and Sinclair, *Collapse and Survival: Industry Strategies in a Changing World* (London: George Allen and Unwin, 1983), 98.

Japanese companies before the first VRA in 1981. Implying that joint ventures directly result from U.S. threats of import protection would be misleading; but Japanese officials and industry leaders clearly indicate that fears of congressional threats convinced them to expand efforts in this area. The greater the interdependence of American and Japanese firms in automobile production and sale, the greater the odds for cooperation.

U.S. threats of protection and retaliation made further joint ventures even more pressing. Once again, U.S. coercion achieved tangible benefits from the Japanese for U.S. domestic industry. At the level of the companies' overall interests, a share in Japanese production and sales improved their profit picture, allowing them to benefit from Japanese design and engineering while enhancing domestic labor opportunities. The willingness of Japanese automobile manufacturers to enter into such arrangements demonstrates their conviction that an accommodative strategy, aimed at increasing U.S. firms' dependence on Japanese industry, would help defuse future protectionist pressure. Moreover, the Japanese knew that they could not continue to expand as an export-only industry. Trade tension between Japan and the United States made such an adjustment even more imperative.

Although mechanisms used to pressure Japan in this sector were different from those used in the steel sector, the two cases raise similar analytical questions about coercive protectionism and reciprocity. My review of the bargaining interaction between the United States and Japan reveals that U.S. protectionism in 1981 was clearly a coercive lever that pressured Japan into the first set of voluntary export restraints. Congressional speeches indicated that one motivation behind protectionist legislation against Japanese car imports was enforcement of reciprocity, but at this point, protection was the crucial factor. This strategy mirrored the coercive protectionism that had characterized U.S. restrictive trade policy before 1934 and mimicked that which had raised its head repeatedly in the steel sector after 1968.

The United States dropped its request for export restraint three years later and based continued market openness for Japanese automobiles on reciprocal access to Japan's other markets, a strategy that lay somewhere between the McKinley Tariff of 1890 and the Reciprocal Trade Agreements Act of 1934: it resembled the coercive, heavy-handed approach of the former while applying the reciprocal access and mutual benefit principles of the latter. That the U.S. market in the early 1980s was relatively open to foreign trade distinguished this ploy from the earlier era, when the U.S. market was relatively closed to foreign trade. Bargaining for foreign trade expansion in the earlier period included the reciprocal promise of wider access to the U.S. market; U.S. policymakers in the 1980s, however, surmised that they could not leverage Japan with what had already been bargained away in previous GATT rounds. Reciprocal access to the Japanese market could be won only with threats of market-restricting retaliatory behavior that, although it threatened established GATT commitments, paradoxically stressed the underlying expectations of mutual benefit that had driven the original GATT reciprocity principle.

This ambiguous situation raises an interesting observation about coercion and reciprocity. When it pressed Japan for voluntary restraints, the U.S. government was responding to domestic protectionist demands to depart from the established liberal trade orientation in this sector, even though Japanese trade practices had not caused the domestic industry's distress. The threat of congressionally mandated import restrictions was clearly a coercive protectionist tactic, not part of a reciprocal strategy. Once Japanese leaders were aware that the United States increasingly based expectations on a definition of reciprocal responsibility in world trade, which included Japanese restraint of exports in the absence of import liberalization, the expectation of reciprocity was interjected into the equation. Consequently, the first VRA can be seen as the product of U.S. coercive protectionism and the accommodative cooperation of Japan, but later VRA renewals were clearly part of a Japanese cooperative reciprocal strategy to deflect retaliatory U.S. pressure with collusive responses.

This behavior influenced the GATT regime in two ways: first, by reinforcing policymakers' preferences for VRAs for solving domestic competitiveness problems and, second, by undermining GATT procedures for enforcing mutual market access. As for steel, bilateral collusive arrangements protected the domestic industry in violation of established GATT norms and procedures; yet this dispute may have had its most far-reaching effect in the increasing U.S. departure from past measures of the GATT reciprocity principle. Frustration over the cumulative asymmetries in market access between the United States and Japan, along with domestic political demands for industry protection, moved U.S. policymakers to consider the issue bilaterally, outside GATT auspices. As we saw in Chapter 4, the GATT has always encouraged bilateral dispute settlement, but the trade-distorting measures that resulted, as well as the collusive nature of the bilateral relationship, undermine GATT regime norms and procedures, weakening its free trade, multilateral orientation.

Canada-U.S. Autopact

Trade between Canada and the United States in the automobile sector differed widely from the Japan-U.S. case. Understanding this North American relationship requires review of historical events that shaped it. During the early 1960s, the Canadian automobile industry, which was grievously uncompetitive, was experiencing serious trouble. Although protected by high tariffs, in 1964, Canada had a deficit in automobile trade with the United States of $620 million.[64] Clearly, maintaining such high duties did not prevent American automobile imports or improve Canadian productivity.[65]

Realizing that the balance of trade in automobile products increasingly favored the United States, the Canadian government initiated a "duty remission program" whereby U.S. automobile exporters could capture a larger share of the Canadian market by increasing company investments in Canadian auto industries.[66]

64. Charles Stedman, "Canada-U.S. Automotive Agreement: The Sectoral Approach," *Journal of World Trade Law* 8 (March–April 1974): 176.
65. Gerard Curzon and Victoria Curzon, "The Management of Trade Relations in the GATT," in Andrew Shonfield, ed., *International Economic Relations of the Western World 1959–1971* (Oxford: Oxford University Press, 1976), 238.
66. Gilbert R. Winham, *The Automobile Trade Crisis of 1980* (Halifax, Nova Scotia: Dalhousie University Center for Foreign Policy Studies, 1981), 88.

Charles Stedman notes that this program, begun in 1963, allowed "manufacturers to import duty-free a value of autos and parts equivalent to the Canadian content of the increase in their exports of these products over the 1962 base year."[67] Because Canadian import duties ran so high and their remission was so valuable, U.S. companies immediately sought a greater share in Canadian operations. This investment effort was further facilitated because most Canadian automobile assembly and parts companies were already subsidiaries of U.S. parent firms. Initially, the Canadian scheme to rationalize its automobile industry by enticing foreign investment and guaranteeing Canadian content looked successful.

As a direct result of this program, however, Stedman writes, the Modine Corporation of the United States filed a countervailing duty suit in early 1964 against Canadian auto exports, "charging that the tariff remission in the new plan constituted a bounty or grant" in violation of the U.S. Tariff Act of 1930 and the GATT. Realizing that an affirmative ruling would completely undermine the duty remission program, the Canadian government negotiated with the U.S. government for a bilateral agreement on automobile trade. At the same time, says Stedman, the Canadian government threatened to "act unilaterally to restrict the Canadian automotive market to products made in Canada if no satisfactory agreement was reached."[68] This Canadian position contained important contradictions. First, as Gilbert Winham notes, the Canadian government wanted an agreement that would "eliminate tariffs and thus create a North American free-trade area in automotive products" to minimize the possibility of future suits against Canadian producers and to provide a degree of certainty for Canadian exports. The government also wanted to impose a "series of restrictions and commitments that bore on the automobile manufacturers themselves" in exchange for free transboundary trade.[69] These restrictions would provide the same benefits to Canadian labor and industry that the previous duty remission program provided.

67. Stedman, "Canada-U.S. Automotive Agreement," 177.
68. Ibid.
69. Winham, *Automotive Trade Crisis*, 88–89.

According to Winham, the so-called Autopact would "guarantee a level of Canadian production of automobiles and original equipment parts as a proportion of Canadian consumption of automobiles."[70] If negotiations proved successful for Canadians, then the assurance of domestic content, which had been the original purpose of the duty remission program, would be exchanged for mutual elimination of import duties. For the United States, then, negotiating would avoid disruptive confrontation with Canada over the duty remission scheme and support U.S. automobile firms. The U.S. government's ultimate goal, however, was to achieve a genuine free trade agreement in the automotive sector and to phase out Canadian content restrictions that were understood as transitional. As Carl Beigie remarked, though, "given the ambiguous nature of this agreement, with formal and informal restraints contradicting in part the free trade implications of other provisions, it was perhaps inevitably destined to be viewed differently in the two countries."[71]

The agreement, signed on 19 January 1965, immediately increased U.S. investment in Canadian production facilities and improved the balance of automobile trade in Canada's favor. With production shifts to Canada, Stedman notes, the efficiency level of the Canadian industry improved dramatically to "more than [double] and exports increased from $36 million in 1968 to $4,625 million in 1972."[72] The United States had always maintained that such an agreement would support the best interests of U.S. manufacturing, even if investment and the balance of trade shifted somewhat in Canada's favor. The U.S. government viewed the Canadian restrictions as transitional and believed that the agreement would prevent the unilateral protective regime that Canada threatened. Moreover, the United States correctly assumed that freer trade, despite Canadian restrictions, would pro-

---

70. Ibid.

71. Carl E. Beigie, *The Canada-U.S. Automotive Agreement: An Evaluation* (Montreal: Canadian-American Committee, 1970), 1.

72. Stedman, "Canada-U.S. Automotive Agreement," 181. The United States obtained a GATT waiver to enter into this preferential agreement with Canada, which required no such waiver because it offered the same treatment to any other exporters willing to undertake the required investment in Canadian production.

duce overall growth for both sides.[73] By entering the arrangement, the United States did avert provoking Canada into a unilateral protectionist policy; but the U.S. view that Autopact restrictions were transitional did not convince Canadians. Six years later, according to Stedman, Secretary of the Treasury John Connolly targeted the Canadian domestic production guarantees "as the principal 'irritant' in Canadian-American relations."[74] Therefore, Autopact expanded automotive product trade between the two countries, but the United States increasingly viewed the agreement as balanced against U.S. interests because of Canadian production guarantees.

The United States International Trade Commission (USITC) reviewed Autopact in 1976 and concluded that "the Agreement as implemented by Canada is not a free-trade agreement, and it has primarily benefitted the Canadian economy."[75] The commission further concluded that only the United States had made concessions and that the Canadian government was in noncompliance with America's understanding of the agreement as it held onto "transitional" restrictions.

At the time that reviewers released the USITC report on Autopact, Canadian competitiveness had clearly peaked and begun to deteriorate. A Canadian government interdepartmental task force, headed by Douglas Arthur, concluded in a report issued in 1977 that deterioration was due to "structural weaknesses" in comparison with the auto industry in the United States. As Ross Perry writes, the report pointed out

> The industry was labor intensive and had a high proportion of unskilled workers relative to its counterpart in the United States; the

73. Stanley Metzger, "The United States–Canada Automobile Products Agreements of 1965," *Journal of World Trade Law* 1 (January–February 1967): 104, as quoted in ibid., 177. Exports of automotive products (vehicles and parts) comprise 80 percent of total Canadian production. Peter Morici, *The Global Competitive Struggle: Challenges to the United States and Canada* (Washington, D.C. and Toronto: National Planning Association [USA] and C. D. Howe Institute [Canada], 1984), 89.

74. Stedman, "Canada-U.S. Automotive Agreement," 179.

75. USITC, *Report on the United States–Canadian Automotive Agreement: Its History, Terms, and Impact* (Washington, D.C., 1976), 21. The USITC reviewed Autopact at the request of the U.S. Senate Finance Committee.

trends in capital investment in the North American automotive industry suggested that more of the capital-intensive activities would be concentrated in the United States; there was little incentive for the vehicle assemblers to obtain parts from the independent Canadian parts industry, and automotive product offshore producers, such as Japan and the developing countries, had a significant labor cost advantage over Canada and the United States.[76]

The report also alerted the Canadian federal government to the fact that Canadian automakers' profitability during the first half of the decade had largely been due to higher prices charged in Canada than in the United States for comparable products. In 1976, this advantage disappeared when the U.S. Treasury Department obtained commitments from Canadian subsidiaries of U.S. firms to price products in parity with American counterparts.

Another potential problem for Canada would result from the Tokyo Round of trade negotiations then underway. Another federal government report issued in 1978 "warned that a lowering of the Canadian tariff on vehicles or parts imminent in the Tokyo Round . . . would reduce the incentive for the Big Three to operate under the Pact and Canada's capability to attract investment or business from foreign vehicle manufacturers via duty remission or abatement schemes."[77] Because of the declining competitive position of Canadian producers, the inability of Canadian firms to charge prices out of line with American prices, and the potential for lower tariffs on automobile imports into Canada, U.S. parent firms were losing their incentive to invest in production facilities across the border. Autopact provisions could guarantee investment in Canada only as long as terms enhanced overall sales.

By the end of the 1970s, the Canadian government knew that its auto industry was alarmingly vulnerable to the world market situation. To further encourage production investment in Canada in the face of growing imports, states Winham, the government in 1978 reinstated the duty remission program for Volkswagen, "despite vigorous U.S. objections," and in 1980 offered the program

---

76. Ross Perry, *The Future of Canada's Auto Industry: The Big Three and the Japanese Challenge* (Toronto: James Lorimer and Canadian Institute for Economic Policy, 1982), 6.
77. Ibid., 7.

to Japanese firms, "but duties were remitted only for exports to countries other than the United States." In addition, he observes, recommendations to the government called for new Autopact negotiations to guarantee that a greater percentage of earnings from Canadian subsidiaries would remain in Canada and that a "designated vehicle importer program be established" that would again ensure Canadian content in Canadian import sales.[78] Ironically, then, Canada's loss of advantages led that country back to the negotiating table with the United States, not U.S. demands that a genuine free trade area be established. But the United States, which had long-standing grievances concerning Autopact, was amenable to a new series of negotiations with the Canadian government, especially after reemergence of the duty remission program.

Talks scheduled to begin in 1980 were canceled before they began because of changes of government in both countries. That year also saw concern rise over Japanese imports to both North American markets, and U.S. parent companies became preoccupied with protection from Japanese imports, which took attention away from Autopact problems. Even so, the U.S. government said in 1981 that renegotiation of Autopact would be considered "only if United States complaints about Canadian policies such as foreign investment and the energy policy were also reviewed."[79] The Canadian government under Pierre Elliott Trudeau found this unacceptable, however, and no serious effort emerged on either side. After that, Japanese exports superseded problems with Autopact for the next several years because the mutual threat from automobile imports made this bilateral dispute subsidiary.

In 1980, Canadian imports of automobiles from Japan rose 151 percent. Instead of concentrating on changes in the fifteen-year-old arrangement with the United States, domestic interest groups and members of parliament turned attention to legislating import quotas and domestic content requirements against the onslaught of Japanese vehicles. As we have seen, similar bills were

---

78. Gilbert R. Winham, *Trading with Canada: The Canada-U.S. Free Trade Agreement* (New York: Priority Press Publications, 1988), 7–8 and 52.
79. *International Canada*, February 1981, 29.

also being introduced in the U.S. Congress, and the U.S. government was coming under pressure from domestic groups to enter into a voluntary export restraint agreement with Japan, despite USITC's negative ruling. In Canada, charges were made that the Trudeau government was, in fact, stalling over parliamentary measures against Japanese imports to see what action, if any, the United States would take. By March 1981 (one month before announcement of the U.S.-Japan agreement), the Canadian minister for International Trade and Commerce stated that discussions with the Japanese for a voluntary restraint agreement had already been initiated. By May, a trade and commerce delegation was dispatched to Japan to negotiate a VRA similar to that reached between the United States and Japan because the Canadian government "was concerned that automobiles intended for the United States might be diverted to the Canadian market."[80]

For the next four years, Canada's relationship with the United States in the automobile sector remained peripheral to the dispute with Japan over both the level of Japanese exports to Canada and Japanese investment within Canada.[81] The North American context within which Canadian policy had to maneuver, however, directly influenced the outcomes of Canadian-Japanese negotiations. Without a doubt, agreements between the United States and Japan and between U.S. firms and Japanese firms directly affected Canada's bargaining position. Moreover, Canada's own duty remission program complicated North American relations.

Canadian policymakers feared a diversion of Japanese exports to the Canadian market because of the restraint on exports to the United States. They also knew that Canada had to compete aggressively for Japanese investment in the domestic automobile sec-

---

80. Ibid., March 1981, 64, and May 1981, 100.
81. A minor exception to this was the USITC ruling that imports of automotive spring assemblies from Canada violated Section 337 of the U.S. Tariff Act of 1930 because of patent infringements prejudicial toward an American firm. Canada objected to the ruling and took its case to the GATT. A GATT panel was established in October 1981, and its report was adopted by the council in May 1982. The report upheld the U.S. position, saying that it complied with GATT Article 20, Section (d). GATT, *GATT Activities in 1983* (Geneva, 1984), 44; and GATT, "United States Imports of Certain Automotive Spring Assemblies," Report of the Panel Adopted 26 May 1983 (L/5333), *BISD* (March 1984), 108–28.

tor. Ontario's minister of industry and tourism, appearing before the Canadian Senate Committee on Foreign Affairs, testified in April 1981 that "Canada had no choice but to compete with the United States for investment opportunities [to attract investment from Japan as well as from the United States itself]."[82] Exclusion of the United States from the duty remission program responded to this underlying and long-standing Canadian concern.

Consequently, two complementary themes appeared again and again in Canadian policy statements regarding trade relations with Japan. First, the Canadian government stressed that the Japanese reduce their automobile exports to Canada in proportion to their restriction on exports to the United States. Arguing that the "North American auto market was one market," Minister of Industry, Trade, and Commerce Gray demanded that Japan offer Canada equal treatment. Second, Canadian officials, with an eye on Japanese investment trends in the United States, linked continued access to the Canadian market for Japanese automobile exports to Japanese purchases of Canadian-made automotive parts and Japanese investment in those industries.

A one-year VRA reached in May 1981 set limits at 174,213 units; when the VRA came up for review in 1982, the Canadian position remained the same. Following VRA renewal in August, pressure mounted in Canada for Japanese investment in the Canadian parts industry. Although there is no evidence of such a promise, the National Democratic party leader in Parliament, Ed Broadbent, claimed that the earlier Japanese-American VRA had "guaranteed production of some Japanese cars in the U.S."[83] Such suspicions attracted the public's attention, and trade relations with Japan were increasingly couched in terms of Canada's competitive position with the United States for Japanese investment. As time passed, Canadian officials appeared less and less concerned about the potential for trade diversion from American-Japanese VRAs. In fact, Canada's twice-proven success at reaching similar accords with Japan gave its government confidence to support future U.S. efforts to obtain export restraint extensions from

82. *International Canada*, April 1981, 79.
83. Ibid., May 1981, 101, and February–March 1983, 13.

the Japanese. Canada had discovered during negotiations with Japan that the VRA with the United States had given Canada greater leverage in bargaining for its own VRA. When the United States announced in November 1983 that the restraint agreement with Japan had been renewed for another year, the Canadian government greeted the news with pleasure.[84]

As was true in the United States, the Canadian bargaining position with Japan was increasingly characterized by efforts to turn the tables so Japan could not achieve *removal* without some concessions. Whereas the United States demanded that Japan open import markets to U.S. products, Canada demanded that Japan invest in Canadian production. Unlike Americans who suffered a substantial trade deficit with Japan, Canada had a trade surplus with that country, which made leverage for further market penetration of the Japanese economy minimal; therefore, the focus of Canadian-Japanese negotiations was Japanese investment and Canadian-Japanese joint ventures.[85]

In February 1983, Toyota announced establishment of a wheel factory in British Columbia. Despite this development, the fact that Canada's trade surplus in the automobile sector "hit a record $3.29 billion in 1983 as a result of strong demand in the United States" and an overvalued U.S. dollar, Canadian officials demanded greater investment.[86] Canada's stubbornness reflected not only concern over competition with the United States for Japanese investment in North America but also a new development in automobile trade. As they invested in U.S. production facilities, Japanese firms created the potential for larger numbers of Japanese cars being exported to Canada from U.S. production sites. Because Autopact continued to allow duty-free access to U.S. cars in proportion to American firm investment in Canadian production

84. Ibid., October–November 1983, 5; and *Globe and Mail*, 27 June 1985, B15.

85. This theme recurs throughout the period of negotiations. See *International Canada*, April–May 1983, 8; and *Globe and Mail*, 17 March 1985, B4; 26 March 1984, B15; and 18 May 1985, B9.

86. *International Canada*, February–March 1983, 13; and *Globe and Mail*, 26 March 1984, B1. The plant opened in 1985. *Financial Post*, 13 April 1985, 40.

and many Japanese investment ventures were made jointly with U.S. car companies, products of these joint deals could enter Canada under the Autopact program. Moreover, nonaffiliated Japanese automobile makers in the United States could circumvent the Canada-Japan VRA by entering Canada from the United States and paying the regular Canadian tariff. This possibility became a reality in 1984, when Honda announced increased exports to Canada—780 in 1984 to 3,000 in 1985—from its facility in Ohio.[87]

As mentioned above, Canada in 1984 removed the U.S. exclusion from the duty remission program offered Japan, allowing automobiles and components exported from Japan to Canada to enter Canada freely as long as the same quantities were reexported to other countries. Because of the proximity and size of the U.S. market, this provision actively encouraged free exportation of Japanese autos into the United States via Canada. Although Canada argued its duty remission program was necessary because "Canada is a smaller economy and not as attractive to overseas investors as the United States," this view became difficult to justify under the substantial trade surplus that Canada enjoyed with the United States on auto parts. Exports *from* Canada to the United States skyrocketed because of preferential access to the American market, revitalized U.S. demand, the high U.S. dollar, and the duty remission program. Whereas Canada had feared export diversions due to the Japanese VER on sales to the United States, it actually benefited from increased exports to America during this period. Added to past U.S. objections concerning Autopact, this policy caused renewed U.S. interest for renegotiating the bilateral auto trade understanding.

When the Canadian government (responding to a report issued in 1985 by the Royal Commission on the Economic Union and Development Prospects for Canada) proposed that a comprehensive free trade agreement be pursued with the United States, the U.S. government was particularly interested in discussing Autopact revisions. Because of Canada's asymmetrical dependence on trade with the United States and its overall deteriorating competi-

87. *Globe and Mail*, 6 June 1985.

tive position in the world market, the commission argued that Canada's economy would prosper most from scale and production rationalization of greater economic integration. This significant departure from 1970s Canadian policy guided the Mulroney government into negotiations for the comprehensive North American Free Trade Agreement.[88] In 1987 the Canada–United States Free Trade Agreement settled many of Autopact's shortcomings as far as the United States was concerned. First, the agreement would completely phase out production-based duty remissions by the end of 1995. Second, it established a new rule of origin, which provided that producers can export into either Canada or the United States if 50 percent of their production destined for these markets in fact occurred within North America. And, finally, the pact eliminated the duty remission programs that had allowed importers into Canada to avoid Canadian duties as long as exports to the United States equaled imports into Canada.[89]

For the United States, the automotive trading relationship with Canada has at times been less than satisfactory but apparently not worthy of major confrontation. The United States was worried less about Canadian imports than imports from Japan, even though imports of Canadian automotive products comprise a significant portion of vehicles sold in the United States or resold in Canada. With integration of the North American industry under U.S.-based firms, parent firms benefit from Canadian production even if domestic labor does not, and none of the Big Three automakers has applied political pressure for import restraints against Canadian subsidiaries. The only time since the 1960s that the United States seriously considered retaliatory trade action against Canada was over Canada's duty remission program for Japanese firms, which served as an export subsidy after 1984 for products entering the United States. The new free trade orientation of the Mulroney government, however, and its North American free trade initiative preempted the countervailing duty suit that had

88. Royal Commission on the Economic Union and Development Prospects for Canada, *Report* 1 (Ottawa: Minister of Supply and Services Canada, 1985), 60.

89. *The Canada-U.S. Free Trade Agreement*, Chap. 10, Article 1001, 1002, and Section 17 of annex 301.2, 12 October 1987.

been considered during this time, and bilateral relations in this sector have remained essentially cooperative.

Conclusions about Protectionist Coercion and Reciprocity in U.S.-Canada Auto Trade

Canada has used coercive threats in the U.S.-Canada relationship in the automobile sector to produce a special bilateral trading and investment arrangement that ensures production locations and employment in Canada. Compared with the U.S.-Japan case, this interesting situation demonstrates that even in a highly asymmetrical trading relationship, the weaker partner can use leverage to its advantage. Canada not only initiated the 1960s dispute with the duty remission program but also got its way with subsequent threats of counterretaliation against a U.S. countervailing duty determination. The United States (via the Modine Corporation) initially used a reciprocal (retaliatory) strategy to counter the duty remission program, but when Canada threatened to close its automobile market to U.S. access, the United States negotiated a compromise arrangement.

The outcome reflected both Canadian and U.S. interests, especially if we accept the U.S. claim that restrictions built into the free trade arrangement were to be phased out over time. In exchange for dropping the countervailing duty suit, the United States received free access to the Canadian market as long as Canada received a percentage of production in the integrated transborder industry. The smaller, more vulnerable trading partner effectively used the potential value of its domestic automobile market to induce a favorable agreement with the larger, more powerful state. The U.S. countervailing duty suit signaled Canada that it could not take unilateral action with impunity, but Canada's counterthreat communicated that U.S. interests would best be served by negotiations. Here again, a collusive bilateral arrangement resulted from reciprocal actions taken in this trade dispute.

Interpretive disagreements over Autopact, combined with Canada's renewed efforts to protect industry and employment, re-

196

kindled the bilateral dispute. After 1984 the United States appeared ready to retaliate with another countervailing duty suit to force reconsideration of duty remission programs on exports to the United States.[90] Canada's adoption of a free trade initiative, however, combined with U.S. readiness to enter into a North American trade agreement, produced a new set of negotiation arrangements, which solved many problems with Autopact and confirmed (although belatedly) the U.S. view of the 1965 Autopact as a temporary arrangement that required eventual rationalization.

Comparisons of Japanese and Canadian Relationships with the United States in Auto Trade

My study demonstrates that dispute outcomes between highly asymmetrical trading partners are not necessarily predictable and that bargaining strategies and the character of market interdependence affect outcomes. Interestingly, the United States pursued widely divergent strategies toward its two most significant trading partners in the auto sector, despite the much smaller size of both partners in terms of economic and political power. The difference in U.S. strategies lies in the different U.S. roles in each trade relationship and in the respective trading partner's strategy.

In the U.S.-Japan relationship, competition over the U.S. market caused the initial dispute. Loss of market share catalyzed demands for protection and pressed the U.S. government to coerce Japan into a voluntary export restraint agreement. In the U.S.-Canada relationship, Canada's loss of market share triggered the dispute. In both cases exporting nations found themselves actively defending their actual and potential interests in the markets of the importing country. Moreover, U.S. threats to retaliate against the export subsidy effect of Canada's duty remission program used market leverage to press Canada into a negotiated settlement, just

90. Paul Wonnacott, "The Auto Sector," in Jeffrey J. Schott and Murray G. Smith, eds., *The Canada–United States Free Trade Agreement: The Global Impact* (Washington, D.C.: Institute for International Economics, 1988), 104–9.

as U.S. attempts to convince Japan to open its domestic market resorted to threatened closure of its own market for any real bargaining effect.

Comparison between these bilateral trading relationships shows that the ability to credibly threaten limited access to one's domestic market generates bargaining leverage, regardless of bilateral asymmetries. This outcome means that both coercive protectionism and reciprocal actions can leverage a cooperative response if the nation employing the strategy can believably use its market as the bargaining lever. Canada and the United States used these strategies effectively, whereas Japan did not. Paradoxically, Japan's integration into global trade has been one-sided, which handicapped this nation's ability to manipulate market access for bargaining purposes. The foreign perception was that Japan was already too protectionist; thus the Japanese government found bargaining reciprocally difficult in any case. Without employing retaliatory strategies, Japan's only viable option was to capitalize on quota rent compensation and resist U.S. pressures while minimally meeting U.S. demands. Japan's accommodative strategy, first colluding with U.S. demands for export restraint and then conceding to demands for broader market access, resulted from the inability to engage credibly in retaliatory threats and from preference for the benefits of accommodation.

Canada's behavior differed greatly from Japan's in dealings with the United States; this contrast suggests that a weaker nation in a highly asymmetrical economic relationship can influence bilateral negotiations to its benefit by using a coercive strategy that threatens to curtail access to domestic markets. Canada's threat to withhold market access effectively leveraged U.S. concessions, thus demonstrating that small as well as large nations can use coercive and retaliatory strategies in interdependent trading relationships if markets are sufficiently important to the larger nation's producers.

The role of reciprocity in this sector is similar to that in the steel case. In the U.S.-Canada dispute, reciprocity constrained Canadian protectionism. Although reciprocal policies were initially reactions against certain Canadian practices, they were not fully executed according to the letter of GATT law. Rather than enforce free trade rules and press Canada into a free trade stance with regard to automobile trade, U.S. retaliation gave the United States a believable bargaining position in negotiations that created and then modified the bilateral Autopact. Although a GATT waiver was granted the United States for deviation from GATT free trade rules, it did not eliminate the discriminatory effect of the bilateral arrangement, not a major issue until the 1980s, when the North American market was clearly no longer isolated from genuine global competition. Moreover, the investment patterns outlined above have continued and, combined with the virtual elimination of auto duties by the United States, have made the North American market very accessible under the Canada-U.S. Free Trade Agreement.[91]

Reciprocity in the Japan–United States dispute played a more ambiguous role. Coercive protectionism, not reciprocity, forced Japan into a cooperative export restraint arrangement with the United States. As we witnessed in the steel case, VRAs allow colluding nations to resolve a dispute bilaterally with mutual benefit, despite violating GATT Article 11. In fact, absence of a reciprocal policy in this sector allowed U.S. threats to close the American market and to coerce a cooperative response from Japan. Initially, U.S. actions were unilateral departures from established trade relations, not reciprocal policies to redress balance in the relationship. Because Japan pursued no reciprocal policy against U.S. protectionism, there was no bilateral check against it.

Later in the dispute, a reciprocal strategy did characterize U.S. policy toward Japan. The issue of market access for U.S. exporters to Japan became tied reciprocally to continued market access for Japan's exporters to the United States, a policy that had no direct precedent in GATT law. Rather than basing agreements for future market access on reciprocal promises abroad, this plan based continued market access from past agreements on immediate guarantees of reciprocal access abroad. To force Japan's reciprocation, the United States threatened to renege on previous GATT commitments. As we have seen, this action in some respects resembled pre-1934 policies more than GATT-sanctioned

91. Canadian import duties remain at 9.2 percent.

avenues for trade negotiation by threatening market closure rather than promising market liberalization for leverage reciprocation.

That the United States chose to pursue this goal bilaterally outside established GATT multilateral trade negotiations undermined the credibility of the multilateral approach and the facilitative institutions. Even so, the outcome of this strategy forced Japanese agreement to certain market liberalizations that coincided with the GATT's larger trade-liberalizing goal. This outcome illustrates the most troublesome nature of the reciprocity dilemma. On the one hand, U.S. actions helped enforce against Japanese free ridership; on the other hand, in the interest of impressing on Japan the expectation of reciprocal market access, U.S. actions have eroded the GATT multilateral process.

7

U.S. Trade Relations
in Wheat Flour

This chapter examines a dispute over wheat flour trade between the United States and the European Community that erupted at the end of the Tokyo Round and has continued to plague bilateral relations through the Uruguay Round. This particular case illustrates a fundamental disagreement over fair conduct of agricultural trade and exemplifies a conscious U.S. effort to use Section 301 retaliation provisions of the 1974 Trade Act to alter E.C. trading practices.

Consequently, reciprocity became a prominent and unambiguous component of U.S. wheat flour trade policy during the 1980s. Prompted by E.C. export practices that put U.S. exporters at a disadvantage, the United States adopted a tit-for-tat strategy to convince the community to cease export subsidization of wheat flour; but U.S. retaliatory efforts escalated bilateral conflict in the agricultural sector without achieving this end. After ten years of disagreement and U.S.-targeted retaliation, the issue remained deadlocked as the Uruguay Round negotiations floundered because of the stalemate over agricultural export subsidies.

This stalemate is not surprising given comparisons between agricultural trade and manufacturing trade over the past forty years. Although trade in manufacturing sectors such as steel and automobiles was facilitated by successive rounds of multilateral trade negotiations and expectations of market access, no cooperative liberal regime ever emerged in agricultural trade from the GATT process. Domestic interest groups were wedded to protection in agriculture long after liberalization had occurred in the manufacturing trade of most GATT members. Consequently, the context for reciprocal relations in agricultural trade differs vastly from that which influenced policymakers in steel and automobile disputes. Generally, national preferences for domestic support policies and complementary protectionism outranked the appeal of an agricultural free market. Most nations pursued various domestic agricultural programs, safely expecting others not to interfere. This practice continued until the U.S. attempted to alter this attitude by pressing for liberal norms and free market rigor in the 1980s. Focusing on export subsidies that the European Community used for wheat flour, the United States retaliated with leverage to force the community to reconsider the policy, a necessary first step to serious reform of agricultural trade under the GATT.

As the paramount obstacle to successful completion of the Uruguay Round, this conflict presents a fascinating case study of the dynamic of retaliation in agricultural trade relations. This issue offers an opportunity to examine both the values and limits of retaliation as trade negotiation leverage in a sector that has not traditionally been governed by the liberal GATT regime and, therefore, has been governed more directly by domestic nationalistic concerns. The agricultural sector has a long history of mutual disagreement over export subsidization and a long-term pattern of mutual toleration for market distortions from each trading partner's domestic price support programs. Consequently, liberal rules and norms governed trade in manufacturing but not in agricultural trade. These circumstances make the wheat flour case particularly interesting for assessment of retaliation as leverage for dislodging an actor from an established mode of behavior that was generally tolerated by others.

Overview of the U.S.-E.C. Wheat Flour Trade Dispute

U.S.-E.C. trade restrictions in agriculture have long been a source of irritation in transatlantic relations. Even though the United States has maintained a nearly consistent record of trade surpluses with the community in the agricultural sector, the latter's restrictive practices make marketing certain products very difficult; among these have been wheat and wheat flour, traditional strengths in U.S. export competition. Furthermore, the European Community has increasingly competed with the United States for sales of wheat and wheat flour to third-country markets. For these reasons, U.S. farmers, millers, and exporters have complained for years that the government should induce the European Community to alter policies regarding these products.

In 1975–76, the U.S. Millers' National Federation requested that the U.S. trade representative consider its complaint against this E.C. practice. The 1974 Trade Act offered a domestic avenue for formal action by granting the president authority to retaliate against trading partners who "unfairly" violated principles of free trade and injured U.S. producers. Not wanting to disrupt the Tokyo Round of multilateral trade negotiations, then considering the proposed International Code on Subsidies and Countervailing Duties of the GATT, the U.S. government delayed action until the code passed. Congress adopted the 1979 Trade Act, thus providing U.S. producers an avenue of representation under the rubric of an internationally recognized institution.

In 1981, the United States filed a formal complaint with the new GATT Subsidies Committee against the European Community's wheat flour export subsidization practices. The two trading partners immediately launched bilateral negotiations to resolve the dispute even as the GATT panel examined the case. When the community refused to alter its export policy, the United States in January 1983 retaliated by subsidizing a substantial wheat flour sale to Egypt, a traditionally European market. The U.S. strategy was designed to win an important European market away from the European Community and thereby to persuade the European Commission to alter its subsidy policy. Europeans protested strongly. When the GATT panel issued its decision in their favor two months later, the European Community demanded financial compensation for the market loss inflicted by the recent U.S. concessionary sale. The U.S. government, which was extremely unhappy with the panel's decision, refused to recant. By using a retaliatory strategy of countersubsidization, the United States had raised the stakes and refused to back away from challenging European agricultural export policy. Consequently, the United States filed another complaint against European pasta exports in June of that year. This time, the panel report favored the United States, but the European Community made no changes. For the next nine years, the U.S. government and the community exchanged threats and counterthreats, rhetoric on both sides charged with resentment, frustration, and refusals to compromise.

Background to the Dispute

The United States itself was responsible for loopholes within the GATT that allow relatively high levels of protection in agricultural products, including import quotas and export subsidies. Because of the U.S. Agricultural Adjustment Act of 1933, which restricted agricultural production levels to stabilize commodity prices, the U.S. government would not allow GATT negotiators to create blanket rules to jeopardize this important domestic program. In effect, production restrictions raised the domestic price of commodities, making some means of protection against cheaper imports necessary. Moreover, primary products exported abroad required subsidies to compensate for domestic and world market price differences.[1]

1. The United States has understood primary products to be those that do not undergo processing beyond the minimum necessary to extract (as in the case of minerals) or harvest (as in the case of agricultural produce). GATT Article 11, Section 2 (c), excepts "import restrictions on any agricultural or fisheries product, imported in any form, necessary to the enforcement of governmental measures which operate (i) to restrict the quantities of the like domestic product permitted to be marketed or produced. . . . (ii) to remove a temporary surplus of the like domestic product." Moreover, GATT Article 16 allows an exception for export subsidies of primary products to the extent that they assist the exporting nation to maintain an "equitable share" of the market. GATT, *BISD* (1980), Article 11, Section 2 (c), and Article 16. For a more complete discussion of the relationship between these two articles of the GATT and the American Agricultural Adjustment Act of 1933, see also Gilbert R. Winham, *International Trade and the Tokyo Round Negotiation* (Princeton: Princeton University Press, 1986), 151–52; and Jimmy S. Hillman, "Evolution of American Agricultural Trade Policy and European Interaction," in Hartwig de Haen et al., eds., *Agriculture and International Relations: Analysis and Policy* (London: Macmillan, 1985), 159–60.

U.S. Trade Relations in Wheat Flour

Unlike progress in the manufacturing sector, Thorald Warley writes, "reciprocal bargaining in frequent major trade negotiations has yielded meager results in terms of improved access to import markets for low-cost agricultural exporters."[2] The chief impediments to trade liberalization in this sector have been due to trading nations' long-standing differences in approaches to domestic agricultural policy, as well as long-standing commitments in most advanced countries to domestic price support systems that distort the market.

The major difference between U.S. and E.C. approaches has been production controls. In fact, Colleen O'Connor charges that "the United States has had to bear much of the burden of production control for the world."[3] U.S. policymakers maintain agricultural prices, particularly for wheat and other grains, at levels above production cost by restricting supply, whereas the European Community, after formation of the Common Agricultural Policy in 1958, offered farmers guaranteed prices by direct market intervention, buying surpluses without, until recently, any parallel effort to restrict production.[4] Consequently, U.S. policy reduced world supply during periods of surplus, and other nations benefited from this reduction without incurring such costs. In fact, evidence shows that U.S. competitors, including the community and Canada, actually increased production and exports to third markets at American expense.[5]

Another area closely related to differences on how to achieve domestic price support has been the European Community's exclusionary import tariff against wheat and wheat products. Unlike the United States, which utilizes quotas and ad valorem tariffs, the community relies on a variable import levy determined by calculating the difference between the domestic price and the prelevy

2. Thorald K. Warley, "Agricultural Trade Policy Issues in the 1980s," in de Haen et al., eds., *Agriculture and International Relations*, 255.

3. Colleen M. O'Connor, "Going against the Grain: The Regulation of the International Wheat Trade from 1933 to the 1980 Soviet Grain Embargo," *Boston College International and Comparative Law Review* 5 (Winter 1982): 230.

4. Brian E. Hill, *The Common Agricultural Policy: Past, Present, and Future* (New York: Methuen, 1984), 19 and 23–25.

5. O'Connor, "Going against the Grain," 244–45, 249.

import price of the commodity at point of arrival and adding that to the import good's price. This system ensures that no matter how inexpensive the wheat delivered from another country, the grain will always be priced as high as that of domestically produced wheat, a very successful policy for excluding competition.[6]

A third area of disagreement concerns the European Community's export subsidization policy, in which bilateral trade conflict in wheat trade has mainly occurred. The European Commission's system for domestic price support as well as other efforts to improve production within the European Community successfully moved the community from net imports of wheat and wheat products to self-sufficiency (the primary goal of the CAP) and then beyond to net exports. As long as the community imported wheat, though not nearly in amounts available in an unrestricted market, the dispute over the variable import levy never escalated to where the United States took countermeasures. When the community began to produce a surplus and dispose of that surplus on the world commercial market, however, the E.C. had to subsidize exports to offset internal policies and import restrictions on the domestic price of wheat and wheat products, which challenged U.S. interests abroad.

The CAP provides a mechanism to bring wheat available for export into a competitive position in the world marketplace by offering export grants to buyers to compensate for the higher E.C. price.[7] The United States has been concerned about this policy for several reasons, most obviously because this makes the European Community a very serious competitor in the world market. The United States has been particularly alarmed with regard to wheat flour, as this country moved from holding 25 percent of the world commercial flour market from 1959 to 1962 to only 9 percent from 1978 to 1981; during the same periods, the E.C. share went from 29 percent to 75 percent. Changes in U.S. export share are equally impressive, from 27 percent of the world's commercial

6. J. Kodwo Bentil, "Attempts to Liberalize International Trade in Agriculture and the Problem of the External Aspects of the Common Agricultural Policy of the European Economic Community," *Case Western Reserve Journal of International Law* 17 (Summer 1985): 357–59.

7. Hill, *Common Agricultural Policy*, 18–19.

exports in 1959 to 1960 to only 9 percent by 1980–81. The European Community, on the other hand, held 25 percent of the export share in the earlier period, which jumped to 80 percent in the latter.[8]

Flare-up of the current trade dispute over community export subsidization has centered around U.S. arguments that such practices, which have been persistent and expansionary, constituted unfair trade to the detriment of other wheat and wheat flour producers. In the face of U.S. concern, the E.C. has explained that such figures do not tell the entire story. In the first place, the community argues, U.S. aid programs (specifically PL 480) that offer needy countries access to U.S. surplus commodities under concessionary credit arrangements are also forms of subsidization. Targeting the CAP is a hypocritical effort to create distinctions that hardly exist, according to the Europeans. In fact, they argued before the GATT Subsidies Committee in 1982 that including the PL 480 program in total U.S. exports would increase figures by 70 percent, whereas including E.C. aid programs in regular exports would cause a rise of only 10.8 percent.

Second, the European Commission points out that U.S. wheat flour is of much higher quality than grain produced in the European Community and that processing to produce such quality—because of such factors as moisture and protein content, presence of ash, and requirements of U.S. bread making—creates additional costs for U.S. millers. The U.S. product is considerably more expensive than its counterpart in Europe. Demand for the European soft-wheat, lower-protein flour has increased, especially in poorer countries, because they can purchase larger quantities at lower prices.

A third reason for U.S. losses, Europeans charge, is that the

---

8. The positions of Canada and Australia, the other major wheat flour exporters, have shown nearly identical losses in favor of the European Community. Australia moved from a share of 20 percent to 2 percent, while Canada went from holding 26 percent to 9 percent. Tables: "Relative Shares of the World Commercial Flour Market" and "World Commercial Exports Crop Years 1959/60–1980/81 (Market Share)." GATT, *Panel Report SCM/42: European Economic Community—Subsidies on Export of Wheat Flour* (Geneva, 21 March 1983), 4–6, hereafter cited as *Panel Report SCM/42*.

U.S. government has carried out certain political positions at the expense of U.S. export opportunities in such markets as Sri Lanka, Egypt, Vietnam, Syria, and Libya. Finally, the European Community has argued that America's PL 480 program encourages purchase of wheat, not wheat flour, which in turn has encouraged lesser-developed nations to improve their milling capabilities to reduce traditional dependence on American milled wheat flour.[9]

Although the two trading partners had prevented an actual dispute until after the Tokyo Round of multilateral trade negotiations in 1979, Americans were adamant from the beginning that E.C. subsidization of agricultural exports be resolved. American worries intensified as policymakers at home became more and more convinced that a demand-growth, export-oriented approach would best solve the ever-recurring farm income problem and make agricultural policy more consistent with a free market economy. The Nixon administration began a clear policy shift away from using production controls toward pursuing foreign markets for America's competitive commodities. The U.S. approach featured complementary components. The first, reflecting the free market orientation of the Republican administration in Washington, called on all U.S. farmers to "plant fence row to fence row" to meet the waiting export demand. The government believed that U.S. farmers had a comparative competitive advantage over other nations' farmers in grain production and that this advantage, combined with high levels of production, would allow them to secure markets abroad.

The second component of U.S. policy sought "fair trade" for U.S. products. On the basis of efficient production, U.S. grain exports would be highly competitive, but as long as other nations used "unfair trade practices" to undercut that natural competitiveness, U.S. farmers would not reap the benefits of their own efficiency. Consequently, the U.S. government actively sought the removal of such unfair practices through two separate tactics, the first of which was the creation of a domestic mechanism to make filing complaints against foreign trade practices easier. The Trade

9. Ibid., 13–19.

Act of 1974, which gave the president authority to negotiate during the multilateral trade negotiations in Geneva, contained specific legislation under Section 301 to provide private individuals the right to file a complaint against unfair trade practices of another nation that jeopardized the plaintiff's trading rights.[10] Second, President Nixon was determined to secure a new, more explicit agreement at the multilateral trade negotiations within the GATT framework to limit uses of subsidies in export trade. This goal was part of the overall U.S. aim to obtain a greater degree of free trade discipline among the contracting parties in Geneva, particularly in the agricultural sector.[11]

Before serious negotiations started in Geneva, the Millers' National Federation filed a complaint with the office of the USTR under the new 1974 act, which charged that E.C. use of subsidies on wheat flour exports had resulted in either reduction or elimination of "sales of competitive United States wheat flour in the markets where the E.E.C. is subsidizing its wheat flour." They asked that the president "eliminate the export subsidies described."[12] The complaint went to the USTR in November 1975; the U.S. government, however, did not want to derail the Geneva negotiations any longer with a dispute between two of the most powerful contracting parties. United States negotiation strategists wanted to ensure that agricultural and industrial sectors were linked so that reciprocal concessions might occur across sectors. Such linkage would enable agricultural exporting nations to exchange tariff concessions on manufactured goods for concessions from importing nations on agricultural products. The concept of

10. USC Section 2411 (1979) amended Title III of the Trade Act of 1974. This section has since been further amended to strengthen the rights of affected industries in that press for retaliation.

11. United States Senate Subcommittee on International Trade of the Committee on Finance, "Results for U.S. Agriculture," *Multilateral Trade Negotiation Studies: An Economic Analysis of the Effects of the Tokyo Round of Multilateral Trade Negotiations on the United States and the Other Major Industrialized Countries* (Washington, D.C., 1979), 5–7, hereafter cited as *MTN Studies*.

12. U.S. Trade Representative, Documents for Section 301 Proceedings, Millers' National Federation, *National Federation Brief before the Section 301 Committee Office of the Special Representative for Trade Negotiations*, 21 November 1975.

reciprocal negotiations across sectors, which is of utmost importance to the former group of nations, would increase their leverage for liberalizing agricultural trade in the broader GATT framework.

Because the European Community was just as adamant that the two sectors *not* be linked, these nations considered the absence of potentially disruptive disputes crucial to any progress toward compromise during the Tokyo Round. As a net importer of agricultural goods with a high level of protection, the European Community did not want to be subjected to the greater leverage that the U.S. proposal would afford agricultural exporting nations. The Tokyo Declaration, which launched the round of negotiations, contained careful language on this subject that allowed flexibility without either side's commitment to change its position. As Winham has pointed out: "For the Americans, the Declaration stated . . . the negotiations 'shall cover . . . both industrial and agricultural products. . . .' For the Europeans, the negotiations . . . should take account of the special characteristics and problems in this sector [agriculture]."[13]

Going into the negotiations, the United States hoped for, but did not expect, linkage of the two sectors in the linear tariff reductions. Coupled with domestic pressure for action against unfair agricultural trade practices, pessimism over altering the structure of reciprocal negotiations—that is, making them transsectoral—made the U.S. executive even more committed to new, more rigid rules to limit use of export subsidies.[14] Thus, officials hoped that limitations on export subsidies could be negotiated

13. Winham, *Tokyo Round Negotiation*, 156–58.
14. In his analysis of the MTN, Winham explained that the pre-MTN period negotiations "resurrected the old lines of division between the Americans and Europeans. The passage of time had not attenuated the differences between the two sides; in fact it had created reasons for both sides to be more insistent. On the American side there was the perception, largely correct, that the U.S. agricultural interests had not gained much from the Kennedy Round, which intensified the demand for a more favorable outcome at the Tokyo Round. The Europeans, however, had more to defend, since by the early 1970s the Common Agricultural Policy of the E.C. was firmly in place." Winham, *Tokyo Round Negotiation*, chaps. 2 and 7.

within the Tokyo Round framework without resorting to special bilateral actions.

As noted previously, the United States was becoming increasingly sensitive to E.C. export practices. Official American agricultural policy on exports became much more growth-oriented at the same time that competition for third-country markets was intensifying. Because the community's subsidized exports were the only means to ensure competitive access to the world market consistently, American policymakers increasingly focused on what they considered unfair E.C. competition. For both trading partners, the issue of export subsidies was critical. For the United States, this one substantive area in agricultural negotiations might produce tangible results for U.S. domestic interests concerned about competitors' unfair trade practices. A consensus on subsidies was just as important to the European Community, but for opposite reasons. The community wanted to clarify the GATT provisions on subsidies so that its policies would no longer be under attack. Delineating acceptable subsidy practices would legitimize them by consensus of the contracting parties who were signatories to the new code. Moreover, the community wanted to clarify the proper usage by importing nations of countervailing duties against exports from nations that used subsidies.[15]

After postponing formal action against the Europeans as long as possible during the Tokyo Round (after the Section 301 petition was filed in 1975), the U.S. trade representative received another 301 petition during the final phases of negotiations. This time, Great Plains Wheat "filed a petition alleging that the E.E.C.'s restitutions on wheat shipped to Brazil lowered the high (domestic) price of E.E.C. wheat to make it attractive in sales

---

15. "The Community has concentrated on trying to clarify when GATT member states may use countervailing duties claiming that the U.S. in particular should go through the normal GATT process of proving injury to its domestic industries before applying the battery of import control measures available to it under the Trade Act. Given both that the Community wishes to retain export subsidies as a CAP trade measure and that it has been the principal target for U.S. trade actions, the Community's stance is not surprising." A. W. Harris, *E.E.C. Trade Relations with the USA in Agricultural Products: Multilateral Tariff Negotiations* (Occasional paper no. 3, Ashford, Kent, Center for European Agricultural Studies, Wye College, 1977), 23.

competition in Brazil with the lower priced U.S. wheat exports."
According to Marsha Echols, the petition argued that "subsidized
Community exports of wheat displaced sales by U.S. exporters in
a third country market, Brazil, and depressed market prices." The
petitioner requested that the executive branch take "counteractive
measures in retaliation for the trade disruption suffered by U.S.
farmers." Among the actions suggested were (1) retaliatory duties
on imports from the European Community, (2) countersubsidies
to carry out wheat export competition on a reciprocal basis, or
(3) an official complaint filed with the GATT. Concerned about a
mutually acceptable agreement with the community on a new
subsidies code, the United States again did not want to take retaliatory action that might disrupt the process or undermine its position. Consequently, the matter was raised in bilateral discussions,
but no attempt was made to take the case before the GATT or
intensify the dispute by retaliating unilaterally.[16]

Finally, agreement on a subsidies code was reached in 1979;
but the code did not accomplish enough in refining definitions or
inserting greater discipline on the allowable use of subsidies for
agricultural exports. Article 10 of the Code on Subsidies and
Countervailing Duties, which addresses export subsidies on certain primary products, commits signatories to "agree not to grant
directly or indirectly any export subsidy on certain primary products in a manner which results in the signatory granting such subsidy having more than an equitable share of world export trade in
such product, account being taken of the shares of the signatories
in trade in the product concerned during a previous representative
period, and any special factors which may have affected or may
be affecting trade in such product." Section 2 of Article 10 further
defines "more than an equitable share of world export trade" as
any case "in which the effect of an export subsidy granted by a
signatory is to displace the exports of another signatory bearing
in mind the development on world markets."[17]

16. Marsha A. Echols, "Section 301: Access to Foreign Markets from an Agricultural Perspective," *International Trade Journal* 6 (Fall–Winter 1980–81): 14–
15.
17. GATT, *Agreement on the Interpretation and Application of Articles 6, 16,*

These provisions, meant to clarify acceptability of and constraints on export subsidies for primary products, left the issue vague and subject to varying interpretations. As Gary Hufbauer and Joanna Shelton Erb state, the new code recognized "for the first time the rights of third-country suppliers in a particular market [and] . . . also enlarged the list of relevant criteria for injury determinations in agricultural cases."[18] More important, as the Subcommittee on International Trade of the U.S. Senate Finance Committee concluded:

> The code does not contain specific criteria with which to measure subsidies and determine when they are excessive. . . . Fluctuations in agricultural production can change a particular country's export level and share of world trade in any one year, and may even influence the level of world prices. Thus, when considering world prices or trade levels it will undoubtedly be difficult in practice to distinguish between the effect of export subsidies and the effects of global and national supply-demand conditions.[19]

In addition, the agreement made no distinction between commercial and aid transactions in the agricultural sector, thus failing to clarify U.S. concessionary credit terms for sale of agricultural commodities under the code compared with E.C. subsidization policies. These deficiencies were highlighted four years later in 1983, when the GATT Subsidies Committee panel issued a report on the U.S. complaint against the community for using export subsidies on wheat flour sales.

After the Tokyo Round produced no obvious progress on curtailing E.C. use of export subsidies, domestic agricultural interests were deeply disappointed. As a direct result, the Millers' National Federation resurrected its Section 301 petition in 1981 against the community's wheat flour export subsidies. When the United States filed the complaint with the GATT, U.S. Trade Representa-

---

and 23 of the General Agreement on Tariffs and Trade (Geneva, 1979), Article 10 (1), (2).

18. Gary Clyde Hufbauer and Joanna Shelton Erb, *Subsidies in International Trade* (Washington, D.C.: Institute for International Economics, 1984), 79–80.

19. *MTN Studies*, 214.

tive William Brock stated "that the agricultural code was so vague that the United States government did not know what it covered." As a result, he continued, "we are taking them [the European Community] to GATT to see if the rules are valid. . . . If not, we are going to change the rules to make them adequate to open markets to our goods abroad."[20] In 1982 a panel of the Subsidies Committee was established to examine the case.[21]

The administration persisted in efforts to solve the problem without resort to retaliation; it hoped to allow the multilateral dispute settlement process within the GATT to function, and at the same time attempted to convince Europeans through bilateral discussions to restrain voluntarily use of agricultural export subsidies.[22] Because neither bilateral talks nor the GATT ministerial meeting had produced results so far—nor had the GATT panel report appeared—the administration was less and less in a position to persuade domestic petitioners that their interests were better served by nonconfrontation. As the president of the Millers' National Federation wrote to Senator John Heinz, "The GATT Ministerial meeting now is behind us and with it the last possible excuse for delay on the part of the U.S. government to address European Community Common Agricultural Policy subsidies through responses outside the structure of the GATT."[23]

When results of the panel report did not appear by the original deadline, the Millers' National Federation offered two proposals for an American governmental "wheat flour export incentive" program to counter E.C. efforts. Targeted at the Egyptian market,

20. Simon Dodds, "United States/Common Market Agricultural Trade and the GATT Framework," *Northwestern Journal of International Law and Business 5* (Summer 1983): 236–37.

21. GATT, *Panel Report SCM/42.*

22. In December 1982, the United States sent a team of negotiators led by Secretary of State George Shultz and including Secretary of Agriculture John Block to discuss major issues of contention between the European Community and the United States. The result was commitment by both sides to a new series of "sector-by-sector" negotiations to begin in January 1983. Emerging from the meeting, Block said, "There will be no agricultural trade war." *Economist*, 18 December 1982, 58.

23. U.S. Trade Representative, Documents for Section 301 Proceedings, Letter, Roy M. Henwood, president, Millers' National Federation, to Senator John Heinz, "U.S.-E.C. Wheat Flour Dispute," 23 December 1982.

the proposals were designed to "have a direct effect against the E.C. and particularly against subsidized French flour sales."[24] Rather than wait for a legal interpretation of E.C. export policies under the GATT framework, U.S. wheat and wheat flour producers urged the administration, or Congress if the administration failed to act, to apply pressure against E.C. trade practices. Only if the United States matched the European Community subsidy for subsidy, so traditional E.C. markets were lost in favor of U.S. exporters, would the community seriously reconsider agricultural trading methods.

Preferring a negotiated settlement but also growing impatient with both the delay of the GATT panel report and E.C. recalcitrance, the U.S. government adopted a like strategy clearly guided by a similar line of thought. On 25 January 1983, the U.S. Department of Agriculture announced the sale of over one million tons of wheat flour to Egypt at a subsidized price. Commenting on the sale, Secretary Block quoted President Reagan's statement that "the U.S. government would not allow U.S. farmers to be 'plowed under by foreign competition.'"[25] In turn, the European Commission threatened to break off bilateral talks and to sue the United States within the GATT for compensation from loss of the Egyptian market. About a month later, writing in response to the Millers' National Federation proposals, U.S. Trade Representative Brock affirmed that "this Administration is carefully examining measures which might be taken to enable our farmers and exporters to compete with the subsidized export of other suppliers. In the case of wheat flour, we have decided to move ahead with an export incentive program similar to that proposed by the Millers' National Federation."[26] That the office of the U.S. trade representative as well as the Department of Agriculture were involved in the decision to sell subsidized wheat flour to Egypt

24. Ibid.

25. William H. Boger III, "The United States–European Community Agricultural Export Subsidy Dispute," *Law and Policy in International Business* 16 (1984): 222. See in particular n. 276.

26. U.S. Trade Representative, Documents for Section 301 Proceedings, Letter, William Brock to Senator John Heinz, "U.S.-E.C. Wheat Flour Dispute," 17 February 1983.

demonstrated a fundamental shift in strategy toward the community.

The panel report issued on 21 March 1983 did nothing to alter the new U.S. approach; in fact, U.S. policymakers felt disillusioned about the GATT dispute settlement process, which solidified the view that the only way to reform E.C. unfair trade practices was through political and economic leverage, not international legal mechanisms. This negative reaction was grounded in two fundamental perceptions: first, that the panel had been grossly irresponsible in deciding that the European Community had not taken "more than an equitable share of the world export trade in wheat flour," as the United States had charged; and, second, that the strictly legalistic interpretation of the subsidies code could not adequately address the dispute.[27]

The former criticism largely reflects the view of U.S. officials who negotiated the subsidy issue with the Europeans, both within and outside the GATT. They believe that the code provided clear guidelines on export subsidies for primary products but that the panel refused to make the logical connection between the European Community's increased share of the wheat flour market (which the panel admitted could not have been achieved without export subsidization) and whether that increased share constituted what Boger calls "more than an equitable share."[28] What most disturbed the United States was the fact that the final decision favored the community, although the panel basically agreed with the United States on the facts of the case: that is, that the European Community was indeed subsidizing its exports; that without those subsidies, E.C. wheat flour would not compete in the world market; and that the community's share of the world market had steadily increased at the expense of the U.S. and others' shares. The latter view is generally the consensus of international legal experts, who maintain that absence of rule definition, coupled with vague terminology, made any other decision by the GATT panel impossible. As Boger asserts, perhaps U.S. poli-

27. Andrew Stoller, United States Trade Representative's Office, interviewed by author, Geneva, April 1985.
28. Boger, "Agricultural Export Subsidy Dispute," 213.

cymakers unrealistically believed that the GATT dispute settlement process would serve U.S. interests in this case, based on the charge that the "United States has an overly legalistic view of the GATT which leads [it] to expect results that are 'literally impossible' from the dispute process."[29]

The European Community, of course, was pleased with the report for several reasons. First of all, the panel agreed with the European view that wheat flour is not a homogeneous product with a "world market price"; therefore, comparing prices of wheat flour from different sources may be misleading. Because U.S. wheat flour is of a higher quality that requires additional milling procedures, it is more expensive than European wheat flour. Second, the panel noted that the community is not alone in using export enhancement programs for wheat flour exports; the United States, it pointed out, uses concessionary credit programs under PL 480 that account for over two-thirds of "its total wheat flour exports." Although the United States attempted to separate commercial and aid-related exports, the panel was skeptical about a distinction that does not account for the role of aid programs as means to develop foreign import markets.[30] Consequently, although the panel determined that export subsidies played an extensive role in the community's foreign wheat flour trade and that the growth in market share could not have occurred without those subsidies, members believed that other factors also affected the commercial wheat flour market in terms of price and demand, which made a determination against the European Community impossible.

Even so, the panel's opinion did not deter the United States from pursuing a second complaint within the Subsidies Committee. This time the United States singled out the community's subsidization of a wheat derivative—pasta—that it maintained could not be classified as a primary product. Under the code, therefore, pasta could not be legally exported with the aid of subsidies. This complaint grew directly out of the wheat flour case. Because the United States had initially leveled the earlier complaint against the

29. Ibid., 215.
30. GATT, *Panel Report SCM/42*, 26 and 35.

European Community on the grounds that an inequitable market share had been taken by subsidies, a late-in-the-game attempt by the United States to include the charge that wheat flour was not a primary product failed on the grounds that it was a new complaint.[31] Guessing this outcome, the United States filed a separate complaint concerning pasta exports because the U.S. position required a clear ruling against subsidization of nonprimary products. Believing this legal position on pasta exports uncontestable under Article 9 of the Agreement on the Interpretation and Application of Articles 6, 16, and 23, the United States filed this new complaint with the GATT Subsidies Committee, and a panel was established on 14 June 1982 to consider the case.

On 13 May 1983, a panel majority "concluded that the E.E.C. subsidies on exports of pasta products were granted in a manner inconsistent with Article 9 of the Code." The United States welcomed this decision that would build the U.S. government's case against the export effects of the Common Agricultural Policy. The June 1983 report did not, however, contribute to a clarification of "more than an equitable share," the major stumbling block in the March report. Moreover, the later report contained a dissenting opinion by one of the panel members, who argued:

> As long as the refund merely equalized the differential between the world market price and the domestic price of durum wheat—the practical effect and the intent of the refund was to enable E.E.C. pasta manufacturers to use domestic durum wheat in the production of exportable pasta products. The refund thus improved the competitive position of the E.E.C. durum wheat production rather than the processing industry and should consequently be considered as a subsidy on durum wheat.[32]

Even though the majority view coincided with that of the U.S. government, there was no consensus, and the European Commu-

---

31. "With regard to the United States' assertion in its presentation to the Panel that E.E.C. export subsidies on wheat flour are *prima facie* contrary to Article 9 of the Code, the Panel was of the opinion that this question did not constitute part of the matter referred to the Panel by the Committee and therefore the Panel did not consider the substantive issue involved." Ibid., 28.

32. GATT, *Committee on Subsidies and Countervailing Measures Panel Report SCM/43* (Geneva, 19 May 1983), 14–15.

nity was by no means stripped of legal justification for exporting nonprimary products at subsidized rates with "upstream" subsidies on primary product ingredients. The GATT Subsidies Committee dispute settlement did little to actually resolve the matter. The United States remained convinced that the CAP's export subsidy violated the GATT, and the European Community remained just as convinced otherwise. As John Filipek points out, the community pressed its position and counterretaliated "by placing tariffs on United States lemon imports,"[33] but retaliation on both sides only solidified their respective positions. The importance that each actor attached to its approach to agricultural trade made both sides unwilling to compromise, and any hopes that the new subsidies code would force a legal remedy were dashed by the ambiguity of the two panel reports.

The administration, which had clearly wanted support under the GATT rules, placed importance on the panel outcomes, but officials had long since decided against appeasing the Europeans in the meantime. According to the reports, the United States had no clear legal (or even normative) justification for retaliatory activity, but U.S. policymakers, members of Congress, and agricultural interests had become impatient with the GATT process. Increasingly, even the most ardent believers in free trade placed bets on retaliation as the only practical means to induce the European Community to revise export policy.[34] Such a strategy was also attractive politically. As Boger explained: "With protectionist sentiment running high in Congress, the most politically satisfying action would be to aggressively pursue more subsidized sales on the world market. In fact, many supporters of export subsidies believe that the United States, with its greater financial resources, could win a trade war with the E.E.C. by using export subsidies." By 1984 a trade war was underway. Instead of reconsidering policy after the U.S. sale to Egypt or letting the situation rest with its threat to sue for compensation, writes Boger, the European Com-

33. John G. Filipek, "Agriculture in a World of Comparative Advantage: The Prospects for Farm Trade Liberalization in the Uruguay Round of GATT Negotiations," *Harvard International Law Journal* 30 (Winter 1989): 146.
34. GATT Secretariat official, confidential interview with author, May 1985.

munity "authorized even greater refunds for its exporters in order to undercut the subsidized U.S. price [in Egypt]."[35]

In Washington, these counteractions merely served Congress's protectionist demands against the community and raised the popularity of a full-fledged subsidy war. As Senator Jesse Helms, head of the Senate Committee on Agriculture, Nutrition, and Forestry, stated again and again in his public speeches: "[The] E.E.C.'s right to swing their export subsidy fist ends at Uncle Sam's nose. At that point, it is time for the U.S. Government to respond in a way that allows U.S. farmers to compete on a fair basis with their counterparts overseas."[36] This sentiment was common. During 1983 and 1984, a plethora of bills to create programs to counter E.C.-subsidized exports with subsidized exports from the United States were introduced. Before the 1984 election, at a time when a rising dollar was making competition abroad increasingly difficult for farmers, legislation for "export market enhancement" was particularly popular. As a result, Congress passed legislation to expand the subsidized credit available to prospective buyers of U.S. agricultural products.

For its part, the Reagan administration coupled targeted sales with highly charged rhetoric to give the appearance of an aggressive countersubsidization strategy. For example, by April 1984, the administration had provided $95 million of subsidized export credits and loan guarantees to countries buying U.S. wheat and dairy products. Although not a departure from past practices, these deals were intentionally aimed at traditional E.C. markets— Algeria, Morocco, and Tunisia. Moreover, they received a great deal of publicity as retaliatory measures against E.C. export practices.[37] Despite U.S. actions and subsequent threats, however, the community actually raised "the maximum export subsidy for cereals, opening the way to the largest quantity of exports" in some time.[38]

By summer 1985, when a new farm bill was under debate in

35. Boger, "Agricultural Export Subsidy Dispute," 230.
36. U.S. Senate Committee on Agriculture, Nutrition, and Forestry, *Export-Equity Legislation Hearings*, 98th Cong., 1st sess., 17 February 1983, 3.
37. *International Herald Tribune*, 21–22 April 1984, 1–2.
38. *Financial Times*, 15 March 1985, 40.

Congress, U.S. administration rhetoric had not changed appreciably and neither had specific tactics. In talks with European farm ministers in June 1985, Secretary of Agriculture John Block stressed the costs of a trade war involving spiraling countersubsidies, but he also contended that the United States did not intend to abandon retaliatory activities unless U.S. policymakers were "convinced by more than just words that agreement could be reached to resolve our trade differences."[39] This U.S. position continued into the Uruguay Round of trade negotiations, a tit-for-tat aggressive policy coupled with verbal pressure for agricultural trade reform. In fact, the United States successfully urged the GATT nations to focus on agricultural trade liberalization as the single most important purpose of negotiations.[40] Even though an agricultural group was established in 1987 to work out proposals for agricultural trade cooperation, however, Uruguay Round progress in this area stalemated. The European Community agreed to the principle of "progressive reduction in support" but also to the view that price supports and attendant export subsidization are valid components of domestic policy and that international price stabilization, not free market competition, should be the goals of a new world agricultural regime. Because the United States continued to take the opposing view, the deadlock that characterized the bilateral wheat flour dispute in the early 1980s illustrated the larger contextual problem that remained, and even though some movement toward a middle ground occured, neither side forfeited its essential position.[41]

Conclusion about the Role of Reciprocity in Altering Established Behavior

In contrast with disputes in the steel and automobile sectors, reciprocal policies in wheat flour trade did not produce coopera-

39. *International Herald Tribune*, 12 June 1985, 5.
40. Filipek, "Agriculture," 146–47.
41. Ray Macsharry, E.C. commissioner, Agriculture and Rural Development, and Julius Katz, deputy U.S. trade representative, presented their respective views in interviews in *Europe*, June 1990, 27–30.

tion, collusive or otherwise; the dispute, in fact, escalated. Although never affecting trade beyond the realm of agricultural export competition, this feud depressed prices and adversely affected other GATT exporters, such as Canada and Australia. Had U.S. retaliatory efforts dislodged the European Community from its export subsidy policy, other wheat-exporting nations would likely have applauded this action. But the ongoing dispute merely made fair competition more difficult.

That reciprocity failed to produce cooperation in this bilateral dispute raises a serious question about its efficacy as a bargaining strategy. Fundamentally, what made the use of reciprocity in this dispute different from use in the other sectors?

Two factors distinguished this case from the other sectoral disputes. First, the regime context was very different. In the manufacturing sectors, a cooperative liberal regime had evolved under the GATT. Trading partners came to expect mutually beneficial trading arrangements, even when free trade was not always politically acceptable. Domestic interests prevented evolution of the GATT in the agricultural sector, however, where trading partners persisted in the general expectation that autonomy in agriculture took precedence over cooperative trading relationships.

Second, competition for third-country export markets, not competition for the trading partner's home market, characterized the dispute in wheat flour trade. The United States could threaten retaliation by subsidizing exports to traditional E.C. markets, but never restricted its own vast market to E.C. trade. In the steel and automobile cases, access to the U.S. domestic market provided the bargaining leverage available to the United States (and to Canada and the European Community in certain instances). In wheat flour trade, partners employed a *like* strategy in a genuine tit-for-tat manner, which kept the stakes much lower than if the United States had threatened to retaliate with limits on E.C. exports to America and may also have affected the efficacy of reciprocal strategy.

This particular conflict illustrates the difficulty encountered when one actor uses retaliation to induce cooperation where no cooperative regime has previously existed and where the retaliator's domestic market is not a component of the bargaining strategy. Although the United States deliberately moved from a policy of persuasion with toleration to one of persuasion with retaliation, at no point in the sequence of interactions did the European Community react with a cooperative response within this sector. In fact, the converse was true: the community escalated the conflict with counterretaliations but also avoided threatening limits on access to its domestic market.

In this case, behavior that the United States targeted was well established, durable, accommodated in the world community for some time, and deeply entrenched in domestic policy. At least in a benign sense, the world community tolerated the behavior for long enough that a "right of use" lent legitimacy and established expectations that the behavior would continue. Thus, the leverage that retaliation might have under different circumstances (e.g., where the policy departs from established norms or expected behavior) was reduced. This case comparison demonstrates that prying decision makers away from a deeply embedded policy is much more difficult than inducing a *return* to previously cooperative behavior.

Adding to this assessment the argument that the U.S. form of retaliation was less effective in the wheat flour dispute than the form of retaliation used by the United States, Canada, and the European Community in the automobile and steel disputes clarifies why U.S. policy failed. The absence of a cooperative regime in agriculture and the firmly fixed nature of E.C. policy in domestic and international politics implied that the United States would have to use even more powerful leverage than that used in the other sectors. But U.S. strategy in the wheat flour dispute actually employed a less powerful weapon. This mismatched situation perpetuated the conflict without altering E.C. behavior.

The ambiguous acceptability of the community's behavior within the governing international regime (the GATT) also reduced the effect of outside leverage by diffusing the impact of domestic proponents' arguments for change in a policy that ran counter to international legal commitments. Ambiguity in the GATT's rules maintained the legitimacy of the community's "right of use" for this long-established behavior. Bystanders, such as Canada and Australia, have criticized U.S. retaliatory strategy because of the deterioration in world grain prices in the 1980s. Also, the risk existed throughout this bilateral conflict that the dispute would escalate into a retaliatory spiral beyond the agricultural sector. Although U.S. and E.C. reciprocal policies contributed to depressed wheat and wheat flour prices, fortunately they did not spill over into other sectors and trigger a general trade war.

As seen, the GATT regime for agriculture, which has been virtually nonexistent,[42] is composed of contradictory rules that reflect the more individual interests of domestic agriculture than the liberal trade tenets of the GATT's founding principles. Had the United States successfully obtained clear-cut guidelines concerning agricultural export subsidies within the GATT legal framework and had it enforced those guidelines on the European Community, a bilateral reciprocal strategy might have shaped a firmer agricultural trading regime. Instead, legal proceedings produced further ambiguity, and the U.S.-E.C. wheat trade conflict ended in the same deadlock in which it began. The Uruguay round of negotiations that the United States hoped would settle the matter stalemated as well, though after nearly seven years with little movement, some progress was made on the issues of production limits and subsidy support.

In 1990 the European Community member states sought to revise the Common Agricultural Policy (CAP) to some extent and in 1992 agreed to some modifications in the community's approach to farm supports and agricultural surpluses. These changes, however, did not constitute a significant difference in overall support policies, because "cuts in subsidies are measured from 1986, when subsidies were at their peak," and observers agreed that the cuts would have a marginal effect on the trade-distorting policies

---

42. Renee E. Marlin-Bennet has categorized trade in agriculture as taking place within a "quasi-regime" that competes with other such nonuniversal regimes. She usefully surmises that "the tensions between and within the components of the quasi-regimes form the political substance of trade disputes." Marlin-Bennet, "A Process Model of Trade Disputes" (paper presented at Peace Science Society International Conference, Detroit, Michigan, 10–15 November 1986). She has further developed this idea in *Food Fights: International Regimes and the Politics of Agricultural Trade Disputes* (New York: Gordon and Beach, 1993).

that caused the trans-Atlantic dispute in the first place.[43] Though modified to some degree by efforts to limit agricultural production, the essential thrust of E.C. policy, especially regarding use of export subsidies, has not been rejected. Thus, the retaliatory policy may have buttressed the U.S. negotiating position with the European Community in the GATT, but after eleven years it has not succeeded in reforming the behavior that Washington found so objectionable.

43. "Agriculture: The New Corn Laws," *Economist*, 12 December 1992, Survey 3.

8

Reciprocity in
U.S. Trade Relations

In the wake of U.S. competitive decline in the 1970s and 1980s, the reciprocity dilemma emerged from debate over the value of retaliation as a means of enforcing fair trade relations versus the costs of retaliation as a contributing factor in undermining the postwar trade regime. Analysts favoring a reciprocal approach to trade worried that tolerating unfair trading practices and free-riding on the GATT open-trading system would encourage one-sided trading relationships, weaken enforcement of norms of fair trade, and appease uncooperative behavior in general. This, they believed, would also effectively make multilateral commitments to liberal trade unpalatable to domestic interest groups that demanded reciprocity abroad.

Others were concerned about the potential negative effect that reciprocal treatment, especially retaliation, could have on the relatively open postwar trading system. These analysts felt that resurgence in the popularity of reciprocity in U.S. trade relations would plunge the United States into pre-1934 protectionism, which in turn could precipitate a 1930s-style global trade war as nations competitively sought reciprocity in a vicious cycle of trade-contracting retaliations. The former approach touted the benefits of reciprocity for enforcing cooperation and fair trade, whereas the latter bemoaned the predilection of protectionist interests to exploit reciprocal policies to the ruin of cooperative trading relations.

My study demonstrates that the reality of U.S. trade policy and bilateral bargaining under the GATT regime lies somewhere between the two views. First, reciprocity and protectionism are clearly not identical. Historical analysis of U.S. trade policy before and after adoption of the 1934 Reciprocal Trade Agreements Act shows that reciprocity can be an instrument of liberalism as well as protectionism and that genuine recognition of reciprocal benefits from trade makes protectionist efforts less viable.

In fact, the most important generalization to be made about U.S. experiences with reciprocity in the last century remains that its incorporation into U.S. trade policy recognized the interdependent potential of trade relations and the vulnerabilities and opportunities that trade relations created. The degree to which this awareness affected trade policy has depended on the dominance of internationally oriented commercial leadership, as well as trade partners' ability and willingness to remind U.S. policymakers of their bargaining and retaliatory capabilities.

During the earliest experiments with reciprocity between 1880 and 1912, protectionist attitudes and restrictions severely limited the scope and effect of reciprocal negotiations. During this period reciprocity in U.S. trade policy generally meant that the U.S. executive was congressionally bound by tight restraints that only tentatively allowed access to certain areas of the U.S. market in exchange for access abroad for U.S. products. Introducing reciprocity into U.S. trade policy represented a positive move toward recognition that to achieve expansion for U.S. producers, some quid pro quo for imports into the United States might be necessary for the bargain. This action also recognized the value of allowing a negotiable tariff, thus sowing the seeds of executive purview in this area.

As long as protectionists dominated trade policy in the United States, however, reciprocity reflected their very narrow, negative attitude toward equivalence of access. Between 1880 and 1912, U.S. experiments in negotiating reciprocal agreements were very limited and highly coercive, based on the backhanded promise of *not* imposing penalty duties on the negotiating partner that conceded to U.S. export demands. Generally, Congress's approach during this time made only two positive outcomes possible. Under

227

successful negotiations, the U.S. trade partner would either protect its exporters from facing extraordinarily restrictive penalty duties on top of the regular U.S. tariff or enable producers to import goods on the duty-free list in an extremely limited number of product categories. On the U.S. side, negotiators secured markets for key American producers who were interested in expanding sales beyond U.S. borders, but negotiations never put domestic producers, except for those in the agricultural sector, in competition with foreign competitors. Congress specified in advance, and thereby controlled, which products would be eligible for negotiations, thus making it impossible for the trade partner to initiate negotiations or define reciprocity on its own terms. In reality this procedure created a highly one-sided approach to negotiations, which distorted the intent and effect of reciprocal agreement.

Although access to congressionally specified liberalization was conditional on meeting Congress's expectations of market access abroad, foreign nations could not expect their access to the U.S. market to be equivalent to that demanded by the U.S. Congress. Moreover, agreements secured under the U.S. trade acts that authorized reciprocal negotiations were rarely ratified by the protectionist Congress.

There was growing interest in U.S. export expansion during this period of U.S. trade policy, but the dominant protectionist view, which did not accept the value of genuine reciprocity in achieving such expansion, limited this interest. Congress refused either to delegate authority over trade to the executive or to trust reciprocity as a tool of trade expansion. The competitive implications of reciprocal agreements were too threatening to U.S. producers at the time.

On examination, reciprocity was not the culprit that made U.S. trade policy restrictive and extortionary during this period; on the contrary, Congress used commitment to restrictive, extortionary policies to manipulate reciprocal negotiations to fit protectionist purposes. As Chapter 2 demonstrates, Congress rejected reciprocal agreements that appeared to threaten this policy. In the pre-1934 period, protectionist interests either circumvented reciprocal commitments or manipulated reciprocal negotiations for extortionary purposes because they were neither internationalist in vision nor pragmatic in views of U.S. manufacturing in the global marketplace. This misuse of reciprocity characterized the dominant, restrictive, and nationalistic approach to foreign trade policy during this period. Even after the United State fully abandoned reciprocity as a condition of U.S. trade relations after 1922, U.S. policy remained restrictive, extortionary, and, worse, nonnegotiable.

To indict reciprocity as inherently protectionist and coercive because of U.S. experiments before 1912 misconstrues U.S. trade policy during this period. Reciprocal negotiations had the potential to liberalize U.S. trade, as President Wilson and his allies in Congress foresaw before World War I denied them opportunity to prove their case. But the general protectionist orientation of most policymakers resulted in their refusal to subject U.S. producers to competition on a reciprocal, mutually beneficial basis.

A historical understanding reveals that as long as protectionist U.S. policymakers were allowed to pursue trade policy autonomously and *without regard for reciprocity*, protectionism dominated. Once they realized, however, that other nations expected access to U.S. markets in exchange for submitting their national markets to U.S. exports, their orientation slowly began to change. But not until the catastrophic repercussions of the 1930 U.S. tariff were enough policymakers and congressional members convinced that U.S. trade policy could no longer be constructed without considering the expectations, interests, and retaliatory capability of foreign nations.

The retaliations of the 1930s disabled the global economy and dealt a crippling blow to U.S. protectionism and the accompanying congressional unwillingness to consider the reciprocal effects of U.S. actions. Clearly, autarky was no longer a realistic approach. Foreign expectations of reciprocity, coupled with retaliatory reactions against the Hawley-Smoot Tariff, demonstrated the presence of a new environment for U.S. trade policy. The interdependent global economy made costs of isolationism unacceptable.

Once key policymakers convinced Congress, in the throes of the Great Depression, that interdependent, reciprocal trade relations made the U.S. protectionist orientation counterproductive,

229

reciprocal negotiations offered a productive avenue for trade liberalization. The post-1934 bilateral negotiations, as well as subsequent multilateral GATT negotiations, proved that trade could be liberalized effectively on the basis of reciprocally acceptable agreements. Commitment to reciprocity proved vital to the public's perception that any concessions surrendered would be matched by market access abroad. To establish legitimacy of a new liberal regime for trade with U.S. domestic interest groups, the reciprocity principle was crucial.

As a founding norm of the GATT regime, reciprocity complemented (though also often contradicted) the principles of liberal trade and nondiscrimination, first, by offering tangible results to domestic interests from negotiations with trading partners and, second, by reflecting a commitment to fairness in trade relations that other principles could not ensure.

Inclusion of reciprocity in the GATT also inserted an enforcement mechanism into an otherwise voluntary arrangement. Bilateral retaliations, in the form of anti-dumping duties, countervailing duties, and withdrawal of concessions in compensation for unfair trade acts, affected calculations of national interest. These external pressures often resulted in moderation or even avoidance of protectionist demands when liberal trade norms alone could not withstand the insistence of domestic interest groups.

The formal inclusion of reciprocity in U.S. trade policy after 1934 and in the GATT after 1948 not only recognized the reality of this new environment but also paradoxically served as a palliative for U.S. domestic discomfort over foreign competition and open markets. The principle of reciprocity embodied the expectation that U.S. concessions would be offered only conditionally upon guarantee of equivalent concessions abroad for U.S. goods. Although the unconditional mfn principle multiplied the market access effect of agreements between principal suppliers, policymakers could always point to the initial reciprocal agreements as proof of the benefits resulting from trade barrier reductions. This, in addition to the promise of trade expansion generally, proved vital for congressional acceptance of trade liberalization. Congress had been awakened to the potential counterproductivity of U.S. protectionism, but that body would not have authorized the executive branch to negotiate bilateral trade-expanding agreements without assurance of reciprocity abroad. Even so, Congress only skeptically and tentatively approved the Reciprocal Trade Agreements Act of 1934, which, for all its groundbreaking success in the area of trade liberalization, pledged not to subject U.S. domestic producers to threatening foreign competition. In addition, the guarantee of negotiations on a reciprocal and mutually beneficial basis allowed Congress to retain authority to protect sovereign U.S. interests when protectionism seemed necessary politically. Under these constraints, the U.S. executive finally obtained negotiating authority to seek reciprocal trade-expanding agreements with other nations.

A number of bilateral agreements, not extensive in scope yet significant in departure from past U.S. trade policy initiatives, were reached after 1934 to liberalize the U.S. market and achieve reciprocal liberalization abroad. Incremental successes of the reciprocal trade agreements created legitimacy and momentum for further liberalization of the U.S. tariff in the post–World War II period. After the war, U.S. leadership used these earlier achievements to create legitimacy for a new regime based on U.S. concepts of fair competition and nondiscrimination in trade.

Here again, reciprocity played a crucial role. The GATT articles included U.S. concerns over unfair trade practices, such as dumping and governmental subsidization of exports, and allowed retaliatory responses to discourage and punish such actions. Reflecting U.S. preferences to retain sovereign control over enforcement of fair trade, the reciprocity principle appeared not only in the preamble, which establishes the general character of member-state relations and expectations, but also in other provisions that allow sovereign nations to ensure balance between themselves and their GATT partners. Examination of the general agreement and the trade regime developed around it reveals that reciprocal behavior between member states has enforced the principle of balanced treatment and mutual benefit. Expectations of mutual cooperation were reinforced by expectations of retaliation when cooperation eroded. In turn, retaliation would return balance to the relationship when warranted by some deviation from the cooperative norm, clearly to keep uncooperative behavior in check.

231

This did not mean that all retaliations and all forthcoming dispute settlements coincided strictly with GATT rules. Sometimes partners have taken "homemade retaliation," rather than codified GATT-sanctioned actions, against noncooperating or rule-violating trade partners; therefore, GATT partners have commonly threatened retaliation as a component of dispute settlement, even when GATT provisions indicated a different approach. The general orientation of the GATT regime, however, has encouraged bilateral dispute settlements, even if outside the formal GATT framework. Therefore, the practice of retaliation and reciprocal bargaining in the GATT regime extended beyond the codified specifications of the General Agreement and became legitimized over time.

Reciprocity was added as a principle of the GATT regime to encourage sovereign nations to submit their markets to greater international competition for the promise of expanded market access elsewhere. This expectation of mutual benefit from multilateral trade negotiations was also reinforced by the understanding that if benefits from negotiations were denied or thwarted by a member state's uncooperative behavior, then the adversely affected nation could retaliate to restore balance, if not mutual benefit, to the relationship.

In other words, reciprocity in the GATT regime could be defined as an *end* of cooperative behavior by member states in the form of mutually beneficial trade relations. Reciprocity also provided the enforcement *instrument* for member nations in their efforts to achieve or maintain mutually beneficial relations. Regime expectations converged around mutual benefit as well as the potential of retaliation if one nation interfered with another's benefits from the arrangement. Reciprocal relations created the incentive for cooperation, whereas potential retaliation provided the disincentive for disregarding the interests of other members. In a very real sense, reciprocity provisions in the GATT embodied the lesson that the United States learned after 1930 about the costs of disregarding trade partners' interests, and these provisions became the fair trade rules of the GATT.

Paradoxically, this internationalist perspective in GATT fair trade principles, based on the interdependent nature of the world

232

economy, used U.S. fair trade law to define acceptable behavior and mutual benefit. U.S. law, however, was unsympathetic to pure free market conditions and international competition, which created two expectations in the United States: that trade partners' rule infractions affecting domestic producers' interests would be handled firmly and punished or compensated and that the United States could not exploit punishment power or pursue protectionist impulses without regard for reactions abroad. America's trade partners could also threaten retaliation to enforce cooperation and mutual benefit. Reciprocity carried a two-edged sword which prevented even the United States from wielding an overly heavy hand in trade politics after World War II and which reinforced fair mutual benefit. When U.S. protectionism threatened GATT cooperative relationships, the expectation of reciprocity and the potential for retaliation helped maintain market access. Although outcomes may not have upheld fair mutual benefit in strict accordance with GATT provisions, expectations of reciprocity encouraged bilateral cooperation.

The character of dispute settlement has also varied with actors' preferences. When disputants favored solutions that coincided with GATT norms and rules, then outcomes reflected this preference, reinforcing the regime and generating further credibility for GATT fair trade law. Often, however, preferences for mutual benefit have superseded those for mutual compliance with GATT rules and nondiscrimination. Therefore, even cooperative settlements have been dominated by domestic political considerations that have favored trade management solutions over free market ones and special bilateral arrangements such as VRAs over nondiscriminatory responses. That is, the use of reciprocal policies alone has not produced managed trade arrangements, but reciprocal policies have facilitated negotiation of such solutions from time to time.

The GATT regime sanctioned individual retaliations against such practices as dumping and export subsidization and tolerated reciprocally acceptable political arrangements that ran contrary to certain general agreement rules as well as against the overarching norm of nondiscrimination. The dichotomy existing between reciprocity and unconditional mfn treatment, given their basis in U.S.

law, made this contradiction inevitable. As trade partners came to prefer special negotiated management arrangements over simple GATT enforcement measures, the contradiction not only represented an uneasy relationship between free trade and fair trade enforcement but also threatened to undermine the original market efficiency norms and cooperative character of the trade regime.

As evidenced in the case studies by the 1970s U.S. producers were beginning to experience the adverse competitive effects of open markets and to turn to the GATT and complementary U.S. trade law for legally acceptable protection. When this fair trade avenue did not seem viable or did not produce high levels of protection from imports, however, they sought to circumvent regime norms and rules and secure protection anyway. This action placed severe pressures on Congress to recapture influence over the trade policy agenda, which in turn strained the executive's liberal trade commitment. The juxtaposition of reciprocal enforcement efforts with protectionism then led to indictments against reciprocity as an inherently protectionist and regressive move. But examination of actual interactions between the United States and its trade partners demonstrates that reciprocity was clearly distinct from protectionism, despite the fact that expectations of reciprocity occasionally contributed to protectionist outcomes.

Review of U.S. steel and automobile trade revealed that GATT reciprocity provisions often provided the reasoning for fair trade enforcement measures aimed against foreign competition. Had U.S. producers and political leaders contented themselves with fair trade retaliations, the original GATT norms would have been reinforced; but when such retaliations did not satisfy domestic producers' demands for protection, they sought other means. When these protectionist demands coincided with demands from the trade partner for alternative solutions to GATT fair trade enforcement provisions, mutually agreeable diplomatic settlements often replaced retaliatory enforcement. These collusive settlements reflected the mutual political interests of the United States and foreign governments who preferred solutions acceptable to each other as well as to their respective constituencies. The irony is that regime-driven expectations of fair trade and retaliatory threats often facilitated cooperation while resulting agreements actually represented collusion against GATT rules oriented toward fair trade and a free market.

At times facilitated by reciprocity, national actors' mutual preferences for bilateral negotiation of trade flows and market management produced such collusive arrangements. I would note, however, that reciprocity could as easily have been an instrument of fair trade enforcement, had the importing nation chosen to pursue GATT-sanctioned enforcement measures. For example, had the United States used strictly retaliatory policies in accordance with GATT rules toward E.C. steel importers, then anti-dumping or countervailing duties would have been imposed to enforce compliance with fair trade rules, regardless of the effect on E.C. steel policy. Instead, government representatives from both trading partners preferred negotiated settlements that allowed assurances of market share rather than regime enforcement. The crucial variable that explains collusive managed trade outcomes was not whether reciprocity was pursued but whether protectionism or fair trade motivated policymakers.

Regardless of motivation, however, the role that reciprocity played in the steel cases and in the U.S.-Canada automobile case reinforced the interdependent nature of trade relations and encouraged cooperative arrangements that maintained bilateral trade flows, despite domestic pressures against them. When the United States or its trade partners took original protectionist actions to secure markets from competition or to coerce collusive bilateral protectionism, the expectation of reciprocity and the fear of retaliation often contained disputes and facilitated settlements even when they did not coincide with liberal GATT norms. Because the European Community refused to cooperate with the United States without some recognition of its domestic policy interests and threatened retaliation to enforce demands, the organization often secured preferential arrangements in comparison with the more passive Japan, which grudgingly capitulated. Although the community's ability to credibly threaten the United States was greater than Japan's, its use of threats prevented the United States from unilaterally pressing protectionism without regard to E.C. interests and expectations. The outcome of the Canada-U.S. automobile dispute also reinforced this link between rec-

235

iprocity and bilateral cooperation, demonstrating that with market access at stake, even the smaller of two trading partners can effectively wield coercive threats in an interdependent relationship but that eventual settlement depends on the reciprocal interplay of bargaining threats and counterthreats.

The comparative case studies in the steel and automobile sectors also show that regime norms continued to guide policymakers to a large degree, despite strong protectionist and coercive impulses. At the height of bilateral disputes between the United States and its trading partners in these sectors, the partners never fully unleashed unilateral protectionism but preferred bilateral collusive arrangements over unilaterally imposed protection. Even when disputes involved highly asymmetrical relationships that favored U.S. power, bilateral settlements were preferred, which verifies that lingering regime norms favoring maintenance of trade flows, international cooperation, and reciprocal responsibility continued to influence policy making in the United States and elsewhere.

In particular, the asymmetrical relationship between the United States and Japan in automobile and steel trade illustrates this choice. Although E.C. retaliatory threats had pressed the United States to consider community interests and demands in reaching cooperative settlements, the absence of those Japanese threats did not cause the United States to embrace unilateral protection when collusive solutions were a viable alternative. By way of explanation, GATT regime norms continued to influence U.S. policymakers' expectations as well as those of U.S. trade partners, even when domestic protectionist pressures were very high. Protectionists in Congress, though very influential, had not forced the U.S. executive to forfeit control over the trade policy agenda, and direct affronts to liberal trade norms and international cooperation were not allowed. Consequently, bilaterally negotiated VRAs, which allowed exporting nations some control over composition, allocation of exports, and the resulting quota rent, were preferred alternatives to autonomous protection. Clearly, regime norms, reinforced by retaliations from those trading partners who were both capable and willing to take action (such as the European Community), continued to influence U.S. trade policy more generally.

236

Although rampant unilateral protectionism did not characterize U.S. actions in these cases, the dispute settlement process demonstrated that original GATT regime contradictions between the reciprocity principle and the nondiscrimination principle had intensified. The underlying tension that had created ambiguity in regime expectations eventually ruptured when the uncomfortable partnership could no longer withstand protectionist pressures.

Reciprocity had enforced commitments to the liberal trade regime but only when trade partners willingly made use of retaliatory measures for that purpose. Reciprocity as an instrument of fair trade enforcement required that both domestic producers and their political representatives accept this use as well as the limited role that reciprocity could play in protecting domestic producers from foreign competition. Coupled with rising protectionism in the United States during the 1970s and 1980s, preferences for protectionist solutions to competitiveness problems overcame those for fair trade enforcement of free market principles.

In regard to U.S. import policy, reciprocity's role in fair trade diminished, although its role in encouraging U.S. export trade enlarged during this same period. The view became increasingly prevalent that the United States should take an active role in opening markets abroad or wresting unfairly seized markets from foreign competitors, which placed new emphasis on reciprocity as a goal in U.S. trade relations and as a potentially useful policy instrument to achieve that goal.

In this study, the automobile sector and the wheat flour sector witnessed this approach to U.S. export trade. In the former, the U.S. effort to secure liberalization of Japan's import policy became intertwined with protectionist efforts against Japanese automobile exports to the U.S. market. Resentful over the absence of reciprocal market access, U.S. policymakers attempted to link continued access to the U.S. automobile market with improvements in U.S. access to the Japanese market across a number of sectors.

In Chapter 6 I examined the United States' mixed motives in threatening a strategy of aggressive retaliation. Clearly wanting to protect its beleaguered automobile industry, Congress pressed the executive to leverage restraint agreements with the Japanese government. But this indisputable move for protection occurred

237

within the context of a general reassessment of the bilateral trading relationship, and U.S. policymakers were convinced that Japan's failure to genuinely reciprocate by offering access to its domestic market contributed to U.S. trade problems. The United States then used potential retaliatory power to leverage liberalization of Japan's market. Although limited, the results generated legitimacy in the United States for this approach to bilateral trade problems and strengthened commitment to the reciprocity principle, but at the expense of the nondiscrimination principle.

These retaliatory threats differed from pre-1912 reciprocal trade policies in two very important respects. First, retaliatory threats against Japan occurred within a much more liberal and interdependent context, in terms of both U.S. policy orientation and trade relationships. Despite protectionist pressures, the necessity and desirability of trade interdependence continued to motivate policymakers, and GATT norms favoring cooperative trade flows and reciprocal market access persisted, though GATT norms favoring free trade and nondiscrimination dwindled in importance. Second, U.S. market openness in manufacturing products was well established by the 1970s, becoming the norm of U.S. import policy rather than the exception. This situation, exactly opposite that of the earlier period, meant that reciprocal bargaining in the 1980s generally required potential denial of market access rather than the promise of market liberalization, as had been the case previously, when the U.S. market was so tightly protected.

Similarly, the wheat flour case demonstrates that U.S. use of reciprocity in tit-for-tat export subsidies to persuade the European Community to forgo its subsidy practices reflected U.S. efforts to punish aggressively behavior considered unfair and harmful to U.S. interests. Reciprocity consisted of matching E.C. behavior with U.S. export subsidies to recapture U.S. wheat flour markets for competitive American producers. As we saw in Chapter 7, however, this effort failed to pry the community away from dumping surplus wheat flour onto the world market at subsidized prices.

Three factors contributed to this failure. First, the E.C. Common Agriculture Policy was deeply embedded in community history and institutional development, which made U.S. reversal of E.C. policies extremely difficult. Moreover, competitive damage done to community flour exports cost no more—and in domestic political terms, less—than the cost of absorbing surpluses internally or abolishing price supports that produced the surpluses. Second, U.S. leverage matching E.C. policies in tit-for-tat retaliation was perhaps less effective than if the United States had threatened to close some important aspect of its own market to E.C. exporters. Certainly, evidence from the other sectoral cases indicates that the significance of market access is a crucial variable in determining the bargaining leverage available to importing nations. Competition for relatively small third-country markets may not have raised the stakes high enough for the community to alter policies substantially. Third, the ambiguity of GATT export subsidy provisions and panel reports regarding this dispute failed to indict E.C. practices effectively and offered no regime-reinforcing legitimacy for U.S. actions. The long-term pattern of noninterference in domestic agricultural policy was difficult to break.

Motivated by the potential effect that reciprocal action could have in forcing the European Community to alter policies, U.S. officials pursued discriminatory, illegal practices that contradicted certain GATT norms but were utilized to enforce others. Again, the global market environment and policymakers' orientation affected the role that reciprocal policies played in this case. Unlike trade in the manufacturing sector, the GATT never fully embraced and embodied agricultural trade in the global trade regime. Failure to create a liberal trade regime in agriculture clearly affected the community's rigid position and decreased U.S. ability to influence it significantly. Reciprocity became an instrument to force fundamental change that the community was not prepared to adopt because political costs of change continued to outweigh by far the costs of maintaining the status quo.

Conclusion

These three sectoral cases verify that reciprocity as an instrument of trade policy has reflected not only the policy orientation of the United States but also the global trade environment of the time. Before the turn of the century, U.S. interest in reciprocity resulted from developing awareness that U.S. economic potential was in part tied to participation in the global economy. Access for U.S. producers to markets abroad offered attractive commercial opportunities; and as long as U.S. negotiators exploited these opportunities without Congress allowing reciprocal access, U.S. free ridership was possible. Not until the international backlash against its free ridership wreaked havoc with the entire global economy in the 1930s was the United States willing to accept responsibility for genuinely reciprocal trade arrangements. By taking the lead to reopen markets and encourage trade flows through bilaterally negotiated reciprocal trade agreements, U.S. policymakers created a new era in U.S. commercial relations.

During the past four decades, that strategy has produced both pluses and minuses for U.S. producers. The global marketplace became less encumbered by trade restrictions, trade expanded, and competition intensified, which placed new emphasis on reciprocity, as a means both to enforce fair competition rules and to encourage better access to markets abroad. Frustrations with perceived unfair trading practices abroad made reciprocal policies, which threatened imposition of trade restrictions, attractive means of leverage in the otherwise relatively open U.S. market. Retaliatory policies that were used to enforce trade norms confirmed the GATT principles of fair mutual benefit and liberal trade. Although these policies proved less effective in altering long-established practices outside the regime, as in the wheat flour dispute, they reinforced the principle that regime expectations might be extended to new areas of trade. Because the renewed stress on reciprocity existed alongside new protectionist pressures, however, reciprocity at times became part of U.S. domestic efforts to circumvent its free trade responsibilities. This again demonstrated that reciprocal measures can be instruments of liberalism and enforcement of fair trade as well as instruments of protectionism and enforcement of sovereign benefit that contradict norms of fair trade.

Policy motivation and international context have determined the role played by reciprocity in U.S. trade relations. Generally, protectionist motivations produced attempts to exploit reciprocal policies, whereas liberal motivations produced mutually beneficial liberal arrangements that maintained trade flows. But even when they attempted to use reciprocity for protectionist purposes, policymakers have found this method less restrictive to trade than autonomous actions. Although this method has often produced bilaterally managed trade solutions that undermine regime norms favoring efficiency and nondiscrimination, a breakdown in trade relations has not occurred and cooperative settlements have been facilitated. Generally, where interdependent trading relationships developed and expectations converged around mutual benefit from trade, reciprocity tended to reinforce cooperative norms and maintain trade flows.

Index

Index

Index

Index